CHINA'S SECOND
CONTINENT

CHINA'S SECOND CONTINENT

HOW A MILLION MIGRANTS

ARE BUILDING A NEW EMPIRE

IN AFRICA

Howard W. French

Alfred A. Knopf · New York · 2014

THIS IS A BORZOI BOOK PUBLISHED BY ALFRED A. KNOPF

Copyright © 2014 by Howard W. French

www.aaknopf.com

Library of Congress Cataloging-in-Publication Data
French, Howard W., author.
China's second continent : how a million migrants are building
a new empire in Africa / Howard W. French.—First edition.
pages   cm
"This is a Borzoi book."
Includes bibliographical references and index.
ISBN 978-0-307-95698-9 (hardcover) ISBN 978-0-385-35168-3 (eBook)
1. Chinese—Africa, Sub-Saharan. 2. Immigrants—Africa, Sub-Saharan.
3. Africa, Sub-Saharan—Emigration and immigration.
4. China—Emigration and immigration. I. Title.
DT16.C48F74 2014
325.2510967—dc23   2013026930

Jacket design by Jason Booher
Map by Mapping Specialists, Ltd.

Manufactured in the United States of America

First Edition

In memory of Mary "Fine Bread" Andoh,

who gave me Avouka,

who begat William and Henry

Alas, journey upon journey
upon journey, we're separated
with thousands and thousands
of miles between us, each stranded
at the other end of the world.
The roads so difficult and long,
when can we possibly see
each other again? The horse
from the north still yearns
for the northern wind, the bird
from the south clings, like
before, to the southern branch . . .

—FROM "JOURNEY UPON JOURNEY,"
    AUTHOR UNKNOWN. HAN DYNASTY CHINA.
    TRANSLATED BY QIU XIAOLONG.

I could not have told you then that some sun
would come,
somewhere over the road,
would come evoking the diamonds
of you, the Black continent—
somewhere over the road.
You would not have believed my mouth.

—FROM "TO THE DIASPORA,"
    GWENDOLYN BROOKS

Contents

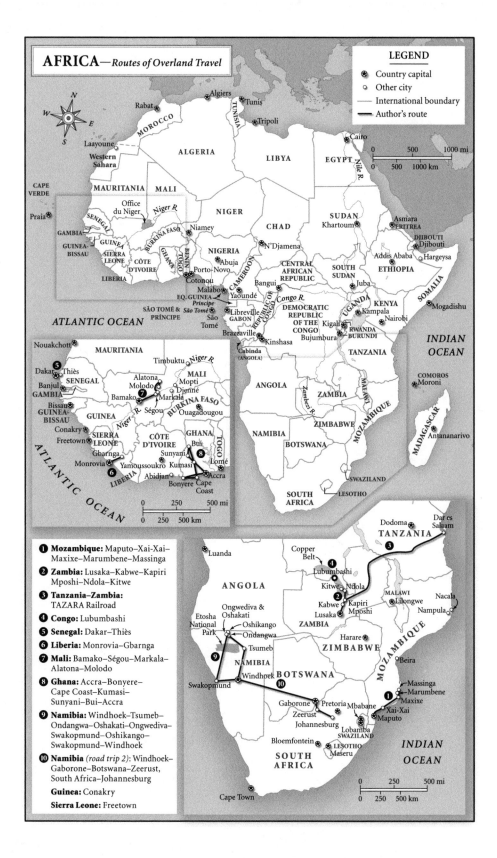

AFRICA—*Routes of Overland Travel*

LEGEND

⊛ Country capital
○ Other city
― International boundary
━ Author's route

0   500   1000 mi
0 500 1000 km

1 Mozambique: Maputo–Xai-Xai–Maxixe–Marumbene–Massinga

2 Zambia: Lusaka–Kabwe–Kapiri Mposhi–Ndola–Kitwe

3 Tanzania–Zambia: TAZARA Railroad

4 Congo: Lubumbashi

5 Senegal: Dakar–Thiès

6 Liberia: Monrovia–Gbarnga

7 Mali: Bamako–Ségou–Markala–Alatona–Molodo

8 Ghana: Accra–Bonyere–Cape Coast–Kumasi–Sunyani–Bui–Accra

9 Namibia: Windhoek–Tsumeb–Ondangwa–Oshakati–Ongwediva–Swakopmund–Oshikango–Swakopmund–Windhoek

10 Namibia (*road trip 2*): Windhoek–Gaborone–Botswana–Zeerust, South Africa–Johannesburg

Guinea: Conakry

Sierra Leone: Freetown

CHINA'S SECOND CONTINENT

Introduction

When China launched its historic opening toward the end of the 1970s, the country and its people not only became the fortunate beneficiaries of astute new policies, but also—crucially—of magnificent timing. The next few years, as they unfolded, would take shape as an era of unprecedented globalization, and no country would profit more from the coming tidal wave of economic change. In little more than a decade, China went from being a poor society with an economy that produced few goods for export and imported little, to positioning itself to become the so-called factory of the world, as we recognize it today.

As great as this era of change proved to be for China and for the Chinese, though, globalization was essentially being carried out on other people's terms, namely those of the United States, Western Europe, and Japan. The economic powerhouses of the rich world sought new outlets for their surplus capital, as well as low-wage labor for their enterprises, allowing them to ply eager Western consumers with ever-cheaper goods. And for both of these purposes, China fit the bill better than anyplace else on earth.

Modern globalization's first great wave has now crested, and is being overtaken by a newer and potentially even more consequential tide. In this new phase, China has gone from being a vessel to becoming an increasingly transformative actor in its own right. Indeed, it is rapidly emerging as the most important agent of economic change in broad swaths of the world.

Chinese banks, construction companies, and other enterprises in ever growing variety conspicuously roam the planet nowadays in search of outlets for their money and goods, for business and markets, and for the raw materials needed to sustain China's rapid growth. As they do so, China is increasingly writing its own rules, and reinventing globalization in its own image, gradually jettisoning many of the norms and conventions used by the United States and Europe throughout their long and hitherto largely unchallenged tutelage of the Third World.

Beijing has achieved this, in part, by engineering a kind of modern-day barter system in which developing countries pay for new railroads, highways, and airports through the guaranteed, long-term supply of hydrocarbons or minerals, thus helping Chinese companies win massive new contracts. In hundreds of other deals, China's Export-Import Bank and other big, state-controlled "policy bank" counterparts have teamed up to offer attractive project financing that is usually tied to the use of Chinese companies, Chinese materials, and Chinese workers.

Africa, more than any other place, has been the great stage for these innovations, and the focus of extraordinary Chinese energy as a rising great power casts its gaze far and wide for opportunity, like never before in its history. Sensing that Africa had been cast aside by the West in the wake of the Cold War, Beijing saw the continent as a perfect proving ground for some Chinese companies to cut their teeth in international business. It certainly did not hurt that Africa was also the repository of an immense share of global resources—raw materials that were vital both for China's extraordinary ongoing industrial expansion and for its across-the-board push for national reconstruction.

As a result, Africa has risen high on Beijing's agenda. Indeed, China's new leader, Xi Jinping, visited the continent in his very first overseas trip as president, and not a year goes by without multiple visits to the continent by several of the country's top leaders, marking a stark and I believe deliberate contrast with the United States, for which a presidential or even secretary of state's visit to Africa is an infrequent event. For China, this kind of attention—what African leaders have called "servicing the relationship"—combined with Beijing's official largesse, is paying off handsomely. China's trade with Africa zoomed to an estimated $200 billion in 2012, a more than twenty-fold increase since the turn of the century, placing it well ahead of the United States or any European country. For a key Chinese industry like construction, meanwhile, African contracts by some estimates now account for nearly a third of its total revenues abroad.

In recent years, developments like these have engendered a lively if often sterile debate about whether China's growing engagement will fundamentally help rebuild Africa, placing it on a path to prosperity, or will result instead in a rapacious recolonization in all but name. In most of these debates the conclusions seem largely predetermined, like so many plodding legal briefs: in reflexive defense of China, or equally automatic skepticism toward the country and its intentions—cheering for the West and celebrating its values, or full-throated schadenfreude over its every comeuppance.

One of the most important and unpredictable factors in China's relationship with Africa, however, has been oddly omitted from most of these discussions: China's export, in effect, of large numbers of its own people who are settling in as migrants and long-term residents in far-flung and hitherto unfamiliar parts of the continent. By common estimate, Africa has received a million or so of these Chinese newcomers in the space of a mere decade, during which time they have rapidly penetrated every conceivable walk of life: farmers, entrepreneurs building small and medium-sized factories, and practitioners of the full range of trades, doctors, teachers, smugglers, prostitutes. It is recent immigrants like these to sub-Saharan Africa who serve as the main focus of this book. I have spent time with them in fifteen countries, large and small, spread widely throughout the continent, and it is above all through their experiences that I have sought to understand China's burgeoning ties with Africa.

States are in the business of making plans, and it is no different with China in Africa. Official lending from Beijing and big projects completed by big, government-owned companies dominate the headlines about the advancing Chinese agenda in Africa. But history teaches us that very often reality is more meaningfully shaped by the deeds of countless smaller actors, most of them for all intents and purposes anonymous. In this vein, each of China's new immigrants to Africa is an architect helping to shape this momentous new relationship. They accomplish this, in part, by helping build networks that loop back to the home country, channeling goods and products and capital via informal circuits that very often escape official control or even accounting.

The historic movement of Chinese to Africa is itself largely driven by word of mouth, by news passed back and forth about a continent that many ordinary Chinese people, even those who reside deep in the hinterland of their country, nowadays speak of in near awe as a place of almost unlimited opportunity. Each newcomer to Africa thus has the potential to become a powerful link in a phenomenon of chain migration that draws relatives, acquaintances, girlfriends, and spouses in their wake. In time, the behavior of these newcomers, the relationships they form with Africans, the way they conduct their business, their respect or lack thereof for the law, for local customs, for the environment, and, above all, for people, will do more to determine China's image, and perhaps even China's broad relationship to the continent, than any carefully planned actions by the Beijing government to build state power and reinforce national prestige.

As a journalist, I observed China's rise from close-up and with fascination, just as I previously witnessed Africa's evolution. China, as almost everyone knows, is the world's fastest-growing large economy. It has tallied 10.2 percent average annual growth over the last two decades, during which time it accounted for 40 percent of global growth. More recently and much less widely appreciated, Africa had also embarked on a phase of stirring growth. According to the International Monetary Fund, of the twenty countries projected to grow the fastest between 2013 and 2017, ten are located in sub-Saharan Africa. Bit by bit, these facts have become closely intertwined.

In Africa of late, I was struck far more than before by the presence of Chinese migrants nearly everywhere I went: speaking at length with ordinary street vendors in Dar es Salaam, Tanzania, poultry farmers and merchants in Lusaka, Zambia, and wildcat copper miners in Democratic Republic of the Congo, and getting to know them well, has powerfully shaped my sense of China.

In their new lands of adoption, Chinese people frequently spoke to me with unaccustomed openness about their hopes for their country and about its problems and failings. I was struck by how Africa, to so many of them, by contrast, seemed remarkably free, and brimming with opportunity unlike home, which they often described as cramped, grudging, and hypercompetitive. For many of them, Africa also seemed relatively lacking in corruption.

Africa is at a critical juncture of its history. This is an era when a combination of demographics, education, and communication technologies have begun to open up possibilities for a number of African countries to break with their poverty and underdevelopment and rise into the ranks of middle-income countries. Already, in the last decade, overall growth in Africa has nearly matched that of Asia, and based on current trends, it is soon expected to take over the global lead.

Africa's population is set to double from one billion to two by the middle of this century, placing most of the continent squarely in a zone known as the "demographic dividend," in which young, working-age people predominate, far outnumbering unproductive dependents, whether young or old. By century's end, demographers predict that Africa's population could reach a staggering 3.5 billion, making it larger than China and India combined.

Growth and development, of course, are not at all the same thing, and it is a safe bet that only the best governed countries—in all likelihood mostly emerging democracies—will manage to leverage natural resource wealth and strong population growth in ways that permit a leap to new levels of prosperity. In many other countries around the continent, greedy and shortsighted political elites will enjoy windfalls from the rising demand for their natural resources, only to squander them; instead of investing sensibly in the training and employment of their own populations, they will spend heavily on dubious prestige projects like new showcase capitals and gaudy palaces, consuming conspicuously and funneling money into foreign bank accounts.

As the population of countries like these soars, their cities will become nightmarishly crowded and instability and even state failure will become chronic among many of them, while their underground wealth is being thoroughly depleted and their environments destroyed. Mid-century will stand out as a sort of twin horizon for Africa, when population growth peaks and when known oil and mineral reserves are exhausted in many countries.

Thus, for some of Africa, the continent's "rediscovery" by China will mirror the lucky timing of China itself a generation ago, when it began its historic opening. Strong new demand and plentiful investment from this big and hungry new partner will fuel growth and dramatically expand opportunities. For the less fortunate, though, China and its voracious appetites will merely hasten an already foreseeable demise.

As Ed Brown, a Ghanaian senior executive at one of his country's leading independent think tanks told me, "This [relationship] is going to determine Africa's future for the next fifty years. The big question is whether African countries are dynamic enough to take advantage, or whether they'll end up being the appendage of somebody else all over again."

My hope here is to shed some understanding on a world being remade through China's important new relationships with the world's least developed continent, and by doing so to lift, however modestly, the veil on the future.

PART ONE
Manifest Destiny

CHAPTER ONE

Mozambique

Hao Shengli and I had been talking for days over a patchy cell phone connection to the farmland he owned in a remote part of south-central Mozambique, where he made his new home. He had come to Maputo, the capital city, to load up on supplies and to pick me up for the long ride back to his plantation.

Hao was barking into his cell phone when his white, chauffeur-driven, late-model Toyota pickup pulled up in front of my hotel. It was clear that he was in a hurry and that he was angry. There was a brisk handshake, followed by a lot more shouting in salty Chinese as he struggled to make himself understood to a countryman whom I could grasp he wanted to buy goods from.

"China is a big, fucking mess with all of its fucking dialects," the shaven-headed, stocky Hao, in his late fifties, said as he hung up.

As I stood there with my bags, already sweating in the mid-morning heat, Hao's frustration caused him to train abuse on John, his tall and sinewy Mozambican driver, who had been coolly smoking a cigarette while he rearranged the supplies loaded onto the Toyota's flatbed.

"You, *cabeza no bom*, motherfucker," he said, the curse word coming in Chinese, as the grizzled immigrant farmer angrily employed three languages in one short and brutal sentence. Having overheard me speaking Spanish to communicate with the driver and assuming it to be Portuguese, he pleaded with me to help him translate. "Could you please explain to this motherfucker where we need to go? We've got to get out of here. We need to be on the road."

A generation or two earlier, the Ugly American had been one of the sturdiest stock characters on the world stage. He was a figure who contented himself with shouting louder whenever he was not understood by the natives in whatever corner of the world he found himself. After just a few minutes with Hao, I felt I had met his Chinese successor.

Over the last ten years, official China had invested hugely in Africa, yanking it away, as many commentators would have it, from the centuries-long controlling grip of the West, while few in that part of the world were paying attention. The foundation for this thrust actually lay somewhat further in the past. The most definitive commencement date was perhaps the state visit to six African countries by the then head of state, Jiang Zemin, in 1996. In a speech at the African Union headquarters in Addis Ababa, Ethiopia, Jiang proposed the creation of the Forum on China-Africa Cooperation (FOCAC).

This turned out to be an important first move in a momentous two-step. Upon his return to China, Jiang gave another speech in the city of Tangshan, in which he explicitly directed the country's firms to "go out," meaning go overseas in search of business. No Chinese leader had ever said anything like that before, and from the very start Africa was clearly a principal target.

Six years later, I was working in China when Jiang's Forum convened triumphantly for the first time, gathering fifty-three African leaders in Beijing. Among China's many pledges, Jiang promised to double development assistance to the continent, create a $5 billion African development fund, cancel outstanding debt, build a new African Union headquarters in Ethiopia, create three to five "trade and cooperation" zones around the continent, build thirty hospitals and a hundred rural schools, and train fifteen thousand African professionals.

By 2013, there was no escaping the notion that Beijing's project on the continent had become far advanced. Because of China's lack of openness, hard data on the country's overseas activities has always been difficult to come by, and nowhere more so than in Africa, whose governments tend, themselves, not to be good at offering up comprehensive or reliable data. But according to Fitch Ratings, China's Export-Import Bank extended $62.7 billion in loans to African countries between 2001 and 2010, or $12.5 billion more than the World Bank. A research group called AidData, at the College of William and Mary, estimated China's total commitments during roughly the same period at $74.11 billion, and put the value of its completed projects at $48.61 billion.

But people like Hao were evidence of something else happening altogether, an even larger-scale phenomenon, one that seemed to be escaping control of the best-laid state plans. Over that same decade, perhaps a million private citizens had chosen to seek a new future for themselves on African soil, and like Hao, many of them had pulled up stakes in China entirely of their own initiative. And as much as anything else, it is the way they have conducted their business—the way they have gone about their investments in land, in industry, in commerce, and of course their general behavior and the human relationships they have formed—that has shaped China's image in Africa and conditioned its ties to the continent.

By the time I met Hao, this "human factor" had already begun to make itself strongly felt in a disparate and far-flung collection of countries. In Senegal, Namibia, Malawi, and Tanzania, protests by local merchants had broken out recently over the influx of large numbers of low-end Chinese traders. In the gold-producing regions of southern Ghana, locals had complained loudly about the arrival en masse of Chinese wildcat miners, who were taking over rich lands and despoiling the environment, cutting down forest and pouring mercury into the soil and streams. And in Zambia, where recent Chinese arrivals have implanted themselves in almost every lucrative sector of the economy, including lowly poultry traders who compete cheek by jowl with locals in African-style markets, the presence of these new immigrants had already become a contentious issue in national elections.

From spending time with migrants like Hao I learned whether Chinese newcomers had come to Africa to stay, and what their impact would be in transforming African economies, how willing they were to integrate with the locals, and what other impact their massive presence around Africa would have. Unexpectedly, I gained a much deeper understanding of China itself.

One usually thinks of China's diversity in ethnic terms. There are minority groups including most famously the Tibetans and Uighur Muslims, whose histories and customs are distinct from the great Han majority, and who see themselves, and are typically seen, as being very much apart. Of course, there is a socioeconomic diversity to the country, as well. It is evident almost everywhere in the widening gaps between the rich, the emerging middle class, and the working-class and poor segments of the population that have made China one of the most unequal societies anywhere. We recognize a kind of political diversity in the country, one mostly represented by a niche population of nonconformist intellectuals and dissidents. They are a favorite topic of coverage by the Western press, which might give the impression that these people's opinions hold great sway, while in fact they represent a tiny fragment of the population, and their views are scarcely circulated.

When I first met Hao, I thought of him as unusual and discounted the possibility that the sorts of ideas he espoused and incarnated could be representative of much of anything beyond his own gruff and often cynical persona. But I would learn that his brand of free-spoken disaffection from the system back home was widespread among China's new emigrants. To be sure, a desire for better economic opportunities was the biggest driver behind their exodus. Still, contributing to the decision for many to take a great leap into the unknown and move to Africa was a weariness with omnipresent official corruption back home, fear of the impact of a badly polluted environment on their health, and a variety of constraints on freedoms, including religion and speech. Many migrants also invoked a sheer lack of space.

This last item had been a big part of the attraction that Mozambique exerted on Hao, and therefore my interest in Hao. The least-explored story of China's newcomers to Africa involved farmers who were buying up land, and Mozambique, a country nearly twice the size of California, with some of the continent's most fertile soils, was wide open to this kind of business.

Hao was a new leaseholder with big dreams of producing lucrative commercial crops. I had met him online before coming to the country and nothing about being new to farming, or for that matter being new to Africa, daunted him. He seemed excited about telling his story, and when I arrived in Maputo he offered to pick me up and take me to his farm.

As Hao and I left Maputo at the outset of our drive together, we passed a big, new national stadium nearing completion by Chinese work crews at the edge of town. I knew it to be a showcase gift of sorts from China to Mozambique, intended as much to make a statement about Chinese generosity and solidarity with the people of this southern African country as it was to host important soccer tournaments, like the upcoming continent-wide African Nations Cup.

China had become an avid practitioner of this kind of prestige-project diplomacy all over the continent. I asked Hao whether a $60 million stadium like this was the best sort of gift in a place with poverty as stark as that of Mozambique, one of the ten poorest countries in the world. His response made clear to me that I needn't have bothered to be so careful with my questions. "Chinese government projects in Mozambique have all failed," he said. "That's because the Chinese *ganbu* [bureaucrats] don't know how to communicate on the same level with the blacks."

As he spoke, he began shaking his head and wagging a stubby index finger excitedly in what quickly turned into a free association rant, one that leaped without warning from his thoughts about government projects to his feelings toward what another group of settlers in another era once would have called "the natives."

"The market capacity of the blacks is pretty bad. The thing you need to know about them is that they only do what they are supposed to do when you are watching them. Otherwise they do whatever they want. On top of that they are very proud. They don't like to lose face." This was my introduction to a kind of casual primary racism by Chinese newcomers toward Africans, which was something I would become well acquainted with.

Soon afterward, in the unbroken green of the countryside, Hao dozed. I engaged John, the driver, by asking questions about the history of his country. My interest was prompted by our crossing of the Limpopo River, a name that resonated with me years after having read about it in news accounts as a strategic dividing line during the long war to liberate the country from Portuguese colonial rule.

"This was an area of particularly heavy fighting," John said. "The liberation war was fought in every little town and village around here. Most of our people had no modern weapons, but that didn't stop us. We even fought the Portuguese with spears."

John's stories went back to the 1930s and to the forced labor practiced by the colonizers, and he peppered his comments with place names and dates. "We were their slaves," he said in conclusion about the Portuguese. "Even now they refuse to accept that word, but our people had no rights at all. We lived at their mercy."

I asked John if he still harbored hard feelings toward the Portuguese, who were now flocking back to his country to escape a debt crisis and severe recession at home. He said no, which surprised me.

"We need to have as many foreigners as we can get here. We need them to come and train us, and if they are able to do that, Mozambicans will prove our capabilities to the world."

Mozambique's war for liberation had been followed almost immediately by another long and bloody struggle, this time between the country's new socialist ruling party and a group of rebels based in the north, who received most of their support from apartheid-style regimes in Rhodesia and South Africa. The second of these conflicts ended in 1992, after fifteen years of fighting, and the extensive use of land mines, and widespread atrocities against civilians, especially by the rebels, had made it one of the most violent and destructive wars that modern Africa has seen.

Since winning the civil war, FRELIMO, the former rebel group turned Marxist ruling party, had introduced multiparty elections, but this had not prevented it from turning democracy into an empty, formal exercise. There was almost no separation between the ruling party and the state, and for years, a small number of well-connected people had been getting obscenely rich, mostly by selling off the rights or access to the country's land and natural resources to foreigners, while the rest of the population toiled, barely subsisting.

In Africa, this kind of equation, a sort of gangster capitalism, had become the common lot of many resource-rich states, and it made pessimism easy to come by. This tragic history helped explain why Mozambique, with fertile land, extraordinarily rich coastal fishing waters, extensive tropical forests, and a generous allotment of minerals of various kinds, remained so poor.

We were making good time now on an empty road, zooming through an open landscape filled with endless low, green scrub. Here and there stood the occasional village whose inhabitants got by from the sale of *piri piri*, the fiery pimento sauce that spiced the daily regimen of freshly caught fish and cornmeal. Otherwise, there were few signs of man or even of his hand.

As I listened to John's history lessons, I wondered how much of this background Hao knew. All I knew of Hao's story was that he had come to this country after the chemicals and trading companies he'd founded in China had lost money in a recent financial crisis. He had told me that a first attempt to do business overseas, in Dubai, had also gone bad, and that he had encountered Chinese agricultural experts who had previously gone on aid missions to Africa and they had planted a very powerful idea in his mind: Go to Africa, where you can acquire good land cheaply.

"I'd never dealt with African people before," Hao said. "At first just coming in contact with them made me feel uncomfortable, their skin is so black. But once you're in contact with them you begin to get used to it. You realize it's just a color.

"I didn't think they were so clever, not so intelligent, and I was looking for an opportunity based on my own capabilities. Can you imagine if I had gone to America or to Germany first? The people in those fucking places are too smart. I wouldn't have gotten anywhere. I don't think I could have beaten them. So we had to find backward countries, poor countries that we can lead, places where we can do business, where we can manage things successfully. If it was the United States, with fucking intelligent Americans, how could we compete?"

At a casual glance, the greenness of the well-watered countryside unfurling before us seemed almost designed to entice dreamers from afar. And given the prevailing idleness of the land and the apparent lack of inhabitants, one easily imagined that all it would take was for a few people like Hao to begin striking it rich here before hundreds or even thousands of other Chinese, drawn by word of mouth—and by the lack of elbow room and opportunity in their own country—started pulling up stakes and peopling the Mozambican countryside.

I already knew that dreams like these were built upon a dangerous illusion. Africa was said to possess as much as 60 percent of the world's uncultivated arable land, which helped account for why the countryside looked so empty and so unworked in so many parts of the continent. But there were a dozen reasons why this was misleading, ranging from traditional farming methods in widespread use across the continent that leave large swaths of land fallow (so as to allow them to recover their fertility), and tenure patterns in which land is owned collectively and control is vested in local chiefs or kings, which until recently had kept land usage under tight rein.

The most powerful reason to doubt this illusion of abundance, however, had nothing to do with such practices, nor even with the past. Rather, it had everything to do with Africa's future. Whatever land was not claimed or routinely worked now was likely to begin coming under heavy demand in the space of a generation, as the continent's population skyrockets.

Hao roused himself when we pulled into a gas station at the entrance to a town called Xai-Xai, and he was quickly back to his non-stop talking self again.

"The most important thing to give your children is not your money. The most important thing is experience, and opportunity," he said, apropos of nothing.

It was an Engen station, part of a big South African chain, and the signs and pumps and even the station building itself were painted in a blinding white monochrome that shone with the brilliance of the sun. The penetration of foreign companies like this into Mozambique represented a huge break from the country's sad past, which had involved enduring war, and essentially having Portugal as its sole economic partner, a monopoly position that enforced the bleakest possible terms of exchange. This meant that almost all of the country's imports had to be sourced through the colonial power at uncompetitive and inflated prices, and that all of its exports in raw, unprocessed goods like cashews and other agricultural produce, tropical hardwoods, and fish would be sold back to Portugal, at prices that Lisbon could dictate.

Whenever there was any meaningful foreign investment it, too, always came from Portugal, one of Western Europe's poorest countries, which had little to spare. Now, though, on the evidence of spanking new Engen stations like this one, and the big new supermarkets and chain stores that had been establishing themselves around Maputo, South African companies and their capital were also irrigating the economy. And as it happened, just across the road from the gas station sat another important sign of change—a dealer of small secondhand trucks from China that sat on a large, walled lot. It didn't look like much at first glance, but I knew better. Here, by chance, was an example of an early foothold that yet another foreign power, this one much further away but incomparably bigger than South Africa, had secured in Mozambique. And just as surely, the farm I was on my way to visit, Hao's new frontier outpost, was another.

Being down on Africa and its prospects has never been difficult, but this scene reflected an optimistic view that was rapidly gaining ground. It held that Africa was in the grips of momentous and historic change, transitioning fast from its longtime status as neglected stepchild of the global economy to becoming one of its most heavily courted regions, and this turnabout was increasingly being driven by Chinese invest-ment and demand. Year on year, China's trade with Africa was growing by as much as 20 percent, and had recently surpassed its trade with both Europe and the United States.

For decades, liberal Western economists had promised that Africa would advance when it could attract deep-pocketed foreigners from richer countries who coveted its assets, and boosted trade, while show-ering the continent with infusions of capital and technology. Some said that Mozambique, where things were undoubtedly speeding up, was already caught up in this process, on the strength of interest from China. The country was finally globalizing, and, they argued, ahead lay progress.

When we pulled out onto the road again after filling up, Hao told me of his early days in the country. He had flown to Maputo alone and wasn't greeted at its airport by anyone. "I didn't understand a fucking word that was being said to me," he said. On his own, he made his way into town and found a flophouse for temporary lodging. Making little headway—he spoke neither Portuguese nor English—he soon gave in to the temptation to call up some fellow Chinese he had found online while still in China.

"I thought if I met a few people I could distract myself a bit, learn about the situation from them, and then figure out how to get hold of some land. But I quickly discovered that not all Chinese people are your friends. The Chinese folks here, or at least a portion of them, a big portion of them, are really bad characters. They are looking for a way to get ahold of some of your money. Yeah, they'll do anything for you, but they won't do anything for free. It's all about money."

Hao fleshed out a picture of how he had naively loaned money to various Chinese people he had met who seemed to have fallen on hard times in Maputo, and had offered to help guide him. A few months after arriving in the country, and having been burned from all of these encounters, he decided to set off alone for the countryside, following the very route we were pursuing northward. When he had traversed two provinces, reaching the south-centrally located Inhambane province, a major focus of the Arab slave trade centuries earlier, he said he contacted the provincial government about acquiring land, and they directed him to local governments. When he found one that was receptive, he set about ingratiating himself to local officials by helping on road and bridge repair projects.

"I took charge of the work all by myself, operating equipment and supervising work crews," he said proudly. "And in the end, I was able to secure a piece of land; a big piece of land."

Big indeed: for a relative pittance he had won control of roughly five thousand acres. The land had been part of a large, abandoned colonial-era Portuguese plantation. A river flowed nearby, and irrigation canals cut back and forth, gridlike, across a fertile plain.

Before doing anything with the land, he said he had been obliged to clear years of heavy overgrowth, wild with thick grasses, weeds, bushes, and vines. Indeed, he had had to cut it back three times, he told me, because after he had done so the first time, using a tractor he had purchased especially for the task, he made the mistake of leaving his fecund tropical earth unattended for too long. Returning from a season of travels around the country, prospecting for business opportunities in other regions, he had been startled to find the place completely overgrown again.

Hao told me that once he had repaired the irrigation canals, he began testing crops on a modest plot adjacent to his temporary dwelling, and with great relish he insisted that everything he tried planting had done very well. Among the many rich possibilities for cash crops, he listed tea, sugar, and tobacco. Above all, though, he was fixated on stevia, a genus of shrub native to tropical parts of the Americas, whose leaves contain a natural sweetener that is widely used as a sugar substitute. The dream, he said, was to export it to the United States and to Europe, selling it to companies like Coca-Cola and Pepsi.

In purely economic terms, Hao knew he had scored a big coup, but it wasn't long before he had other things to worry about. He hadn't invested much thought into who lived on the land or controlled it before he came along, or even who his neighbors were. After a period of warm enough hospitality, the people from nearby villages began to question him about how he had gotten ahold of the land and asked him for compensation, with some of them claiming the area was an ancestral holding.

"The local people are really not friendly. They are peasants and they resent the idea that the government took their land and gave it to us. They have no land for themselves. They're not comfortable. They are working for us, and they are not comfortable with it. In fact, the Mozambique government has given us land, but it's not forever. After a few years, once we've put the land to good use, perhaps they will take another tack and try to reclaim it from us, but we've got our own ideas; we're also making plans."

The first person plural had been creeping into his banter, but only now did its significance become clear.

"Right now I am bringing my children here," he said. "My older son, my younger son, eventually my daughter. I'm taking them out of school in China and bringing them all here. Within the next ten or so years we need to raise enough money, and then if my son has a lot of offspring with local girls, my two sons, in fact, if they've had lots of children, well what do the children become? Are they Chinese or Mozambicans?"

Hao issued a deep, mirthful laugh at his own cleverness, as he told me his older son already had a live-in girlfriend. Then he proceeded to answer his own question. "The mothers are Mozambicans, but the land will be within our family. Do you get it? This means that because the children will be Mozambicans they can't treat us as foreigners. If need be we can even put the property in their name, protectively, but it will remain ours. It will be in my clan."

Yes, but what would become of these children of his? I asked. Forgoing education ran counter to one of the strongest cultural stereotypes of the Chinese, their famed obsession with the betterment of their offspring through ever more schooling.

"Chemistry, physics, mathematics, they don't really require such things, wouldn't you say?" Hao responded, brushing off my question. "English is what they need. What we need to focus on is foreign trade, and all they need for that is a calculator; a calculator, plus the ability to speak languages. That way they can do business and deal with customs officials."

By now, Hao was bubbling over with enthusiasm for his scheme. "I can use my little daughter to be my translator," he said. "I'll let her study for a couple of more years and then bring her here."

I pointed out that his young daughter wouldn't be fully literate in her own language when she came to Africa, a sacrifice many other Chinese would find inconceivable, but he brushed this off, too. "There are too many people already who know how to write Chinese," he said, and laughed again.

Hao said that his older son had been with him on his newly acquired land for about half a year now. His younger son, fourteen years old, had joined them a few weeks earlier. "The older boy is doing fine already," he said, with evident pride. "He's doing a lot of training."

"Training?"

"I'm guiding him," he said. "It's not hard physical labor. I have to encourage him, have him fool around a bit, catch some fish, shoot a gun, hunt some birds. Boom, boom! That way he'll be happy. He already shoots well."

I told him that his son's experience seemed to mirror the way youth were treated in the Cultural Revolution, when schools were closed and young people were "sent down" by the millions to work alongside peasants in the countryside.

"Exactly! That's how I was raised. I was sent down and it changed me for the better. Young people in China today no longer learn how to *chi ku*," he said. His expression, one of the most basic to Chinese popular culture, literally means to "eat bitter," in order to endure great hardships. "I want my son to become a real man, a worthy person."

I asked Hao how many children he had and he answered five, a stunning number in a country where most families were officially limited to one child. Perhaps sensing my reaction, he said, "I've got three wives. That's not counting the ones who haven't given me children."

Hao was proving to be a man with a strategy for most everything. When I asked him how it was possible to be married to three women in China, his face broke into a wicked grin. "I can't be married to them legally all at once, but we've made arrangements. I divorced the first one to marry the second one, and divorced the second one to marry the third, who is quite young. I remain with all three of them, though, and have given each of them a company to run in her own name. The Fujian wife has my Fujian business, the Henan wife has my Henan business, and the Shandong wife has my Shandong business, and they're all happy. Every year or two I'll go home and see them. I don't bother them. I don't interfere in their lives. I don't worry about them spending money or even cheating on me. They're very happy."

I imagined that he had done the customary thing among many successful middle-aged men and gone for youthful beauty, marrying a trophy wife, but he shook off that suggestion. "My first two wives were quite good-looking," he said. "It wasn't until I got a little older that I came to understand that this was the least important consideration. The third time, I married the smartest woman I could find. She has a real genius for business. Everything she gets involved in does well."

Hao's problem was that it was proving impossible to persuade her to join him in Mozambique, not to mention to live on a homestead in the middle of nowhere. He had also tried hard to persuade his brother, a low-level Communist Party official in Henan.

"He's not willing to come here. He is a man without goals. Drinking, that's about it."

Hao had also tried cajoling several friends to come, offering to pay their way and even provide jobs for them.

"For most Chinese people, if they have enough to eat and a little money in their pocket they are satisfied," he said, the disgust palpable. "They're not ambitious. They have no sense of adventure." In my experience, that had certainly not been the case.

I was curious about the response of Hao's sons to his scheme to secure control of his new land through a kind of sexual colonization. I waded into the subject delicately, asking if his older son had had girlfriends in China before.

"In China my son didn't know anything about girls, nothing at all. He'd never had a girlfriend."

How then had he managed to choose one here so quickly?

"There is no standard. It's enough that she be willing. Any girl must be willing to cook and to wash clothes. She is there to serve us. We'll teach her and if she does well, then great. If not, we won't need her anymore.

"The other thing, of course, is to have children. Lots of children. That way we'll have people who can serve in each and every occupation we need, you know? Successors."

"You mean members of your family?" I inquired, just to be sure I was hearing right.

"Yes, they will all be members of the family: drivers, salespeople, foreign trade agents. No matter what we need, we'll have it. There will be nothing we can't do."

"So does this mean you'll stay here forever?" I asked him.

"That's the way things stand right now," he said. "But soon, I will also be bringing in some Chinese farmers and agricultural experts. I'll have them help me run things." He told me that the Chinese man he had trouble finding in Maputo that morning was one of the people he was trying to recruit.

A couple of hours after filling up, we dropped John off at the main square of Maxixe, a little drive-through town that nonetheless enjoys a status as economic capital of Inhambane. John, who was from Maxixe, spoke happily about being able to sleep at home with his family after several days away. His main employers, a group of road builders from Henan, like Hao, who shared a house just off the narrow main road, were in Maxixe, too.

Night was falling fast, and I enjoyed a rare chance to stretch my legs and take pictures amid a lively street scene filled with merchants and customers haggling furiously as townspeople hurried to make their last evening purchases. I spied a Chinese couple I thought to be in their early thirties who ran a shop set diagonally across from a small and jewel-like old colonial-era church.

They told me they were natives of Fujian, a mountainous, hard-to-farm, and hence historically poor coastal province in southeastern China that has generated a disproportionate number of Chinese migrants overseas during the last two generations. They said they had been in Maxixe for a couple of years already, selling a wide assortment of goods, including candles, cigarettes, simple medicines, soft drinks and beer, pots and pans, and cheap toys. The window of their little shop sat behind rebar reinforcements. It gave the place the feeling of a cave.

When I caught up with Hao, where John had parked the pickup, just down the street, I was invited into the home of his Henan friends. He introduced them as his *lao xiang,* an expression Chinese use to refer to people from their hometown or region, a concept that resonates deeply for many overseas Chinese. There were four of them, living in a modern, one-story villa with a large living room and kitchen in the back, from which emanated the very distinct aromas of a home-cooked Chinese dinner. In the living room, which had the cluttered and slightly unkempt feeling of a frat house, two men and a woman were hunched in nearly identical poses over laptop computers, each at his own cheap desk, connecting with friends in China via QQ, an Internet message and phone service, near universally subscribed to among Chinese, that combines features of chat and Skype.

I secretly hoped that we would be invited for dinner. The traditionally generous hospitality I was accustomed to from Chinese people seemed to make this a safe bet, but no invitation came to pass. Hao talked business with one of the Henan road men in an adjacent bedroom and then we were on our way, with Hao now at the wheel. His banter picked up again as he spoke of the utility of having friends, especially *lao xiang* like this, living nearby.

"I've only gotten sick once since I've been here, but it was malaria, and it was a very bad case," he told me. "I usually come through this town once every week or so, but there was one time when I didn't show up for a long while and I'm lucky that they came looking for me. I was laid out flat on my back at my farm, all alone, sweating and shivering there in my own vomit. They took me right away to the hospital, and I'm told that this saved my life."

I asked him about the Fujian couple who operated the little shop I had visited and he mumbled something in halfhearted response. Why hadn't he even paused to exchange pleasantries with them? "We're just not the same," he said, with the impatient look of someone explaining the obvious. "Everyone knows Fujian people are no good."

When I expressed surprise that they had set up shop in such a little place, Hao laughed gruffly and said one could find Chinese people in every town in Mozambique, and even in most of the country's villages, and that the majority of them were Fujianese.

There was an irony in Hao's stereotyping. Among Chinese, people from Hao's own Henan province bear one of the heaviest stigmas: of a reputed propensity for cheating, dishonesty, and quarrelsomeness. Hao himself frequently referred to the toughness of Henan people, usually while bragging about how he feared no one and would never back down in a dispute. But later, whenever I told a Chinese person that I had met a businessman from Henan in Mozambique, it was likely he or she would respond with a little cringe, as if bracing for a negative story that would tar all overseas Chinese with a broad brush; others tried to disarm me with jokes about the supposed roughness and ill breeding of Henan people.

The totemic statistic thrown around about recent Chinese migration to the continent, even though it had no firm source, was one million over the last decade. The Chinese government's statistics about the country's involvement with Africa were in fact both sparse and vague. High on my list of priorities was an attempt to determine if that number was roughly accurate.

Hao was driving on a road hugging the Indian Ocean coast which was lit brightly by a full moon. Not having eaten since breakfast, I interrupted Hao's storytelling to ask if we could stop for food. He protested, saying that since there was little traffic on the road, if we pressed onward, we would arrive soon.

This exchange took place as we were entering another town perhaps half an hour beyond Maxixe. Hao insisted he didn't know the place, but warned that we were unlikely to find anything to eat there. At that moment, just ahead of us, I saw three men standing in a cluster talking by the roadside. Impulsively, I asked Hao to pull up alongside them. When he did, I opened my window and asked, in Spanish, if there were a small restaurant or a place to buy snacks nearby. The man closest to the pickup peered into the vehicle through my window and, seeing Hao, exclaimed that there was a Chinese woman right here in their little hamlet who kept a shop and sold food. It wouldn't be difficult to find, he insisted, pointing to an unlit dirt road on the other side of the highway, which he told us to follow until we reached another path that would lead us to the rear of the buildings we could see in the middle distance. I thanked the men and we turned off the highway as instructed.

There was no obvious sign of a shop when we reached the darkened, sandy lot behind the buildings we had been directed to. I knew Hao's patience was running thin, so I jumped out of the car and called out *Ni hao, ni hao,* in what felt like a desperate, even comic bid to raise a response. As I stood in the bright glow of his headlights, Hao began honking his horn, as much at me, I thought, as at anyone who might be lurking inside the lifeless-seeming buildings. The instant he relented, though, noises could be heard emanating from a plain one-story house off to the side of the lot. *"Shenme shi,"* came a Chinese woman's voice with a sibilant accent, suggesting a southerner. It was full of irritation. "What's going on?" she asked.

Another moment later, a woman of medium height in her late twenties appeared in the doorway and began unlocking a second metal, cagelike security door. Her hair was cut very short and she was dressed in cutoffs and a white-and-pale-blue soccer jersey against the warm and damp evening air. Startled, Hao jumped out of his Toyota and approached rapidly. "I pass through this town all the time, and I didn't know there was a Chinese person living here!" he exclaimed. "I'm traveling with an American journalist who is trying to meet Chinese people. He would like to interview you."

It was a rushed, awkward introduction that I would rather have handled myself, and the woman responded with a curt, "No, thank you," and began to turn on her heels.

"It's not an interview," I said hurriedly. "I'd just like to exchange a few words with you. How long have you been here?"

She answered, "Two years." I asked whom she had come with, and then she repeated her initial question, with more annoyance: "What's going on here?"

Worried our encounter was about to end I tried desperately to loosen her up, telling her that I had lived in Shanghai for five years, and that I pegged her voice as that of a southerner.

"Yes, I'm from Fujian," she answered. "From Shantou."

"That's a city I've visited several times," I told her, hoping to establish a connection. I could make out the noise of a TV playing inside her house and apologized for disturbing her. "Are you watching something good?" I asked.

She said she was watching DVDs from back home, and added that living alone there was little else to do.

I expressed admiration for her pluck for getting by in such a remote little place like this by herself, but she refused the compliment. "It's nothing," she said. "I'm just a trader."

Hao told her I was looking for food, but she said that all she had was potato chips and other such snacks. That didn't do much for me, and besides, I wanted to hear as much from her as I could before the encounter was over.

The young woman told us that she sold electronic goods, household supplies, odds and ends. How had she decided to come to Africa, or to Mozambique? I asked.

"I came with my mother, but she has gone back. We discovered the country online. It seemed like a stable place. They seemed to be friendly to Chinese people."

These were answers I would hear hundreds of times in the months to come as my own picture of the numbers of recent migrants from China to Africa began to fill out.

"How's business?" I asked her, bombarding her with questions in quick succession now, hoping to prevent her from breaking off the conversation.

"Not so good."

"How did you end up in such a tiny place as this?"

"They didn't have any shopkeepers," she said. "I only had enough money saved up to open a small shop. I couldn't afford a bigger store in a city."

"How do you get your supplies? Where do they come from?"

"I don't have a car. I rely on other people from Fujian to help me. There are folks driving north and south all the time, and they keep me resupplied."

She told me her little settlement was called Marumbene, and I asked how many people lived here.

"Not many," she said.

"Ten thousand?"

"I don't think there's that many people here. Who knows?"

"Are the people friendly?"

"I didn't come here to make friends."

Things continued this way between us for a bit more.

"Do you miss home?" I asked.

"I'm talking to people back home all the time on QQ."

"Can you speak the local language?"

"I speak Portuguese well enough to get by. The black people here have their own language. I can't speak that."

"Why did you leave China?"

"I had to make a living," she said, turning and disappearing into her house without so much as a wave or a word of good-bye.

As soon as Hao and I got back on the road, he expressed annoyance that I had made him stop. He said he was tired and he complained, cursing the whole time, about having to drive at night. He'd spent most of the day trying to impress me with his professed Henan toughness. Now the dark roads were making him nervous.

I tried to change his mood by coaxing stories out of him about his life and past. From his age and from his references to "eating bitter" during the Cultural Revolution, I knew Hao to be a member of the Lost Generation, a group that included people in their late forties to early sixties who had grown up in the bygone era of the iron rice bowl, with its expectation of cradle-to-grave socialism. When China opened up and turned capitalist in the early 1980s, members of that group were too old to recover from the deprivations of the most radical period of Maoism, which had lasted from 1966 to 1976. It was a time when higher education, and even secondary school for many, was interrupted and the country was plunged into political and social turmoil. Unlike the overwhelming majority of his age cohorts from undistinguished back-grounds, though, Hao had thrived in spite of his generation's unlucky timing.

As he warmed to the subject of his youth, Hao told me that his formal schooling had ended in junior high school. He had been a neighborhood tough, and then a member of a gang, and had segued from that perch to become the leader of a brigade of Red Guards in his native Henan. In his early twenties, he said his group was tasked with smashing Buddhist temples, burning religious books and scripture, and destroying their relics.

"I've beaten up a lot of people in my day," he said, matter-of-factly. "I may look old, but even now I don't fear any fucking man."

Now and again, Hao made references to God. After our last stop, when I'd asked him for the first time how he had decided to come to Africa, he replied tersely, "God's plan." It wasn't so often, in my experience, that Chinese people resorted to divine explanations for things. Most often when Hao had invoked God, it seemed less the voice of reverence than it did the kind of punctuation the word takes on in much English-language profanity. I asked him if he believed in a deity, and if he had any remorse or fear of punishment for the violence and destruction of his past.

"A God surely exists, but I figure it's like this," he answered, now waxing philosophical. "With so many people to watch over, he must be very busy. He's already working himself to death. Do you think God has time for me?"

The full moon had risen high in the sky, chasing off the blackness Hao had so feared, and we had begun slicing through little townships every few minutes as the population density of the area increased. There were drive-by glimpses of prayer vigils in clapboard churches; smoky, ramshackle saloons filled with garrulous drinkers; women sitting by the roadside wrapped in printed cloth, hunched, half asleep over storm lanterns as they awaited nighttime buyers for their wares. All this activity signaled a city was nearby.

Hao soon announced with relief that we were about to enter Massinga, the nearest city to his farm. I returned to the question of how he had chosen to settle in Mozambique in the first place.

"I went to an African trade fair in Fujian province and there were lots of Chinese businesspeople there," he said. "I got excited by all the talk of business opportunities in Africa. Later, I figured my English is no good, though, so I got the idea that if I went to an English-speaking country, English being a popular language, Chinese people would be everywhere.

"Mozambique is a Portuguese-speaking country, though. This might bring me luck. I'll be damned if I understood Portuguese, but damnit, I figured, neither do most Chinese people in general, so what the fuck? There must be great undiscovered opportunities there, and I won't have to be constantly looking over my shoulder for other Chinese people coming to compete with me, cheat me out of my money, or steal my ideas."

If God had a plan for Hao, as he liked to say, his own criteria for a Promised Land sounded strictly practical. It should be a place not only where opportunity reigned, but crucially, where Chinese people were few. Outsiders are awed by China's extraordinary economic growth over the last thirty years, during which time its GDP had increased tenfold. But along with that growth has come cutthroat competitiveness and grinding stress in daily life that many find unbearable, and which drove many Chinese to leave the country. Time and again, Chinese told me they did not fully realize *how* oppressive things were at home until after they had left. Living in Africa, they said, it felt as if a lid had been removed from a pressure cooker. Now they could breathe.

Hao was the first person I had met, however, who had chosen his destination in Africa because he believed there would be few Chinese there. He was a new kind of frontiersman, and I would meet many others like him. Collectively they challenged another common image about the Chinese, who were held to be a reflexively insular people who constitute self-enclosed communities wherever they go.

As we pulled into Massinga, Hao announced, almost sheepishly, a major change of plans. Instead of driving straight to his homestead he had decided to have me sleep at a cheap hotel instead. He had been unable to reach his son, he said, to make sure there was dinner waiting for us, and by dropping me off, I'd be sure to have an evening meal.

We were both exhausted by the time we reached the roadside hotel, a sprawling and charmless one-story affair, hidden behind a high cement wall, that doubled as nightclub and brothel. I dragged my bags into one of the hotel's shabby rooms and unpacked a bit. Before locking the door and rejoining Hao, I pulled the windows to my room closed to keep out the swarming mosquitoes and sprayed the place with insecticide.

I found Hao pacing in the courtyard. The two of us sat outside at a cheap plastic table with an exposed bulb that dangled above us and ordered a late dinner. While we waited for the food, he asked me at least for the third time that day about my itinerary. I told him I'd just been in Ethiopia, which produced a look of deep puzzlement, and that the next country I would visit was Namibia.

"What is Namibia?" he asked.

I drew him a crude map in my spiral notebook. "Ethiopia is up here," I said, pointing to the continent's northeastern shoulder. "Mozambique is here. And Namibia is over here. It's on the Atlantic coast." Hao wanted to know how far away that placed Namibia from where we were. Several hundred miles, I said.

I started to fill in the map to show him some of the other countries I planned to visit. When I sketched Senegal's position, at the continent's furthest point west, I decided to give him a little more context and added Europe, tracing its downward slope toward Africa that culminates in the Iberian Peninsula.

"Here is Portugal," I said, which produced another look of confusion. He asked me what Portugal was exactly. It was the colonial power that once controlled Mozambique, I told him. As he nodded, still looking uncertain, I added that it was the place where the Portuguese language came from.

He knew that Mozambique had been a European colony, a *zhimindi,* but he had not known it had been Portugal's colony. "I thought Portuguese came from Brazil," he said.

I drew South America on the map for him, separated, as one would expect, by a large blank expanse for the Atlantic Ocean, and told him that Brazil, too, had been a Portuguese colony.

Hao began making some connections, thinking of Macau, the tiny formerly Portuguese enclave near Hong Kong. "Son of a bitch," he exclaimed. "You wonder how the fuck little countries like Portugal controlled so many big, faraway countries? It's just like the way the Europeans carved up China, I suppose." After a pause, he asked: "Where is America?"

I sketched North America onto my crude and now crowded map, and Hao was astounded to learn that it was not of a piece with Europe, as he had always assumed.

Hao's geographical curiosity waned and the conversation shifted back to his African ambitions, which apparently went far beyond his new farm. "I've got lots of other plans, lots of projects," he said. "I want to open a beverage factory. I also want to produce tea for sale and for export that will be grown on our own land." There was also talk about building a charcoal-processing factory that he had already broken ground for two hundred kilometers further to the north. It would produce honeycombed braziers for cooking. At first, he said, these would be sold only here in Mozambique but later, he speculated, the export potential back to China, and perhaps around the world, would be very great.

By the time Hao took leave of me it was pushing eleven. He said he would be back for me very early; could I be ready by 7 a.m.?

I set my alarm clock for 6:30, but was awake by six, my sleep shortened by the sound of women drawing water noisily from a spigot near my window. I had a quick, cold shower, which was all that was on offer in the dingy bathroom, which was so small there was hardly space to stand between the toilet and shower stall. Then I pulled my things together quickly and lugged my suitcases out to the restaurant area so that I would be ready to leave the instant Hao pulled up.

I was surprised to find the sunshine so powerful at this early hour as I sat down to take coffee, a half loaf of French bread, and fried eggs for breakfast. As I ate, a young girl entered the hotel courtyard with a bucket on her head, soon followed by a woman doing the same thing. They squatted by the faucet a few feet from my window and took turns filling their buckets and hoisting them atop their heads before gingerly duckwalking back outside, as rivulets of spilled water trickled down their torsos.

Hao appeared at the hotel entrance a little before seven, wearing his now familiar grumpy expression as he beckoned to me with a wave of his hand that suggested impatience. As we headed out, in the light of day I could see for the first time that the place I'd slept, Allegre, was a truck stop hotel, evidenced by the tractor-trailers parked all around the entrance. At this early hour a stretch of road in both directions was given over to a lively street market, and there were hundreds of people in the streets, including traders who were already touting their wares and uniformed children on their way to school.

As we drove northward out of Massinga, Hao's talkativeness of the previous day had been transformed into clipped and almost grudging answers to my questions. After we were waved through a roadblock at the northern edge of town, he pulled over suddenly. He said he didn't enjoy driving, and asked if I would take over. With me at the wheel, we proceeded in a vaguely eastward direction down a graded trunk road, which soon led us past a tiny settlement where a cluster of people by the roadside gave us a halfhearted wave.

Beyond this dusty outpost lay a world of dense, tangled bush punctuated now and then by a neatly swept clearing, where there was a solitary shack made of brilliant sheets of aluminum.

The road had narrowed considerably and the smoothness of its first leg had given way to an obstacle course of divots and tree stumps and the occasional peasant balancing huge loads of scavenged wood atop his head. Hao instructed me to stop up ahead, where I could see the road cresting beneath a stand of oil palms in the distance. When I reached that point, we came upon a group of men sitting and standing in conversation among themselves at the edge of a cleared field. Hao stuck his head out of his passenger's side window and began barking in his unique and polyglot pidgin: *"Ganma, ganma, zheli, trabalho, ganma? Wei shenme?"* What are you doing? What are you doing? Here, work. What are you doing? Why?

The local men gestured off into the distance and answered that someone else was paying better now. This was a showdown over wages, a walkout. "Why should you pay us differently?" one of the Mozambican men said, challenging him.

Hao grew excited and started to curse. He was saying, mostly in Chinese, that he was not going to raise their pay. The two sides went back and forth like this for a few minutes. Hao was sweating profusely, wiping his brow with a hand towel. "Forget it. I don't need you," he said. "I'll find other workers." With that, the men picked up their belongings and trudged away, heading off in the direction we had just come from.

Hao laughed even as he continued to swear. "Africans like nothing better than to get together and complain," he said. "My son told me we don't need these people any longer, though. Why should we pay them more?"

From that point on, the path grew steadily rougher, forcing me to twist and turn sharply. Then, less than five minutes later, with no forewarning from Hao, his new homestead appeared around a bend. At his instruction, I parked the pickup right there in the clearing, a few yards

from the temporary dwellings that he now called home. They were two
shacks, really, thrown together roughly with poles, canvas, straw mats,
and whatever other cheap materials were at hand. The French would
call this kind of place a *campement*. We climbed out of the vehicle into
the heat and light.

Next to one of the dwellings a thin, dark-skinned woman with long
braids stirred a pot slowly over three stout sections of roughly hewn
tree branches that smoldered in a pit. Off to the side, another young
woman, heavyset, buxom and short-haired, squatted sullenly by what
I took at first to be a small creek, washing pots and pans in the stream.

Hao walked over and removed a burning twig to light his cigarette.
He did not introduce the women to me. A minute or two later, a plump
boy of about fourteen emerged from one of the huts, buttoning his
shirt. Hao identified him as his *"lao er,"* or second son, as he called him
in lieu of a name. "Old number two."

Like us, the boy was sweating heavily. It was only 8:30 a.m. but I
guessed the temperature was already well above ninety degrees.

"Where's your brother?" Hao asked him.

"He's gone hunting," came the reply.

The boy, whose name I would later learn was Chuan, had sensitive
eyes but wore a put-upon look that suggested a difficult relationship
with his father. Indeed, moments later, as Chuan wandered to the edge
of the clearing, not quite far enough to be out of earshot, Hao began
grumbling about him.

"While Little Fatty is lying around playing fucking games, his
brother is off hunting. That's what he should be doing, too. I need the
boy to grow up and to get with it."

I felt bad for Chuan, and at the risk of playing the meddler suggested to Hao that it takes time to grow up.

"I want to introduce him to girls, but he has no interest at all," he
said. "He's too soft. He doesn't understand anything."

Moments later, a junky old sedan lurched into the clearing. It was
the older brother, Yang, who emerged with a triumphant air, carrying
a shotgun and a pheasant, which he hoisted upside down by the feet.
When he approached, I said *"Ni hao,"* and there was a moment's pause
while he registered that the foreigner has addressed him in Chinese.
"Ni hao," he said, but nothing more. Yang, whose hair hung thick and

wild, almost shoulder length, fairly strutted about the clearing shirt-less, with his sinewy build and wispy facial hair.

While Hao looked on with evident pride, Yang delivered the bird to the thin woman tending the fire, tapped her butt in a gesture equally playful and possessive, and then ordered her to deplume the bird and prepare it for lunch. Before she could begin, he barked at her again, this time to say he was thirsty and to command her to chop open some coconuts. *"Mais, mais, mais"* (More), he demanded, as she lopped off the top of first one, then two other coconuts. He emptied them with gusto.

Without explanation, the father wandered off, which gave me a chance to introduce myself properly to the boys and talk with them. Yang confirmed that he had been there for six months. I asked him how he liked it.

"It's too hot," he said, answering without hesitation. "I wanted to cry when I first got here."

I wanted to know about his girlfriend, whose name, Delima, I had overheard in their conversation. She had disappeared to the other side of the hut with her friend.

"The women here are too black. Actually they are different colors, different shades of black, but to us they are all dark."

Yang said in China he had never had a girlfriend. I asked him how he had met Delima, and he ignored my question.

"When I first got here I discovered that the girls fear us," he said. "The blacks think that Chinese people eat humans!" He recounted his first day in the area, when he stopped amid a street crowd in Massinga and lowered his car window only to have people run away in fear. I could only imagine his perplexity. For thousands of years, Chinese had called people on their frontier barbarians, and now the stereotype had been reversed.

It was not easy to get the boy to engage with me. He preferred to emulate his father's coarseness in ordering the women about and administering playful slaps and threats of harsher measures, which pro-duced sulking in the short-haired girl and game retorts from Delima, who knew better how to defend her ground.

The younger son, Chuan, seemed more thoughtful, but he was just as hard to draw out, and spoke with me in substance only when no one else was around. In those rare moments I learned that math was his best subject, that he missed his favorite TV shows, and that he longed to go back to school in China.

Hao now beckoned to me in the distance, eager to show me around the place where God's plan had landed him. Out back beyond the huts lay his experimental garden, a handful of acres where he was already growing stevia, tea, and a variety of Chinese vegetables. He plucked some of the stevia leaves and crumpled them in his hand and urged me to taste them, which I did; the effect they produced was an instant and overpowering sweetness.

We circled back around the huts and wandered into a large open plain, all of which he said was his. The dark, pliant soil was criss-crossed with irrigation canals, one of which I'd mistaken for a creek. Hao pointed out the concrete blocks that could be seen here and there sunken in the muck of the channels. He explained that they were the remnants of a system of locks that had been built by the Portuguese when they controlled the land before independence.

"They built all of this and then they left it," he said in evident puzzlement over why anyone would give up land so rich. "When we first arrived, even our tractors had trouble passing here. I had to employ a lot of blacks to clear the fields, and I had to clear them three times before the bush would finally yield." With that, he fixed me with a fierce expression and offered his best measure of himself. "Some of the Chinese who have come to work the land in this country under sun this strong have failed," he said. "Others before them have failed, too. But for me, there is no such thing as failure. I am no ordinary man."

Hao was walking briskly now, leading me in the direction of a structure that loomed in the distance, perhaps a half mile away. The site was shaded by a few large trees, and several African men could be seen milling about. As we walked, he announced the place would be his new home—a house being built on a grand scale. He had employed the principles of feng shui in selecting the site and in orienting the building. Once the home was completed, he said, others would be built nearby, houses for his sons and their families and housing for managers who would come from China.

The outer walls of the house were already standing about ten feet high around most of the perimeter. As we entered the site, Hao grew animated again, shouting at the workers, threatening to dock the pay of those he had found sitting in the shade, cajoling others, and delivering commands about where to place the window frames to the thin, shirtless man of about twenty-five who seemed to function as foreman.

As I walked through the small grove of trees that would eventually provide shade for the house's entrance, I encountered a man who had just wheeled a heavy load of sand into place with a wheelbarrow. His body glistened with sweat. When I asked about his job, he immediately began grousing. Within a minute or so two other workers had joined him, and they echoed each other's complaints. They didn't mind so much that Hao was a hard taskmaster; it was the pay that rankled. I did the math quickly in my head when they gave me a figure and found that if their numbers were true, Hao was employing eight men on the site for nine hours at just under $10 a day total.

A few minutes later Hao and I walked back to the *campement* together. I asked him how much the workers were paid and he proudly gave me the same numbers they had. It became clear he saw this as a mark of his good fortune and business sense, as he recounted a story about buying coconuts.

"Did you know coconuts cost 1 metical here and 15 in Maputo?" he said, laughing. "Big or small, it's all the same. Well, the people selling them sometimes come to me and ask for 3 meticals, and then 2, and I shake my head and refuse. Finally, I'll walk away, but they always come running after me and I get them for 1 metical apiece!"

When we reached the huts, lunch was nearly ready and the fragrance of the freshly killed bird and the sauce it was stewing in hung sweetly in the air. When Hao saw me taking pills for a bad chest cold, he went into his dwelling and reemerged with a big jar of thick, dark honey, which he said he had bottled himself. He swore it was the only "medicine" he used, apart from tea, which he drank constantly, and he urged me to swallow a couple of large spoonfuls three times a day.

Hao and his boys wandered off to the other side of the huts, which left me alone with the women for the first time. The two shared a single wooden chair a few feet from the fireplace, where they sat to keep an eye on a pot of noodles. Admira, the plump one, had looked angry ever since she was spoken to roughly by both Hao and Yang. Delima was pure equanimity, though, and gave away little behind her enigmatic smile and intelligent eyes. I asked them in my makeshift Portuguese if the Hao family were good people. "I don't know," Delima answered so quickly that it seemed to foreclose any follow-up.

In the event, the others appeared in the next instant and called for lunch, which we ate sitting together in the sweltering heat. I was given a mug of hot tea and a plate of food that was delicious; the women had adopted Chinese cuisine remarkably well. Yang finished his plate first, filled his mug from the little stream by the hut, and drank the water in one draft. I had seen tiny minnows in the water, along with insects skating on the surface. Such a practice couldn't be safe, I thought. Hao dismissed my concern out of hand. "In small quantities it can't harm you," he said.

Chuan, the younger son, had remained quiet the whole time. When he had finished eating he promptly disappeared with his brother, and as the women began to clean up, I peppered Hao for more details about life here.

"How do you celebrate Chinese New Year?" I asked.

"We don't," he answered; they had forgone the most important holiday in the Chinese calendar.

The original plan had been for me to stay on at least one night, and maybe two, with Hao and his family, and then to ride back with him to Maputo. Within the space of a few minutes, however, something had stirred in Hao to make him suggest that he take me back this very day. I wondered if I had offended him somehow but I couldn't find any cause. I was surprised and disappointed, but I made no attempt to resist. An hour or so later he and I piled back into the pickup with Admira, still looking sullen, riding in the middle of the front seat, between us.

As we bumped along the winding access road to his spread, with me again at the wheel, Hao told me we would pick up John at Maxixe and that he would hire a car to bring him back to the *campement*, allowing John to drive me back to Maputo. I didn't feel comfortable probing the change of plans and tried instead to explore the marriage questions that Hao's land scheme were predicated upon. How did one go about finding a wife here and what did the ceremony of marriage entail in rural Mozambique?

"It's very simple," he said. "You choose a woman and then you go and present a gift to her father—a little money, some cloth, some alcohol. You can buy a woman here for as little as 4,000 meticals [about $12]. That's all it costs."

I asked if he had some kind of relationship with Admira. "Yes, there's a bit of a relationship," he answered. Hao went from this admission straight into a discussion of sex with local women, calling it "different" and "strange."

"With Chinese women you have to caress her first, get her in the mood, you know; produce water," he said. "The ones here are not like that. You just make love to them straight away. It's no problem."

When we reached Massinga he wanted to make a quick stop in the midst of the same crowded street scene that had greeted us early that morning outside my hotel. When he climbed out of the pickup I was left alone with Admira, who had sat silently through our whole conversation, which had been in Chinese, sparing her. I turned toward her and asked if she had feelings for Hao, and she replied "No."

What about her friend Delima? Did she have feelings for Yang?

"I don't know," came the reply, more an evasion than an answer. "I just know that she won't marry him."

I asked Admira why this was, and she said, "Later," which seemed to indicate that it wasn't safe for her to talk with Hao nearby. At that point a market girl of about sixteen approached the car and began chatting with Admira in a mixture of Portuguese and the local language. She told Admira to ask Hao for 20 meticals for her, and then with a little complicit smile she raised her request to 50 and then to 100 meticals.

When he returned to the car the girl was still standing by his door, blocking his entrance. "*Shenme shi?*" Hao asked, roughly. What's going on? Admira told him the girl was her little sister and needed 100 meticals for an important purchase. Hao reached in his pocket and separated a couple of crunched-up bills from a balled wad and handed them over, exclaiming "motherfucker" in Chinese as he closed the door.

The return drive to Maxixe was far quicker than it had been the night before. On the way up the only scenery I'd seen was the low, quicksilver clouds at sunset that wafted swiftly by, borne on a steady, comfortable breeze. But in the brilliance of daylight the town was revealed to me as sitting beside a broad, turquoise bay, and as we entered Maxixe, I noticed a sign proclaiming that it sat astride the Tropic of Capricorn.

John was waiting for us at the house of the Henan road builders and took over at the wheel. After we filled up with gas, there was another sudden change of plans. Hao wanted me to hitch a ride back to Maputo, allowing him to return home with his car and driver. Again, I was taken aback but in no position to argue. Indeed, all in all, though he had revealed some of the qualities of a monster, he had been more than generous with me.

Hao jumped out of the pickup at the edge of town, where half a dozen tractor-trailers were parked and tried to talk their drivers into taking me aboard. After having no luck with them he tried flagging down a couple of trucks that rumbled by. There was much cursing, and amid his frustration he ordered John to pursue one of the trucks with the pickup and cut it off. John simply sat there, nodding to the music that was playing loudly in the cab. He had either not understood the command or he had coolly decided to ignore it.

"Motherfucker. Motherfucker," Hao sputtered at each escaping truck, jumping up and down as he cursed. I couldn't understand his agitation. I climbed out of the pickup and walked onto the road-bed, where I made a hailing motion to an approaching truck. When it stopped I asked the driver if he was going to Maputo. He said yes and immediately assented when I asked him if I could hitch a ride in exchange for a small payment. He pulled his old blue Freightliner off to the side of the road.

I returned to the pickup to collect my bags. Gathering my camera and backpack from the front seat, I pressed a modest sum of money into Admira's hand, which produced a soft smile on her hitherto taciturn face. I handed my bags up to the man who had been riding shotgun in the truck and then turned to the others to say my good-byes. I repeatedly expressed my gratitude to Hao for his hospitality, which he brushed off, saying, "It's nothing. It's nothing." Then I embraced him. For the tiniest instant he appeared to recoil but then accepted the gesture. I did the same with John, who had been good company throughout the ride up. Then I climbed aboard my new conveyance and waved good-bye as we lurched forward, the first few feet of a 375-kilometer drive to Maputo.

CHAPTER TWO

Behold the Future

The road north out of central Lusaka quickly transitions from a world of impressively broad avenues and fancy new commercial districts to a stop-and-start tour of desolate, overcrowded slums. There, half-dressed young men sit around glumly, seemingly lacking the motivation in the face of persistently high unemployment to even bother looking for work. When at last one reaches the highway that leads north to the Copper Belt it is the oncoming traffic that makes the strongest impression. It consists mostly of van after jam-packed van full of poor Zambians. They are overwhelmingly young and desperate to get off the land and they arrive in the capital with dreams of remaking their lives in the big city.

When most people think about China's relationship with Africa they reduce it to a single proposition: securing access to natural resources, of which Africa is the world's greatest storehouse. As one of the top copper-producing nations, Zambia, a landlocked country in southern Africa, is doubtlessly a very big part of that story. Today, China alone accounts for 40 percent of global copper demand. But there is a more farsighted motive, one overlooked in almost all the speculation about China's ambitions in Africa: to cultivate, or perhaps even create, future markets for China's export-oriented industries, markets that could one day pick up the slack from the aging consumers and debt-ridden economies of the West and of Japan.

Chinese diplomats, trade officials, and business executives all confirmed that, as did ordinary migrants who had pulled up stakes in places like Chengdu and Guangzhou to move to this continent. They were betting their personal savings that they could make a better living hitching a ride on Africa's future than they could back home, despite the torrid pace of China's own economic growth. Was this irrational exuberance on the part of these restless Chinese, or had they grasped a trend pointing to momentous change in a faraway part of the world long before the West had caught on?

Zambia had been in the vanguard of this gigantic movement of people. Chinese had been coming here in substantial numbers since the 1990s, earlier than to almost any other country on the continent. By now they numbered 100,000 or so by some estimates, making them one of China's biggest migrant communities in Africa. Only time would tell, of course, if this popular Chinese bet on the continent's future would pay off. What is known, though, is that a variety of economic indicators show that the fortunes of large numbers of Africans are improving dramatically and will likely continue to do so over the next decade or two, only faster. This is happening as a result of a variety of factors, especially increasing trade among Africans, and an intensification of services, including telecommunications, banking, and transportation. As a result, in the last decade, Africa's collective middle class, numbering over 300 million people, has grown larger than that of India.

Across the continent, investment in education is booming, and according to the United Nations, enrollment in secondary schools jumped 48 percent between 2000 and 2008, while enrollment rates in higher education grew by 80 percent. In 2013, meanwhile, the World Bank attributed 60 percent of Africa's economic growth to strong consumer spending. As a consequence of changes like these, the African Development Bank predicts that by 2030 a large number of African societies will be dominated by lower-middle-class and middle-class majorities.

A strong hint of the changes sweeping the continent can be seen in the fancy shopping malls that are proliferating in places like Lusaka. In one of them on a Saturday night I watched in fascination as scores of teenagers took over the scene for a period of several hours, displacing the housewives and other middle-aged customers who usually enjoyed the run of the place. Their mastery of the latest teen styles from rich Western countries couldn't have been more complete, down to the fancy boxer shorts they wore under drooping trousers, elaborately stenciled skateboards, and Major League Baseball caps worn carefully askew.

These were mostly the offspring of diligent working-class parents who had provided their children with much better educations than they enjoyed themselves. Along the way, they have not only acquired modish new clothing and mobile phones, but also new aspirations. They want to become lawyers and doctors and pilots, and listening to many of them reminded me of nothing so much as the old American dream.

Lusaka offered even better evidence of the rise of a new African middle class, though. It could be found in the booming way that housing was being built throughout the city, and it couldn't be built fast enough. In Kalingalinga, a working-class neighborhood I had remembered from years past for its almost narcotic lethargy, people were now laboring furiously everywhere one looked, crouched on the ground breaking rocks with hammers, hauling cement, sawing wood, and laying the foundations for new houses. Scenes like this are being played out all over the continent, which is urbanizing at a pace unequaled in human history.

This helps make sense of the bet that China's migrants are making, and it has nothing to do with hope or idealism or any ideology. It was an updated version of the dream that drew many Westerners to China a little more than a century ago, despite appalling poverty and widespread unrest in the country. If one could only sell a bolt of cloth or a pair of shoes to every adult in a country that large, an untold fortune could be made. This is a good time to be in Africa because the door and window frames and roofing materials and bathroom fixtures and plumbing and electrical systems that millions and millions of new homes will require constitute fabulous new markets. The continent's rapidly rising population means lots of new mouths to be fed, lots more people to be clothed, devices and appliances and goods of all kinds to be sold. And as the Chinese livestock breeders, produce farmers, clothing importers, and car and motorcycle dealers I met in Lusaka had come to realize to their happy astonishment, no other big outside players in the world besides the Chinese have fully understood the opportunity this represents.

"You could see the future right away here," Hu Renzhong, a pig and poultry producer, told me. "Food was expensive and people didn't have enough meat to eat. They couldn't afford it. The land was good, though, and back then it was still cheap."

Hu received me one morning at his mansion farmhouse on the outskirts of Lusaka, offering me a seat in the marble chill of his enormous living room, before taking me on a long walking tour of his acres and acres of hog-breeding pens and sprawling, temperature-controlled chicken hatcheries, all impressively modern and minutely organized. He had come to Zambia from China's Jiangxi province in 1995 as a twenty-two-year-old simple laborer, but soon got into business for himself, raising chickens at first with another Chinese immigrant. It wasn't long before the two had struck it rich, buying land and building ever-bigger houses.

"Things had started developing really fast back home, and a lot of people tried to tell me I'd made a mistake," he said. "But I've never really looked back."

I wanted to drive far to the north into the Copper Belt to see for myself how Chinese employers and Zambian workers were getting along. Zambia was not just ahead of the curve in Africa in terms of receiving large numbers of Chinese migrants, it was ahead, too, in having their presence spark political debate, labor trouble, and even unrest. It was easy to believe that this would be the shape of things to come across the continent. As China scaled up its presence on the continent, more and more Africans were working for its companies, and in the Copper Belt, where the newcomers were particularly thick on the ground, Chinese bosses had developed a reputation for rough and dangerous conditions, low pay, and punishing hours.

That Zambia had become the leading edge of China's push into the continent was the result of a political coincidence. China's official embrace of Africa had roughly coincided with a radical transformation of this country's political economy. In the early 1990s, Zambia had gone in a blink from being a socialist-minded, effective one-party state to a multiparty democracy that embraced the standard economic prescriptions emanating from the West, and Washington in particular. Practically speaking, the country's change of economic direction required wholesale divestment by the government of its monopoly control of major industries. As elsewhere in Africa, as countries applied the prescriptions of the International Monetary Fund and World Bank, this meant the selling off of national telecommunications and power companies, and the opening up of commerce and agriculture to foreign investment. But in Zambia, where copper had always been king, it meant above all privatizing the country's mines.

This began occurring at the precise moment when the new Chinese "go out" policy was gathering momentum. This was the blunt watchword that Beijing gave to Chinese state-owned corporations, and the provincial governments that often controlled them, to begin scouring the globe in search of business opportunities. And because Zambia was largely ignored by the West, the pickings were plentiful and often seemed easy.

Against such a backdrop, it would not take long for an initial trickle of individual Chinese prospecting for business to become a vigorous stream. Word of mouth quickly spread in China that Zambia was open for business, that it was stable, that its people were "gentle," and that its government was friendly toward Chinese. This last element was due at least in part to the lingering gratitude in Zambia for the immense gesture of solidarity extended by China with its construction of the TAZARA Railway in the 1970s. The railroad gave the country an outlet to the sea via Tanzania and reduced its dependence on a hostile South Africa that was still governed under apartheid.

After seventy miles or so on the road north out of Lusaka, my driver, Brian, and I reached Kabwe, the first city along our route. Its name means "ore" or "smelting" in the local language, a reference to the lead and zinc that was discovered by the British at the turn of the last century, decades ahead of copper. The mid-morning light was still gentle and it burnished the saturated hues of the storefronts that were strung out along the main strip and busy with foot traffic. If one could replace the automobiles and their fumes with horses and stagecoaches, this little town might have made a great set for a Western, I thought, amid pangs of regret over not pausing.

Less than thirty minutes later we reached Kapiri Mposhi, which I'd first visited two years earlier, traveling by train from Dar es Salaam. This dust-blown crossroads, the terminus of the TAZARA Railway, announced itself by the hand-stenciled billboards that crowded the roadside at the city's edge. They touted the prices of cheap, hostel-style lodging, and, for those who couldn't afford even that after a long rail trip, campground-style lavatories offering the relief of cheap showers.

At the approach of traffic women crouched by the roadside hoisted aluminum platters full of peanuts in their shells, while men raised squawking hens for sale. A little bit further, beyond the road's tarry apron young girls watched over displays of papaya and potatoes, while wrinkled old women nearby busied themselves selling big sacks of charcoal for cooking.

The Chinese-built line's tracks stopped a few miles short of another railroad that also passed through the town. This one had been built seventy years earlier by the British, at the height of their power, and was part of Cecil Rhodes's grand imperial dream to lay railroad tracks from Cape Town to Cairo.

If the British never managed to quite pull off that feat, they satisfied an important interim strategic goal nonetheless: bringing rail to the cusp of the world's most extensive copper reserves. Kapiri Mposhi was the gateway of the Copper Belt, where in 1895 an American explorer named Frederick Russell Burnham, at least an indirect source of inspiration for the Hollywood film character Indiana Jones, had discovered geological formations similar to copper deposits he had seen back home. In his prescient report to the British South Africa Company, he called the deposits "probably one of the greatest copper fields on the continent," and went on to note that "The natives have worked this ore for ages, as can be seen by their old dumps, and they work it today. . . . The natives inhabiting this part of the country are skilled workmen, and have traded their handiwork with all comers, even as far afield as the Portuguese of the West Coast and the Arabs of the East. These natives, being miners and workers of copper and iron, and being permanently located on the ground, would give the very element needed in developing these fields."

Before that could happen, though, Britain and Belgium's King Leopold II, whose Congo Free State lay to the immediate north of the British South Africa Company's holdings, needed to agree on where to place the dividing line between their territories. Unable to resolve their dispute, they submitted it to the king of Italy, whose country was not a player in the region at all, with the result that Leopold was awarded a "pedicle" of land the size of New Jersey that juts southeastward into present-day Zambia like some drunken mapmaker's baroque flourish. The Italian king based his decision about where to draw the border on the watershed of the region's three great rivers, the Zambezi, the Congo, and the Luapula, and on the fact that after murdering the ruler of a large and powerful regional kingdom named Msiri, Belgium had moved faster to consolidate its claims to land in the area than had Britain.

This frenzied imperial jousting during the Scramble for Africa left what would eventually become the independent nation of Zambia with its odd, bent dumbbell shape—like two countries fused together with a tiny waist to join them. But the significance of this perverse mapmaking goes far beyond any such curiosities. Only later would it be discovered that the Italian king's border ran through the heart of one of the world's richest copper deposits, dividing the mother lode into two unequal parts, with the far bigger share going to Congo.

During my visit, with elections near, Michael Sata, the longtime opposition leader and presidential candidate, was making loud and frequent claims that Zambia was being cheated by the big foreign companies that controlled its mines. Given that Sata had denounced Chinese exploitation of Zambians in a previous, failed campaign for the presidency, most guessed that even though he had toned things down this time around, it was the Chinese he had in mind.

It was a little after 1 p.m. when we were stopped at a police roadblock at a big intersection, where trucks ground to a halt and dust and diesel fumes filled the hot and heavy breeze. This was Ndola, the capital of the Copper Belt. The heart of the city was built on a tidy grid, with tall jacaranda trees with their lavender flowers in bloom on most every block. We passed a golf course that sat idle in the stifling midday heat, followed by an old polo grounds, and then a squash club, one after the other.

Ndola announces itself as an old colonial mining center and staid company town, an impression that only deepened as we penetrated a residential area where the comfortable middle-class villas of managers sat at a respectable recess from the street behind impeccable lawns. Later in the day, when the sun's intensity had ratcheted down a bit, I could see Chinese people on the golf course.

We were heading for a meeting with Yang Bohe, who ran a large copper-processing plant at the edge of town. Access to it was mediated by a heavy steel gate and by three ferocious-looking junkyard dogs, and when he heard them snarling at me, Yang emerged from a dark, hangarlike building to greet me. I had spoken with him a few times from Lusaka, and he had always sounded gruff, hurried, and a bit put upon. In the process, a picture had formed in my mind of him as one of the rough-and-tumble types from China's interior cities I had often met in Africa. They were all grit and no polish, hayseeds driven to quit the poor Chinese countryside and determined to make it by whatever means necessary.

Like Hao Shengli in Mozambique, the sixty-two-year-old Yang's formative years had come during the Cultural Revolution. However numerous they were, the idea of going off to remake one's life in Africa struck me as an offbeat or counterintuitive choice for people in the newly affluent younger generation that followed them, especially to those who lived in the rich cities of the east coast. But for members of China's Lost Generation like this, it beckoned as a rare chance to make up for missed time.

"People of my age either become laborers without knowledge, or they decide to learn something new by themselves," Yang told me early in our conversation. He was speaking English, very rare for the Chinese people I had been encountering in Africa. He spoke it slowly, almost painfully so, and not at all well. At first I thought, uncharitably, that this might have been intended to impress his Chinese subordinates who roamed in and out of listening range during the hours we spent together at his plant. But as his story unfolded, I understood why he might cling so fiercely to his acquired tongue. As a teenager during the Cultural Revolution, he had been "sent down" to the countryside from his native Chengdu and placed in the care of a teacher who had also been banished from the city. The older man spoke English and was a closet Christian, and at considerable risk to himself he secretly got Yang started in the language by giving him three pages torn from a Bible every day to commit to memory before burning them.

"I would spend fourteen hours a day studying, hiding in the mountains so that I could learn without getting into trouble," he told me. "These many years later, people ask me, 'Do you believe in Jesus? How did you manage to do these things?' And I tell them that all along I have only believed in myself. I have no theory, no education beyond two weeks of middle school. Everything else, including the English, I have learned by myself."

Yang's Bible studies in the rugged mountains of Sichuan would utterly change the trajectory of his life, but their effect wouldn't be clear until two decades later when, in the early days of the "go out" policy, English speakers were suddenly at a premium. This won him work with engineering and construction companies, and he spent several years in the Middle East translating technical plans and presentations on big projects.

Yang arrived in Zambia in 2002 on a three-year contract with one of the biggest players in construction in Africa, the China Road and Bridge Corporation. In Zambia, Road and Bridge had a contract to renovate the water supply system in Ndola. While translating technical documents, Yang became curious about the green rocks he noticed in the soil wherever the company laid new pipes. The rocks were well known among locals as malachite, and he discovered their green color was due to their high copper content. Since they were so abundant, Yang got to thinking about how to make money from them, so he sent samples off to acquaintances in China, who confirmed his hunch that the copper was concentrated enough to extract ore from, and more important, to make money.

"I decided with my friends that we could use very simple firing methods to make copper ore. Five thousand years ago, man was already smelting copper. The technique was almost the same, and the cost was very cheap," he told me. "But before we tried this, no one in Africa had used copper oxides for smelting copper."

Yang's newly formed company, Tianfen, brought a veteran engineer from China to direct the smelter construction and for a year he and Yang lived and worked side by side. "He had the experience, and I learned from him, and helped him with the English."

Later, when Yang's passport was approaching expiration, he returned home to Chengdu in order to renew it and to see his family. A big government contractor successfully recruited him to work on a water treatment scheme that was part of the gigantic Three Gorges Dam project, but Yang continued to dream of returning to Zambia to be on his own and to make a fortune. After two years, he linked up with an Australian businessman of Chinese origin who provided the start-up capital he needed to build a copper smelter entirely on his own.

Yang had always made a religion out of self-reliance, and he had taken copious technical notes throughout the years he had spent working with engineers. In 2005, in the space of four months, he completed his first smelter, which he designed and built himself. It had cost $625,000, an amount he said he recovered in less than two months of operation. But as we walked through the complex, he didn't brag but rather emphasized his good luck.

"When we started producing, the price of copper was $2,800 a ton, but while our first shipment was still on the sea, the price shot up to $5,000," he said, chuckling with delight. "Right now, it is about $9,000."

Luck has been fundamental to the history of the Copper Belt from the very start. But busts have always followed tightly on the heels of booms, and only the smartest and most fortunate of players have thrived over the long term. The Chinese had ridden the last and perhaps wildest wave of this phenomenon, pouring by the thousands into the Congolese Copper Belt, which began at the border just a few miles from Ndola, and setting up shop all over the countryside surrounding the city of Lubumbashi. These small, private operators were chasing the same fat windfalls that Yang had enjoyed. They cobbled together crude furnaces to produce copper concentrate, and they paid Congolese desperate for work a pittance to dig up the earth on whatever parcels of land they could secure control of. The countryside was denuded of trees in the process and toxic industrial wastes were dumped into ditches or poured onto the open earth. When the bubble inevitably burst, almost all of the small Chinese operators, and even some of the bigger ones, left virtually overnight.

Together, Yang and I climbed rickety, soot-covered scaffolding. From the top I could see the full extent of his creation, as well as the difference between his operation and those of the fly-by-nighters. His complex had grown to include four smelters, all of which he built, as he shepherded his company from one success to another, planning and strategizing cleverly and keeping costs low enough to ride out the down markets.

Most of his ore came from Congo, where he had also built two affiliated smelters. Its unusually high concentration made it cheaper. His pitch coke, too, came from the cheapest source he could find, Zimbabwe, less than two hundred miles away across the wasplike waist of this country.

Down below us as we spoke, in the shade of a large tree, a team of Zambians loaded charcoal pellets as thick as artillery shells into a tractor-pulled wagon. They would be used to stoke the furnaces that burned here night and day. Under the supervision of a bored-looking Chinese employee, another team loaded bricks onto the bed of a pickup truck. Yang said proudly that he also made his own bricks, using the ash from his smelters. "This is a competitive market, and I knew this would save us money." The bricks were being put to use almost as quickly as they could be produced in the construction of yet another smelter, this one, with a chimney thirty meters tall, the biggest here by far.

Yang stubbed out a cigarette and led me into another long, hangar-like building that buzzed with activity. It housed one of his smelters, but functioned like an assembly line, with workers constantly shuttling in supplies of charcoal pellets both by conveyer belt and by wheelbar-row. The fuel arrived alongside an elevated platform where the furnace sat, and from below workers tossed the pellets up to those who manned the smelter. It was their job to stuff the pellets into like-sized round holes in the sides of the furnace's edifice, reminding me of nothing so much as movies I'd seen of submarine crews loading torpedoes into their tubes for firing, only at a much quicker pace. The furnace roared, not just with the light and heat of its merciless blaze, but with a loud, angry growl.

Had I been willing, Yang would have had us linger longer around the smelter. It was clearly his pride and joy. Within a fifteen-yard perimeter, the temperature was all but unbearable to me, but that was not the main reason I began suggesting with ever-greater insistence that we move on. Rather, it was the air, which hung so thick with particulates that, on this dazzling afternoon, the hangar might as well have been moonlit. Worried about my lungs, I gathered the bottom of my T-shirt and drew it to my face, fashioning an improvised filter. Not one of the workers, men who would spend hours at a time in this environment, wore a mask, or any other specialized clothing. Some lacked even gloves and helmets.

When we emerged from the other end of the structure, Yang took me to the base of the new smelter he was building. The chimney, which was newly completed, towered over the scene, but the edifice that would house the giant furnace was still being built. There, as Zambian workers hauled bricks into place or simply looked on, two Chinese men in broad-brim straw hats and coveralls slathered the structure with cement spackling and lay bricks carefully into place. They both had a salt-of-the-earth look to them, and they eyed me warily as they worked and Yang and I spoke. The only communication between them and the Zambians who handed them bricks consisted of one-word commands: "Next," or "Wait," or "No."

One of the most common complaints among Africans about China's economic activity on the continent is that Chinese companies bring their own workers to carry out their projects. Critics hold that this practice extends down to the commonest of laborers. Two years earlier, Michael Sata had told me angrily, "We don't need Chinese to come push wheelbarrows in our country."

Hiring patterns like this have contributed to the birth of a persistent urban legend. It holds that Chinese companies are using prison labor to carry out their projects around Africa. This legend helped Africans make sense of why workers like the two bricklayers I'd encountered looked so rough-hewn. It explained to them why Chinese laborers lived such regimented lives, traveling in their own groups to and from work sites, and residing in confinement barracks. And it helped explain how Chinese companies could seemingly always come in with the lowest bid on a project. How, after all, could anyone compete against construction companies using prison labor?

The rumor has no basis in truth, but it nonetheless impeded a more serious discussion of Chinese hiring practices in Africa, whether involving big state companies or smaller private ones, like Yang's. Most African countries have long suffered levels of unemployment that are orders of magnitude higher than what people in most developed countries are accustomed to. Beyond questions of hiring, there is the problem of transfer of skills that will never take place so long as foreign workers fill even the most rudimentary of jobs.

With this in mind, I asked Yang about the two Chinese bricklayers, and for the first time he became defensive. "That job is not as simple as it looks," he said, as we walked away from the smelter. "We have to recruit from China, and it costs us a lot of money, because they only come for three months at a time, and we must pay them very well." When I asked him how much, he said $1,500 a month, which was roughly twice what a similar tradesman's wage would be in China, and easily ten times what even a skilled Zambian might make.

When asked why he couldn't find or even train local workers for such a desirable job, all Yang said was: "We take care of our Zambian workers, too. In all of my years here, not a single complaint against us has gone before the labor board." When I asked him how much his Zambian workers made, he said 1.5 million kwacha per month, or about $300.

Yang took me to the building where I had first met him and showed me a small, bonded warehouse where there were one hundred tons of his product, so-called blister copper. It made little impression on me until he casually said that the modest jumble of squat, messy pyramids of dull ingots lying there in the dimness, where they awaited export to China, were worth several million dollars.

When we sat down to talk over tea, Yang brought up his relationship with Africans, or with Zambians specifically. He said he was at ease with the local people he dealt with. He even expressed a love for the country, for the land, and for the opportunity it had given him.

"If you give a Zambian a piece of bread and someone comes along, they will share it. I don't think among yellow people or white people you can find that trait; well, maybe a little, but only very rarely. They treat orphans the same as their own children. No difference. Everyone is equal. This is their best quality."

When I asked Yang about other Chinese in Ndola, I was surprised by his response.

"I don't talk to the other Chinese here," he said. "I mind my own business."

He allowed that sometimes newcomers from China would knock on his gate and he would politely give basic pointers if asked, but he did not socialize with other Chinese and didn't go out of his way to do business with them, either.

"Whenever the police come here, or the inspectors, or the tax people, or anyone asking questions, I tell them that we are an Australian company, and not a Chinese one," he said. "And if they keep asking questions, I show them the papers."

I was prepared for him to tell me, as so many other Chinese businesspeople in Africa had told me over the years, that he was being unfairly singled out, harassed and extorted. Instead, he clearly averred that there was far too much shadiness among his compatriots, and that it sometimes brought about guilt by association.

Yang believes it will take between fifty and a hundred years before Zambia becomes developed. "You will need to see good education for three generations." I objected that the local copper, the source of 70 percent of the country's foreign exchange, will not last that long.

"The copper will be gone, but they have land. They are rich in land, and Zambians have good bodies. The problem is they cannot work hard." It was the commonest of prejudices, and its delivery, as a simple fact, seemed to answer my earlier question about why he brought semi-skilled workers all the way from China.

The next morning, I set off to visit the site of the huge new 45,000-seat stadium that China was building in the city. We drove through a residential neighborhood where I noticed signs for a Chinese restaurant, and for a medical clinic called "Dr. Shang's Surgery." The contours of the new stadium wheeled into view, with its sleek, sloping white roof. A large white sign with distinctive black lettering that read "China Aid" stood out in front of the stadium. Facing it directly across the road stood a huge billboard of a smiling President Rupiah Banda, accompanied by one of his campaign slogans, "Your Money at Work."

China is patently suspicious of a Western agenda driven by questions of democracy and human rights, but that doesn't mean it is indifferent to African elections. The balloting here was less than three months away, and crews were rushing to put the finishing touches on the stadium so that it could be inaugurated before the vote and enlisted in the incumbent president's campaign, just like the Chinese-built, 159-bed Lusaka General Hospital that had recently opened. For a week, national television had been filled with breathless reports about the hospital and with footage of the presidential ribbon-cutting ceremony, in the company of the Chinese ambassador, Zhou Yuxiao. Michael Sata had abandoned his attacks on China since the last vote, and President Banda was running on a platform that might as well have been called "Friendship with China: It Delivers."

We parked in the lot of the construction site and I walked up to the entrance gate, where heavy trucks were maneuvering in the mud as they loaded and unloaded supplies. A company sign in Chinese, written in bright red characters, loomed above the entranceway and I addressed the first man I encountered, asking in Chinese if I could approach a bit closer to the stadium to take some pictures.

"Yes, yes, go, go," he replied in English, his tone almost hostile. I made my way to a second perimeter about a hundred yards distant. There, three young African workers manned a second entranceway, a low, makeshift fence that commanded access to the stadium itself. In the distance beyond, a handful of Chinese workers in hard hats could be seen walking around the circumference of the immense structure, examining its exterior and gesticulating as they spoke.

"The stadium is almost finished, isn't it?" I asked the African workers.

"That's what they say," came the response from the nearest worker, a skinny man in his mid-twenties who squinted at me from beneath a billed cap.

I asked what they did on the site, and they said they were painters, which explained the heavy spackling stains on their coveralls.

"How do you like your jobs?"

"Working for the Chinese is no good," said the worker who had already engaged me. His name was John. "They are terrible."

I had come to expect complaints by African employees of Chinese companies. But I played devil's advocate a bit, saying they had been lucky to get jobs like these.

The pushback was swift. All three workers grew animated as they vented over their low pay and routine thirteen-hour workdays. They complained about the harsh way they were addressed by their overseers, who they claimed threatened them with firing or beatings. And they said the Chinese taunted them, saying that their complaints would go nowhere because the stadium project was a favor China was doing for Africa, and it was being built as the result of an agreement with the Zambian government.

John was vehement on the subject of workplace safety, so much so that it hinted at something very personal. Indeed, he told me that two Zambian workers had been killed on the site recently while mixing chemicals, following the instructions of their Chinese supervisor, who stood there looking on. He claimed the fire had been started when the foreman flicked a cigarette butt at the workers after an exchange of angry words.

John reached down on the other side of the barrier and produced a sheaf of laminated documents that included pictures of the dead men, one of whom was John's best friend, photos from the scene of the fire, and a copy of his friend's worker ID. John complained that the Chinese wore protective gear when they worked with volatile chemicals but that Zambian workers were forced to do without. "Even this morning, we had to mix chemicals in the same old way."

I became aware of someone shouting to me in the distance, and when I turned around I saw that it was the Chinese man at the main gate whom I had spoken with briefly. He was gesticulating in a way that conveyed impatience, ordering me to leave the site.

I thanked the workers and wished them good luck. When I reached the Chinese man at the gate I tried to engage him. How long had he been here? I asked him, drawing an evasive, "Not long."

"Since the stadium will be finished soon, are you going back home soon?"

"No," he said. "We have other work here."

He began to wave me away now, shooing me no differently than he would have an annoying fly.

"You allowed me into the site. Why are you being so unfriendly now?" I asked.

He responded to me in English again with another guttural "Go, go, go. Foreigners come here to make trouble. They are always looking for ways to harm China's image."

Later in the day we visited a Chinese metallurgy plant called Shanghai Mining, one of dozens of such copper-working industries sprinkled throughout the Copper Belt. It is in the industrial zone on the other side of town, tucked away behind a heavy gray steel gate and high cement wall. I had an appointment there with a Zambian worker, John Kasonde.

Kasonde was tall and thin and in his mid-twenties. Among his first words, when he had settled into my car, were, "The Chinese are no good. But because we are in Zambia, where there is a big unemployment problem, we don't have any choice. But they don't treat us like people. They work us too hard and their jobs and their money are both no good."

As Kasonde explained his job, it became clear he was by no means a lowly worker. Shanghai Mining produced copper concentrate by crushing and processing metal-bearing rock. In his seven months at the company, he had risen to the post of a shift supervisor. He told me that before coming here he had never encountered Chinese people nor even heard much talk about them.

After we had spoken for a while, Kasonde excused himself to return to the main building. Fifteen minutes later he returned with Chola Warren, a young man he thought would be an interesting person for me to talk with. I invited Chola to take a seat and we drove off, parking in the lot of a nearby shopping center to talk.

He was a twenty-year-old with chiseled features and strikingly dark skin. Although his clothing, a black-and-gray herringbone jacket and dark shirt and trousers, was the worse for wear, it dignified him beyond his years. Speaking in a soft voice, he said that he had been forced to drop out of school in the ninth grade when his father died. His mother had died two years before that, so he had become the main provider for five siblings.

This he had managed as best he could through a series of odd jobs—physical labor that had run the gamut from loading and unloading heavy trucks, farm work, and, most recently, a copper-processing job at the Shanghai Mining company. His stint here had lasted only a month before he quit.

"We worked very hard but they don't give good money," he said. "If you worked one week they would pay you 50,000 kwacha [about $10], but you cannot survive in Zambia with 50,000. The safety, it is very dangerous. And then there was the food, which was not good. Every day cabbage and little tiny fish."

Chola said he had not been told up front how much he would be paid. The Chinese foreman had instead told him, "You work first and then you will see the money."

On his first payday, a Saturday, a Chinese manager with a cigarette dangling from his lips appeared before a group of workers and peeled each man's allotted earnings from a wad of bills, one by one, Chola said. There was no discussion; later Chola was told that the Chinese man didn't even speak English. When he approached an African supervisor afterward to voice his dissatisfaction, that man berated him and said that he had no business complaining.

Work began at seven each morning, Chola said, and on days when there were large quantities of crushed rock to be processed, the African laborers were denied lunch. No overtime was ever paid. Chola had many things to be unhappy about, but he spoke with an even tone throughout. One grievance, nonetheless, seemed to stand out above all the others.

"The dust and the fumes that come from the copper concentrate are just too harsh," he told me. "The smells are very strong and the work clothes we have do nothing to protect us." He described the way he and others used little bits of torn cloth to stuff in their noses to ward off the chemicals.

"The Chinese people themselves wear different clothing, though, and they wear special gloves to protect their hands when they handle the chemicals. They wear masks when they enter the room where I worked. But we, we had nothing."

I asked him if he had ever lodged a complaint with the government or with the country's labor board, and he said no. I asked why, and he said: "I don't know, but I don't think the government can help us, because it is the government that is bringing these people here as investors."

I asked Chola what he planned to do with himself, and he said he was on his way to a truck depot to see if he could land a day's work at a loading dock. "With the piecework I can make 50,000 in a day," he said. "That's what the Chinese paid me in a week."

The next day, I set off from Ndola to Kitwe, a drive that once again took me past the Chinese stadium site and the smiling campaign poster of President Banda and onto a highway that boasted two lanes in each direction. Ndola is the political capital of the Copper Belt, but with over 500,000 people, Kitwe was Zambia's second biggest city and this region's incontestable economic heart.

The undulating thirty-mile stretch of smooth tar cut through commercial tree nurseries and livestock farms that teemed with grazing horses, and then stretches of tall, golden grass rendered dry and crackly by the seasonal lack of rain. For the entire drive, the road was shaded by the huge power transmission lines that glinted in the sun high above the highway, suspended between gigantic steel towers.

Almost no African country has resolved its problems of supplying power for their populations, including relatively wealthy South Africa. Instead, power outages of twelve, fourteen, or even sixteen hours a day are common. In the euphemistic language of African governments these daily events were called "load shedding," rather than blackouts.

But in the Zambian home of Big Copper, enormous mines and smelters run twenty-four hours a day. A heavily capital-intensive industry like this will not be denied. Its thirst for energy has to be slaked. Its productivity is measured by the hour and its output is bought and paid for by powerful industrial corporations in faraway lands that brook no interruption to their supplies. As we drove, here and there at ground level, villagers burned their dried fields, overgrown with tall grass, producing intense but controlled fires that crackled and fumed with thick black smoke.

This divided highway was the only one of its kind in all of Zambia, where, as in so much of Africa, the two-lane road remains king. So Brian exulted in the chance to freely pass other vehicles, pushing his little Toyota hard along the long, shimmering straightaways.

Kitwe soon hovered on the horizon, revealing itself in the form of a peculiar all-black mountain that fumed with trailing columns of smoke. It loomed far taller than any building in sight. To enter the city was to drive around the mountain, which reveals itself to be an immense slagheap. It belonged to the city's biggest mining operators, and as if to flaunt their power, they had placed this monstrosity—many stories tall and at least as big at the base as five football fields—smack dab in the middle of town.

During the early decades of copper mining in Zambia, the industry was controlled by the British colonial regime. Later it was dominated by private British and South African capital. Prices for the metal soared in the 1960s and early 1970s, and by 1974 Zambia was as rich on a per capita basis ($614) as Brazil, Malaysia, South Korea, and Turkey. After independence in 1964, Kenneth Kaunda, the country's founding father, confronted an issue that has challenged every leader of Zambia ever since: how to capture more value from the country's main natural resource in order to fund development and improve the lives of the poor.

Kaunda's first approach was to try to raise taxes on the two main mining operators of the time, but these firms, Selection Trust and the Anglo American Corporation, strongly resisted. Kaunda responded by nationalizing the industry in 1969, following a constitutional referendum, and thirteen years later merged the two big national operators to form Zambia Consolidated Copper Mines.

Kaunda ruled the country until 1991, and during his long years in power the government's record of economic management came to be widely seen as disastrous. Many would say this was more a matter of ill-conceived socialist policies and poor management rather than high-level corruption, the common bane of resource-rich African countries. There was something more at play in the sharp economic decline during the Kaunda years, however. The second half of his long tenure coincided with tumbling world prices for copper. As a result, by 1994, in the space of twenty years, Zambia's per capita income had fallen by nearly half, to $384.

To climb out of this hole, Zambia's second president, Frederick Chiluba, privatized the copper industry in 1997. He hoped this would provide a cash-strapped government with an infusion of capital in the immediate term. Chiluba was also wagering that private management for the mining sector would be more effective and open the way for badly needed new capital investment and modernization by foreign investors.

China, whose economy was already becoming a powerhouse by then, pounced on the opportunity presented by the privatization of Zambia's copper industry. Its first big move was in Chambishi, a city that flirts with the Congo border, just thirteen miles beyond Kitwe.

There, the state-owned China Nonferrous Metal Mining Company bought the mothballed Chambishi Copper Mine, once one of the crown jewels of Zambian mining, for a mere $20 million.

One can hardly fault China for seizing on a great bargain, but for Zambia, the auctioning off of its most lucrative economic resources at fire-sale prices constituted another big stroke of bad national luck. Copper prices were still depressed and the government's state of near bankruptcy at the time meant that Zambia had little negotiating power. Edith Nawakwi, who was the Zambian finance minister at the time of the sale, said that the country was pressured by its more traditional partners to accept this pittance. "We were told by advisers, who included the International Monetary Fund and the World Bank, that . . . for the next twenty years, Zambian copper would not make a profit. [Conversely, if we privatized] we would be able to access debt relief, and this was a huge carrot in front of us—like waving medicine in front of a dying woman. We had no option [but to go ahead]."

The new Chinese owners poured over $100 million into rehabilitating and modernizing Chambishi, where production resumed in 2003. By 2008, the Chinese buyers had reportedly recouped their investment. And by 2010, according to the Chinese newspaper *Southern Weekend,* the Chambishi mine was producing a regular profit.

Right from the start, though, there was trouble between the new Chinese owners and their Zambian employees. Human Rights Watch, in a report published in 2011, put it this way: "Almost immediately after production began [at Chambishi] in 2003, the Chinese companies faced complaints about labor abuses, particularly low pay, poor safety conditions, and union busting. While some of the anti-Chinese vitriol seemed to reflect racism fueled by cultural differences, the Chinese companies were—and, as this report shows, remain—the biggest violator of workers' rights among Zambian copper industry employers."

These tensions soon went beyond grumbling. Less than a year after the start of operations, a blast at a Chinese-owned explosives factory attached to the mine killed nearly fifty Zambian workers. It was the biggest industrial disaster in the country's history. What is worse, Chinese managers were reportedly seen fleeing for cover moments before the blast, not having bothered to warn their Zambian employees or sound any alarm at the first signs of danger.

As anger toward the Chinese swelled, the Zambian government promised to investigate the blast, but having done so much to attract Chinese investment, and to tout its virtues to the population, its efforts came to nothing.

The following year, protests broke out at the Chambishi plant over salary and workplace safety issues after the company failed to make good on back pay that was due to workers under a new collective labor agreement. On July 24, 2006, protesting miners vandalized equipment and beat up a Chinese manager. The following day, after rumors spread that mine security officers had shot a worker dead, a group of angry miners made their way to the living quarters of the Chinese managers. There they were met at the gate by a Chinese supervisor they knew by the name of Qiu, who opened fire on the crowd with a shotgun, reportedly wounding six workers.

The government promised to investigate, once again. The firing of some of the protesting Zambian workers was upheld, and no Chinese were punished. Indeed, the results of the investigation were never released.

The Chambishi incident took place against the backdrop of the 2006 presidential election in Zambia, one that pit the then incumbent, Levy Mwanawasa, against the rabble-rousing leader of the opposition, the aforementioned Michael Sata. As I said earlier, Sata was able to establish his candidacy by leveraging anti-Chinese sentiment in the country, which had never been higher. He ridiculed the government for supposedly bartering away Zambia's sovereignty and for allowing Chinese people to behave as they pleased, and he spoke of the Chinese as exploiters and new enemies of the country. (As we've seen, he changed his approach later.)

By that time, rumors had already firmly taken root among poor and working-class people across China that sub-Saharan Africa was an El Dorado, and Chinese traders who had scraped together enough money to try to remake their lives on African soil had already become a common sight in the urban markets of Lusaka. There they famously sold chickens alongside local market women, or flogged the cheap toys, shoes, and electronic goods that were flooding in from China. Sometimes Chinese hawkers could even be seen working the traffic lights at busy intersections. They were far from the only target of Sata's nationalist trash-talking, but China alone rose to the bait and became his helpful foil.

Ordinarily, China pledges not to interfere in other countries' internal affairs, a traditional pillar of its foreign policy. But worried by Sata's rise, Beijing fumed darkly about punishing Zambia if he prevailed. Sata lost the 2006 election badly, but mounted a second bid for power scarcely two years later, in a special election that followed Mwanawasa's sudden death in office. This time, he toned down his anti-Chinese rhetoric, and even went so far as to pledge that Chinese investments would be protected in Zambia. Still, he narrowly lost to Banda.

During a visit to Zambia in 2009, I went to see Sata in his seedy downtown party headquarters. He made no pretense of striking a sympathetic posture, as so many politicians do when dealing with the press. He greeted me by saying that he had very little time for my "kind," then he picked up the telephone and began making calls. When he finished doing that, he called for the morning's newspapers and began scratching lottery tickets to check his numbers as I spoke.

When he eventually began to engage, though, one didn't necessarily need to agree with Sata's message to feel that there was something refreshingly forthright about it.

"Our [Chinese] friends are too numerous, and we know their resources cannot sustain them," he told me. "Zambians do not need foreign labor being dumped here. The Chinese are scattering all over the world, but there is no such thing as Chinese investment, as such. What we're seeing are Chinese parastatals [state-owned companies] and government interests, and they are corrupting our leaders."

In October 2010, there was another shooting incident, this time at the Collum Mine, a privately owned Chinese coal producer in the south of the country, not in the Copper Belt. Thirteen miners were wounded, two of them seriously, when during a protest organized by the Gemstone and Allied Workers Union of Zambia, shouting employees of the mine converged at the entrance, pressing against the closed gates. From the inside, two Chinese supervisors fired fifteen rounds at the men with their shotguns. After their arrest, the two said that they were frightened and were attempting to disperse the crowd. They were charged with attempted murder.

By consensus, the owners of the Collum Mine treated their workers horribly and paid them well below the legally mandated wages. Already, in May 2006, the minister for the Southern Province and pro-Chinese ruling party member, Alice Simango, paid an impromptu visit to the mine, following complaints that workers there were being subjected to slavelike treatment.

After the shooting, though, President Banda clumsily tried to calm the waters with a far-fetched statement that convinced many that his government had sold out.

"I don't like what happened there and the law is definitely taking its course," he said. "Let's be careful that we do not single out people. Every day, people are shot by Zambians, are shot by white people, are shot by the Americans, they are shot by everybody."

Banda was tiptoeing around an issue that even Chinese bloggers who operate under censorship were not shy about. When news of mine unrest in Zambia reaches China via the Internet, there is no shortage of Chinese voices to denounce abusive practices of Chinese companies.

"When [the Chinese businesspeople] treat Zambian workers the same way [they treat] Chinese workers, the consequence is different," wrote one blogger after a violent incident. "They think all human beings can be treated in this way. [But] Zambians will not stand for it. How much longer will Chinese stand for it." Another wrote, "While Westerners like exporting their ideologies, Chinese like exporting exceedingly low labor standards. Then, tragedies result."

The Lusaka rumor mill had it that President Banda's party, the MMD, was receiving substantial support from China. Such things are very difficult to prove. Even absent a money trail, though, the flow of those big, showy projects, with completion dates that so often converged around the election season, seemed a sure signal of China's support for the status quo.

I had come to Kitwe to see Rayford Mbulu, a political ally of Sata, who was running for a parliamentary seat representing the city. I had to cool my heels quite a while, though, at our assigned meeting place, a downtown intersection, before he arrived riding shotgun in a big, late-model, chauffeur-driven Land Rover, and signaled that we should follow him. After fifteen minutes we pulled into the Lions Club, which was housed in a series of low-slung buildings surrounded by shade trees and an ample, sloping lawn. We looked in vain for a quiet meeting room and settled on the bar, where a television blasted Al Jazeera far too loudly.

Mbulu had a very full résumé in Zambian and African union organizing, including serving as president of the country's mineworkers union from 2006 to 2010. He maintained that he had been forced out of that post by Banda because the Chinese had complained about him.

"I think there have been no new agreements reached since I left my position at the union," he said, by way of extra bona fides. "I think I know what is going on in the mining industry, and it does not give us a lot of comfort to tell you that there is a lot of government interference when it comes to the relationship between labor and Chinese employers."

"We tend to overpoliticize the Chinese in our country," he said, uttering words that could have been spoken by President Banda himself. "It must be appreciated that Zambians like investment, and investors can come from anywhere, so long as they respect us."

Mbulu, a compact and tightly wound fifty-one-year-old, is more than well spoken and, at moments, downright forceful. At heart, though, his message is very simple: Chinese employers treat Zambian workers unfairly. In the pursuit of its interests, China was corrupting the political process in Zambia. And new Chinese investment had done nothing to help Zambia capitalize on its finite supply of natural resources.

"In terms of pay, many Chinese companies run at the bottom of the scale," Mbulu said. "Our interest is that there be a positive trickle-down effect for the workers of this country. There must be a positive trickle-down effect because to have policies skewed totally in favor of profits has been a negative for our country.

"You have people working in mines for as little as $100 per month, whereas the basic basket for workers in Zambia at the moment requires almost $700 to live—and that is the minimum. Look at the disparity here.

"When we are negotiating [these issues] the government says please let the Chinese set up. Let the investors set up. Well, [during privatization] the Chinese were the first to come to our country, in the year 1999, and twelve years down the line, looking at the copper prices, where it is selling at almost $10,000 a ton, can't we expect the workforce to get a reasonable salary and reasonable social security, with proper infrastructure, proper human capital development?"

What about the projects that China was building in the country, and the effects of growing Chinese investment on the economy? Mbulu dismissed this all as "gratification" for the ministers and other officials involved, and likened China's diplomacy to the buying of influence— on the cheap.

"From the year 2000, when we were selling off our industries to them, we became a compromised society. Our politics were driven by their finances. Now it has become a habit. We in Zambia, we are not poor people, but we have crowned ourselves with poverty. Government is moving about with a bowl in the hand, begging. Everything you see the Chinese building, that stadium, another one that is coming up in Lusaka, it is all flattery."

Mbulu had spoken at a fast pace right from the start, switching with scant segue from one subject to the next, but now he was racing.

"The Chinese government is doing two things. They are investing, of course, doing good business for themselves, with almost all of the money going back to China. But they are doing something else, as well. They are offloading their excess population. You can see this in Kenya, Malawi, basically all over the continent now. I've been to China and I know how they live. It is overcrowded there. There are too many of them in their own country, and they are doing this to decongest China."

Michael Sata won election a few weeks later, defeating Banda and his MMD party, which had ushered in privatization and managed to hold on to power, albeit never winning an outright majority of the vote, since 1991. Mbulu was named deputy labor minister.

Just days after the vote, workers at the Chinese-owned Chambishi Copper Mine received a surprise in the form of double payments. For one worker, Hedges Mwaba, who was interviewed by *The Christian Science Monitor*, this represented an 85 percent raise.

"What is weird is that I got two pay slips," Mwaba said. "It looks like the Chinese had prepared for any outcome of the election by printing two pay slips for us for the month of September. If the incumbent Movement for Multiparty Democracy [MMD] had won the presidential election, we would have been paid our old meager salaries. But we got almost double the money because the opposition Patriotic Front led by Michael Sata won the election."

Sata's first diplomatic audience was granted to the Chinese ambassador, Zhou Yuxiao, who promised to assist the new government in making sure that Chinese investors respect Zambia's labor laws. Sata's reported reply was: "When your countrymen adhere to local laws, there will be no need of pointing fingers at each other."

"My dear Chinese brothers and sisters," the new president said at a luncheon, "Zambia welcomes you, because we are all-weather friends."

In families one can't choose one's siblings. Within regions one doesn't choose one's neighbors. And if you are one of the world's leading producers of a critical industrial resource like copper, in the end you can't really choose your customers. China and Zambia will just have to get along.

CHAPTER THREE

Friendly Gestures

Senegal, like Zambia, occupies a particular place in the unfolding story of Chinese migration to Africa. If Zambia had been way ahead of the curve in terms of Chinese emigrating to seek their fortunes in mining and in agriculture, Senegal, in West Africa, had been a pioneering destination in petty trading and commerce, a sector that would prove immensely popular among Chinese newcomers, indeed the most popular of all.

Chinese shops have become commonplace sights in the streets of cities big and small across Africa, but their ubiquity is deceptive; it masks just how recent a development this has been, and how incredibly fast they have spread. Dakar, Senegal's capital, was different, though. The presence of petty traders from China had already begun to be keenly felt here by the late 1990s, years ahead of most other big African cities. And just as in Zambia, the sharp and sudden rise in the numbers of these newcomers had provoked a swift backlash from the population.

Senegal had always boasted one of Africa's most vibrant merchant cultures. The country's boubou-wearing traders had long colonized street corners in New York and many a European city, where they sold clothing, gadgetry, and assorted tourist fare. But in 2004, Dakar's traders woke up suddenly to the alarming notion that they were in turn being colonized by Chinese who seemed to be taking over the retail sector. Large protests followed in Dakar, with the striking Senegalese traders demanding government action to protect them from the Chinese newcomers.

From time to time ever since, tensions like these have resurfaced, but they have never again reached a crisis level like what was seen in 2004, and therein lies an interesting tale.

On my most recent trip to Dakar, one morning I made my way into the center of the city to the Place de L'Indépendance, a long, rectangular, formal "square" set on a gently sloping hill that dominated the plateau, the heart of the old colonial city and the furthest point west in continental Africa. The Place's bottom end pointed in the direction of the port and toward the terminus of the old imperial railroad that tied together what was once called the French Sudan, an expanse of territory that stretched unbroken all the way to present-day Chad. The old station itself, with its frilly ironwork, was designed by Gustave Eiffel, a sure statement of Paris's attachment to its colonial possession.

The Place that I knew had traditionally functioned as an immense roundabout, and the streets along its two long sides had always boasted the most prestigious addresses in all of downtown Dakar. The old French-era buildings on this stretch were built to overhang the sidewalk, providing cool shelter from the intense sun during the hot parts of the year for the affluent types who came here to conduct their business.

When I stepped into the shadow of the overhang on this morning, though, I discovered that the shaded walkways had been taken over by the lowest form of street commerce. Since my last visit, this once elegant, gently downward-sloping promenade had degenerated into a dusty souk.

Here, men hoisted socks aloft on one arm and belts on the other. Boys waved cheap, pirated DVDs for sale, while girls held up undergarments. Others sold cigarettes by the piece from opened packs. There were more vendors of mobile phone airtime than anything else.

How had things gone so badly wrong in Senegal? Dakar was filling to the transom with futureless youth, most of whom, like my taxi driver, seemed incapable of speaking French, the language of government. They were crowded into every space, striving, strolling, hustling, hawking, or simply lounging, and countless more of their kind— equally short of education, of skills, and of prospects—were plotting their own route from the dusty, overfarmed countryside to the city to join them.

In Lusaka, similar scenes spoke to me of African promise. Here, though, the knowledge that by century's end there could be nearly as many Africans as Chinese and Indians combined felt almost paralyzing. How will these new multitudes be educated? How will they be housed? Who will provide their health care? How will they be fed? And if the center cannot hold in a place like Dakar, what will become of Africa's countless even-less-well-organized cities?

That morning, I went to see Li Jicai, a kind of informal leader of the Chinese community in Senegal. When I entered his downtown office, which occupied a marble-floored executive suite, I found him seated behind a desk at the far end of the room, busy on the phone, discussing business in very good French. He was wearing a business suit, and his slick black hair, parted crisply on the left side, shone as brightly as the high polish of his shoes. When Li joined me he immediately recounted his experience of over twenty years in the country.

Li had been one of the fortunate few Chinese who gained entry to higher education just as universities began to reopen at the end of the Cultural Revolution. The common practice back then was for the authorities to assign students to a specific course of study, leaving individuals little say in the matter. China was just beginning to open up to the world, and its planners were aware of the stark shortage of people trained in other languages, and Li was deemed fit for a place in a French program at Beijing's prestigious Foreign Studies University.

During his time there, he learned a bit about the history of France's African colonies, and knew that Dakar had been the capital of the French empire. "I imagined Dakar as the Paris of the region," he told me. But when he mentioned to people back home that he was thinking of setting off for Senegal, absolutely no one had any idea what he was talking about.

From the start, he said, his dream was making money in the import-export business. "When I first came, I sensed that trade was very poorly developed. I sold clothes. I sold shoes. I sold merchandise. Basically, I sold whatever I could. For me, understanding Africa became a matter of understanding economics. It was my teacher."

And a good teacher at that. Li was either too modest or prudent to speak in any detail about money, but he is clearly a very wealthy man and the owner of all sorts of businesses.

"Most of the trade was in the hands of Lebanese who went to Hong Kong to buy their goods. It's not like that anymore. All you have to do is go online to see the goods, and you can make your purchases via email."

The Lebanese in French West Africa were one of the continent's great comprador communities, the dominant traders, local investors, and financial middlemen between the colonies and their colonizers. In East Africa, it was South Asians who had most famously played this role. In a few other places, it was Greeks or others. Li was being coy in making it sound like the Internet had led to the demise of the Lebanese here. In truth it was the Chinese who had been steadily muscling in on them. Through no coincidence, the timeline of this story neatly matched his own experience.

"Back then there were very few Chinese who were doing foreign trade, too," Li said of his early postgraduate years. "Nowadays, though, even in [a place like] Senegal there are Chinese people present in every sector—private businesspeople. Nowadays, even peasants come here from China [to do business]. It's not the same as before."

Li said that people from Henan had quickly established themselves as the largest Chinese community here. There had been a big construction project in Senegal years before, involving another African stadium, and a company from Henan had been the main contractor; many of its workers had stayed on, forging new lives in the country.

The phenomenon of laborers staying on at the end of their contracts with big public works companies is likely the biggest single source of Chinese migration to Africa. Workers would arrive from a given locality in China and discover there was good money to be made in some corner of an Africa they had never before imagined viable. Soon, they were sending word back home about the fortunes to be made there, or the hospitality of the locals, or the wonders of the environment, or the joys of a free and relatively pressureless life. In short order, others would follow.

Li said the 2004 protest against Chinese traders had not been a big deal. He said the government had eventually calmed the waters and in the end defended the Chinese merchants.

Why would they do such a thing, given the risk of backlash from an angry population?

"Because this is an open country, a friendly country, a country that respects the rule of law and believes in treating everyone equally."

What he didn't say was that there was a counterstrike by an association of Senegalese consumers, who were angered at the thought of an end to cheap imports. Some say Chinese merchants had paid the counterprotesters to demonstrate, others say it was the Senegalese state that had handed out the money.

Through the neighborhood that is home to many of the new migrant traders from China runs Le Centenaire, a broad ceremonial avenue consisting of two lanes in each direction. Almost incongruously, one side of the road is completely lined with small, ramshackle stalls divided one from the next by blue tarpaulins. When I visited, goods were laid in front of them, right there on the ground in the middle of a smoothly paved carriage lane. There, Senegalese hawkers tended to plastic and tinsel jewelry and other frippery on the asphalt under the watchful eye of the recently arrived merchants from China who manned adjacent stalls.

From just beyond the carriage lane, I walked the entire length of the strip, observing the interactions between the Chinese and Senegalese and found them unremarkable. The Chinese were the bosses, just as the Lebanese had been before them, and as such they would emerge from the shadows of their stalls from time to time to give instructions to their local underlings who were flogging merchandise laid out on the ground. When customers approached their stalls, the Chinese haggled with them in the simplest of sentences, sometimes using a single word or two in an approximation of French. A few of them, though, had a good grasp of Wolof, the Senegalese lingua franca.

I approached a Chinese shop where two men looking profoundly bored propped themselves on their elbows on the countertop and peered out onto the scene. *"Ni hao,"* I said to them, before asking deadpan in their language, "Are you Chinese?"

They fit Li Jicai's description of the Henan exodus almost perfectly.

Liu, one of the men, had experienced good fortune after he arrived in Dakar nearly five years earlier and set up his first retail stall at Le Centenaire. With money coming in hand over fist, he had decided he could use partners, and invited Li, his brother-in-law, who came with his wife two years later to join him. "It's a lot easier to make money here than in China," he said matter-of-factly.

By his own admission, Liu had made no effort to learn French, and had done little else to integrate himself with Senegalese.

"There is no future in Africa; no future for development," he said, giving vent to a surprisingly dim worldview. "How will they develop with the kind of education they have here? Look at China. We are putting people into space. We are developing our technologies. We are inventing things and competing with the rich countries. But these people, they are impossible to teach, whether it is how to run a business, or how to build a building, or how to make a road. They just don't learn."

Li was fresh-faced and slight of build, and dressed in a knockoff Lacoste polo shirt, like the ones their shop sold. He had little to say about the big picture and showed no interest in speculating about the future. His concerns were close to home and personal.

"It's very dangerous here," he said. He had been mugged while opening the shop. He had been mugged while closing the shop. And he had been mugged on his way home, too. Things had gotten to the point, he said, where he went virtually nowhere without at least one other Chinese person to keep him company. "What kind of people are these?" he asked me. "Have you ever experienced anything like this [in China]?" (I was moving about Dakar alone and without any great concern for crime. I was also carrying an expensive camera and no small amount of cash.)

Li confided his belief that Chinese people were being singled out as targets, a common refrain.

An unskilled class of petty traders from a fast developing and much more powerful country like China steadily filtering into a society like Senegal, which had its own deep commercial culture and was suffering through a phase of stalled economic development, was bound to cause problems. This is not to excuse any individual act of crime or violence, but rather to suggest a useful pause for reflection among both the Chinese and the many African governments that have adopted a laissez-faire approach to this kind of migration, with neither side having bothered to think much about possibly combustible outcomes.

In Zambia, Fred Mutesa, a former finance minister, told me that whenever his government sent delegations to Beijing for talks, in at least one session they would be leaned upon to maintain relaxed immigration policies toward Chinese. The language, he said, wasn't particularly subtle either; something along the lines of: *We are making so many friendly gestures to your country, building roads and stadiums, etc. We would consider it a friendly gesture if you did not enforce such strict immigration controls on our citizens.*

This reminded me of the historic 1979 visit to the United States of the Chinese leader Deng Xiaoping during Jimmy Carter's presidency. Deng was seeking most favored nation trade status for a newly reforming China, which under American law required that a country not prevent its people from emigrating freely. When a member of Congress pressed Deng on this point, he replied: "Oh, that's easy! How many [Chinese] do you want? Ten million? Fifteen million?"

In 2011, the United States suddenly roused itself to become involved in the issue when the assistant secretary of state for African affairs, Johnnie Carson, engaged with a group of Tanzanian journalists via teleconference. Carson's advice for Tanzania, and implicitly for the rest of the continent, was to regulate Chinese migration, along with the hiring practices of Chinese companies, more tightly.

American diplomats had been slow to understand the scope of the change being driven by Chinese migration to Africa. The phenomenon had been flagged in State Department cables as early as 2005, with diplomats identifying the budding, large-scale movement of people from China to Africa as part of a campaign to expand Beijing's political influence and simultaneously advance China's business interests and overall clout. These early, classified warnings also spoke of the spread, via emigration, of Chinese organized crime, particularly in smuggling and human trafficking. For the most part, however, it seemed that American diplomats were still in search of the right voice, the right message. All too often, Washington struck a paternalistic tone that came across as: *Listen up children, you must be careful about these tricky Chinese.* Carson's message wasn't far from this. "It is important to African governments that they hold Chinese companies to higher standards than they hold American and European companies," he said. "American and Canadian companies will hire most of the local people and train them and not bring along their own people."

I spent another hour or so walking around on the strip at Le Centenaire to get a stronger sense of how business was faring for the newcomers and how well they had managed to adjust to life here. Li Jicai had warned me about the false impression that the majority of these petty traders were making it in Senegal. On the contrary, he said, most of their dreams ended up crashing in fairly short order, leading them to return home.

One after another, merchants filled me with stories of skimpy margins, of hassles with the police and customs agents, and of crime. And as they did so, the anecdotes about friends they knew here who had returned to China piled up quickly.

Among the many people I spoke with on this subject was Chen Rui, who ran a karaoke establishment, the Dynasty Bar. The ground floor of the building, not far from Le Centenaire, was unfinished, with walls made of exposed cinder blocks and a floor of rough cement. The streets outside were swarming with *bana bana,* a common West African term for roving traders, and all manner of people out and about buying and selling things. I made my way up an iron-railed staircase and found Chen waiting for me at the top, where she whisked me through a dimly lit space with a high wooden bar and into a private room. There, it was darker still, with red-and-gold wallpaper and low, overstuffed black divans.

Chen was a twenty-six-year-old *mama,* as the Chinese would call the female boss of any nightlife establishment that offered karaoke and massage and perhaps more. Dressed in black from top to bottom, she was of medium height and handsome. Her prominent cheekbones were accentuated by her heavy black eyeliner, and by her hair, which she wore pulled back in a severe ponytail. And her right nostril was studded with a diamond. She spoke modestly about her place before adding with pride that she had built it herself. "I did it with my own eye, my own sense of art," she said.

Chen, who was also from Henan province, described what she called a restless youth in Kaifeng, a northern city of about five million people. She was a decent enough student when she applied herself, she said, but she was always a bit rebellious. "My mom was very strict, but the more she tried to control me, the freer I behaved."

Her mother was a *xiao ganbu,* a low-level official, and her father had owned a small restaurant. The family was financially stable growing up, she explained, but by the time she finished junior high school, she had already begun to sense that her prospects in Henan weren't great. When the SARS epidemic swept China in 2002, sparking waves of panic, people abandoned public places en masse, and her father's restaurant, like thousands of other public establishments, was forced to close.

Once the epidemic had passed, she fled home for distant Guangdong, where a cousin had found work in the country's booming and intensely competitive southeast. Hers was the dream of an entire generation—simply put, making money—and when she got to Guangdong, she felt excited to have a paying job.

"When the restaurant failed, I started thinking of going out and finding some work," she said. "My cousin was working in Guangdong, so I asked her for help and what I found was an entertainment company; a really big bar. While I was applying for a job there, filling in the forms amid lots of other applicants, a manager, a woman, called me into her office.

"She said, 'What kind of work do you want to do?' I told her I didn't know what kind of work I could do, and she said, 'Well, why don't you work in the customer care area?' I told her I wasn't sure. I didn't have any experience in that sort of thing. I wasn't sure I could do it. But she said, 'Why not just give it a try and see?'"

Chen worked there for nearly half a year. The words she used for "entertainment company" strongly suggested the sex business, just as did her words for customer service, and her demure way of framing the conversation had strongly suggested providing sex. She was making $500 a month, which was very good money for a girl in China with her education, but the job was physically depleting, soul-killing work. She confided to a man that she was eager to go overseas.

"He asked me if I had a passport, and I said yes. Three days later, unbelievably, I had a visa. I had no choice. It had all started sort of as a gag. I didn't really imagine it was possible. I felt like I didn't have a choice at that point, so I said to myself, Well, you'll just go, then. It all happened just like that."

A week later, at age eighteen, she landed in Dakar, alone. The man who brokered her journey to Africa delivered Chen into an awaiting job in a small but busy restaurant/bar run solo by a man from Henan. The broker called him his brother. "My job was to help his brother keep the bar," she said.

Chen no doubt skirted many important details in her story, but in its broad contours her experience bears a strong resemblance to the stories of many thousands of Chinese women trafficked both inside their country and overseas. In one country after another, they worked in restaurants and in the "entertainment" business, where they have effectively become indentured servants by virtue of arrangements not unlike those I heard from Chen.

In Maputo, I met a twenty-four-year-old masseuse whose working name was Wang Fei. She had been in the country for two years, and claimed never to have had a meal outside the parlor where she lived and worked. Her boss, who feared seeing her disappear and losing his investment in her, wouldn't allow it. When I spoke to her, Wang was counting the days until three months hence, when she said she would have finished paying off her obligations to the salon owner, and could return home to China.

In Chen's case, after a year or so, once her boss's daughter back in China had entered college, the bar owner's wife arrived in Senegal to help him. Chen worked alongside his wife for a time but then decided to return home, and had the means to do so.

"I didn't think I would come back to Senegal. I was still quite young," she said. "I looked upon the experience as just an adventure, like something for fun. In fact, Dakar in those early days was really boring. Pretty much everything was lacking here, and I thought even a county seat somewhere in China must be more interesting. But when I got back home, there wasn't much for me to do, so I changed my mind."

Chen said what brought about her change of heart was a surprise phone call from her former boss. He told her he was suffering from hypertension and from fatty liver disease and had decided to return to

China for treatment. "He told me that if I wanted to take over the business, he would sell it to me. So that's how I came back a second time."

Chen worked to pay down the outstanding debt on the original owner's loan, then decided to find a new location, which she completely renovated. She said she had spent about $100,000 to do so. She now employed four Chinese girls, three Senegalese female entertainers, a couple of cooks, and security guards. Her clientele consisted mainly of Chinese men.

"Now and then, locals will wander in," she said, adding that she had one Senegalese friend who came by fairly often. "Maybe it's because the food is too expensive. I think it is reasonably cheap, but for most blacks even eating a hamburger is a luxury."

After a brisk start serving traders, like those I spoke with at Le Centenaire, or crews from the big Chinese shipping vessels that made call at the port nearby, her business had dwindled, because other enterprising Chinese had set up shop much closer to the docks.

Dakar has grown tremendously since she first arrived, and the city was pricing itself out of a lot of port business; companies carrying cargo for inland destinations preferred cheaper cities along the coast. "Blacks don't understand doing things little by little. They don't know how to do business. If you don't want a lot of ships to come, then you don't want to make a lot of money, am I right?"

Chen said that she wouldn't remain in Senegal very long, but there was no real sense of what she might do with her life. "I can continue for another year or two, then I'll want to return home. Maybe I'll do something else, some other work.

"Here, once you hit summertime, it's a real horror. That's because day after day there's no electricity. It's so hot that at night, when there's no power, it's impossible to sleep." In a typical twenty-four-hour period, she said, one could go for twenty hours without power. "Even in the cool season, like now, when we're not using much electricity, it cuts off. When I think about this I'm just disgusted. Can't these people even assure basic minimum conditions for the people?"

To hear her tell it, life was insufferable here, and yet she continued to suffer on. The explanation lay elsewhere. Early on, making a profit in business here was easy, but now there were Chinese people everywhere one looked in Dakar, and lots of them were taking losses. And Chen confided that she had essentially remained single during her seven years in Senegal. The selection of Chinese men, she said, was too thin, and African men, it was clear, were not an acceptable option.

The year before, though, she had financed her twenty-two-year-old brother's emigration to Senegal and was helping pay his way through college, at the University of Dakar. He was studying French, and wanted to do business in Africa.

Each time I talked with Zhang Yun on the telephone he seemed genuinely warm. I was now looking forward to meeting him at his metallurgy factory in Thiès, forty miles into Senegal's arid interior.

I hadn't bargained for what those forty miles might actually entail when I confidently hired a taxi and negotiated a day rate. The driver scarcely spoke French—I had learned never to assume it in Dakar any longer—but he understood enough of what I was saying to express surprise when I told him I wanted to leave at 8 a.m. and be back in Dakar by 4 p.m. Yes, it was possible, he admitted, but it seemed like he was trying to tell me something.

We rode an elevated highway on the way out of town, speeding past a big stadium of recent vintage and then into an industrial zone. I smiled at the ridiculous thought that we might need more time for this trip than I'd bargained for. If anything, at this rate I feared we would be in Thiès too early.

The scenery that scrolled out before me catalogued the many ways Dakar had grown, molting and metamorphosing two or three times since my last visit. All about, new roads were being laid and older streets being widened or dug up to allow for new drainage systems or other improvements. There were young people everywhere along our route, mothers and often fathers dropping off children at day care centers, older kids in blue-and-white uniforms who made their way to school single-file or in clusters by the roadside.

After a few minutes of driving, though, the grand highway that had seemed such a harbinger of rapid progress proved to be an illusion. First came a couple of detours in a nearby suburb, and in the next instant we were plunged into a scene that would have been very familiar to me twenty-five years earlier, were it not for the immensity of the traffic. Cars were crawling bumper-to-bumper in the mid-morning heat through sandy townships where the roads became so narrow that two cars occasionally couldn't pass in opposite directions without one of them straddling the curb. I started noticing the same recurrent pedestrians slinking by in their boubous and plastic sandals, block after block. One of them was a droopy-eyed vendor who managed to clean her teeth with a chew stick as she walked with a tray of peanuts on her head.

Things continued this way for at least an hour, allowing me to study at leisure the tiny mosques that proliferated along the roadside, along with the tailor shops, hair salons, and water vendors. I glimpsed into courtyards where women and girls bent over little charcoal stoves or crushed and ground tomatoes and hot peppers into sauces using pumice stones in preparation for lunch. There was very little I could say to the driver that he could understand, but I monitored him out of one eye nonetheless for signs of clucking vindication. This trip along a fake highway now seemed to symbolize everything that was wrong with and disappointing about Senegal: lots of projects that got started but never finished, and a precedence of image over substance.

When the road finally opened up we found ourselves on a typical two-lane African highway, meaning a meandering, sporadically potholed, unlit affair with kilometer markings but no guardrails. On either side of the road lay a broad, arid plain that was broken here and there by bare hills. There were few villages in evidence, and from the looks of things, it hadn't rained in ages.

The heart of Thiès was a jewel of perfect tidiness and order. Its basic contours had changed little since colonial times. The city had never been overrun by mushrooming population growth because people had other destinations in mind, Dakar first, and then Europe, whether this meant legally joining relatives who were already in France, or making the perilous journey north across the Sahara and into Libya, Algeria, or Morocco, before attempting to cross the Mediterranean by boat. Untold thousands died this way, but that had never stanched the flow.

I called Zhang to get specific directions to his metallurgy plant. He answered the phone promptly, and with the same accommodating tone. I told him where we were.

"Ayaa!" came his reply. "I am in Dakar, in my office. I've been wait-ing for you here."

When I informed the driver that we would be heading directly back to Dakar, he must have thought it was some kind of gag. Perhaps I was trying to prove my absurd point that one could drive up and back within the prescribed number of hours.

I met Zhang at the gas station nearest to where I was staying, in a neighborhood called Mermoz. He had come with two other Chinese, one of whom was a young woman who was driving his small vehicle. The woman, whom I assumed to be in her early twenties, was in fact ten years older, and had been working for Zhang in Senegal for years. The other passenger was a Chinese man who had arrived in Senegal for the first time that very afternoon.

At my apartment, a modern, sparely decorated affair that belonged to a West African friend of mine who worked for the United Nations, we sat on couches in the living room as the sun set fast, and got down to talking. Zhang's story was complicated and took time to unravel.

Like Yang Bohe, in Zambia, he had first come to Africa as a trans-lator, working for a state-owned company in Madagascar. Watching carefully, learning obsessively the whole time, he stayed on when his contract expired and opened up an electronics goods store, eventually becoming one of the biggest sellers of TVs, computers, mobile phones, and the like in the country.

He hadn't needed to borrow money to get the start-up capital to open a big store because he had sold goods on margin as a middleman for other Chinese businesspeople until he had amassed the necessary funds. In due time, for a man who had grown up as a member of the lower middle class in Chengdu, he found himself making very large sums of money. He also found himself increasingly bored.

With a small fortune in savings at his disposal he got the idea for the first time in his life to take a vacation. He first went back to China and then went to France—he had studied French in university in China—essentially as a tourist. But traveling around idly and spending money soon left him bored again. "I couldn't get used to it," he told me. "There was nothing to do."

Zhang pursued an MBA in a French business school but sure enough, with time, this bored him as well. He was coming to understand that restlessness was in his nature, and brimming with new ideas about business, he planned a return to Africa.

What had led him to Dakar in 2007, he said, was a chance encounter with a Senegalese man who told him that his country had recently severed ties with Taiwan and established relations with China. "He told me that Chinese people were still very scarce in Senegal, and that there were lots of opportunities there. Later, he called me from there and said I should come, so I came."

Zhang's first venture in Senegal revealed little of the boldness that was to come. He opened a downtown restaurant almost right away, followed by a business importing cheap goods from China, and then a retail shop. "Later, I began doing a few other things," he added modestly, "then I started to do metallurgy."

This remarkable transformation had started during his first job as translator at the state-owned company, which was a construction firm. "Our company had built a sporting complex, and now our project was involved in building housing, so it was very natural for me to experience such things. I was constantly listening. I was studying, I was watching, and with time I was able to learn a few things. After absorbing them, it was time for me to go somewhere and try my hand. There were a few Chinese engineers and technicians whom I could recruit. That way I could resolve the problem of inexperience."

Like so many of the stories of Chinese success I'd heard in Africa, Zhang's path revealed a combination of keen intelligence, opportunism, and sheer chance that put people in the right place at the right time and primed them to take advantage of their circumstances. There were also ties of solidarity that often favored trust and mutual aid between Chinese in a faraway and unfamiliar land. It was through just such trust that Zhang had gotten his start in trade. In lieu of lending money, other Chinese had extended their goods to him via a system of informal credit.

In his own companies, Zhang began to favor other Chinese over Africans with that same trust.

In either Madagascar or Senegal had he forged any partnerships with Africans? "Basically no," he said. "Finding good collaborators isn't an easy thing," he added, although obviously there was more to it than that.

Bosses like him, and I'd met plenty of them, relied on Chinese engineers and technicians, and they recruited fellow Chinese investors from afar, often after a single meeting, or sometimes with no prior meeting at all. Such as they existed, partnerships with locals rarely went beyond influence trafficking by well-connected local elites. Under circumstances like these, it was difficult to imagine how any robust transfer of knowledge or expertise could arise that might directly benefit Africans now, or even at any point in the near future. Zhang and others like him inhabited a new Chinese world under construction. Africa was just one backdrop among many, where new opportunities lay and where lots of money could be made.

As little space as Zhang's way of operating offered to Senegalese, he said there was scarcely more hope for other Chinese who might be tempted to follow the route he had taken either. Thousands more would continue coming, but the path from petty commerce to big wealth was already closing for Chinese here.

He spoke of Chinese merchants like those at Le Centenaire as little more than poor slobs and losers. Dakar was a harbor, a crossroads, a port city with an outward-looking population, he said.

The Senegalese, he insisted, were already moving up in commerce, already trading for themselves in places like Dubai and buying directly from China, notably in Guangzhou, where more than 100,000 Africans now lived. The processes of empire are almost always bi-directional, and in this sense the recently formed Guangzhou community is classic. As had happened with other rising world powers, China was not only depositing people in a region where it sought influence, but people from that region were simultaneously depositing themselves in China.

By virtue of these sorts of experiences, Zhang felt Africans were increasingly well positioned to compete with the low-level Chinese traders, most of whom he said didn't have any idea what was about to hit them. The men working the stalls at Le Centenaire had contemptuously described the locals as scarcely capable of learning and self-improvement, but they were deluding themselves according to Zhang.

"Since 2009, I've basically stopped doing simple commerce altogether," he said. "The golden period had already passed for that. Basically, the people doing that now can't make it. The competition is too fierce, and [the Chinese have] no advantage."

There is no way to validate Zhang's prognostications. The class of Chinese traders he spoke of was hardly limited to Le Centenaire, or even to Senegal. I have seen their lot in urban commercial scrums in some of the most desolate and unpromising places on the continent, sweating it out in tiny cagelike shops in Harar, with its Death Valley–like weather, near Ethiopia's border with Somalia. I have seen them in downtown Lubumbashi, in southern Congo, where Chinese salesmen walk around with vest pockets full of $5 and $10 mobile phones of the poorest imaginable quality. And I have even seen them selling individual cigarettes at street intersections in Dar es Salaam, Tanzania.

I also knew that Zhang, by now, was far removed from that kind of gritty world. He'd surfed from one golden moment to the next, from one end of his African experience to the other. Still, he was all self-deprecation, until we got around to talking about his dealings in real estate.

He claimed that his construction company had built such a big presence in Senegal that everyone in the country knew about it. Its best-known project could certainly not have been more prominent. Despite being a relative newcomer to construction, this former vendor of microwaves and TVs in Madagascar had won control of one of the choicest pieces of real estate in the capital. It was a gigantic plot of land that sat along the seaside corniche at the very edge of the old and heavily congested *plateau,* or downtown, where roads had been laid by the French during colonial times, and where most of the standing buildings dated from that era, as well.

His land was halfheartedly sealed off from the road by plywood boardings, and on some of them one could read the stenciled words "Dakar CBD." From one end of the site rose the gray minaret of a modest neighborhood mosque, and at the other end the start of the veritable downtown commenced. The lot seemed vacant and idle of all construction.

President Abdoulaye Wade fancied himself a great builder, but he had a remarkable knack for approving prestige projects that became public relations disasters. The most notorious of these was the Dakar Renaissance Monument, a 160-foot-tall statue that depicts in the bygone, heroic Stalinist style a man, woman, and child, striding forward, their gazes fixed toward the sky. When it was inaugurated in

2010, it was touted as the tallest statue in the world outside Asia and the former Soviet Union, but far from embracing it as a point of national pride many Senegalese regarded the monument, which was built by a North Korean company, as a vain and grotesque waste of money. It didn't help that people said the figures in the statue were modeled after Wade's own family.

The next most infamous of Wade's projects was perhaps the "tunnel" that he had built on what most people felt was an already perfect corniche. It was a shallow underpass, really, and given that it didn't dip beneath any intersecting roads, most people regarded it as at least as pointless as the giant North Korean bronze. A good road had been dug up at great expense so that for a length of about fifty yards, people could utter, Think of that. Dakar's got a tunnel now! In their enthusiasm, Wade and his builders had neglected to consider that digging a structure like that so close to the ocean might bring about the infiltration of seawater, which it did. Soon after its opening, the underpass was plagued with leaks and had to be patched with plaster and filled with sandbags, and ultimately, reengineered.

Zhang's prize was just a stone's throw down the road from the tunnel, and it, too, had trailed controversy ever since it was announced. His plan was to build a giant office, residential, and commercial complex— seven large steel-and-glass structures in all—along the lines of the central business districts, or CBDs, that have become common in almost every big Chinese city. Its centerpiece was to be a thirty-two-story tower. Zhang told me that the total investment would be 200 million euros.

The Senegalese press attributed the idea for the project to Wade, who, speeding down the corniche on his return from an overseas trip, told aides that something ambitious should be done with the site in order to spruce up the city. Within a few months, a Pakistani investor came forward with the idea to build a modern residential complex on the site, but press reports say the man died before anything came of his plans.

Despite never having built anything comparable in scale, Zhang mysteriously won the rights to the land. Soon afterward, he had the site razed by bulldozers in the middle of the night, a tactic employed by many developers in China, where murky, noncompetitive deals are struck all the time between builders and local politicians. There, the lucrative back-scratching around real estate deals takes many forms, including having the city use police and even thugs to expel residents from freshly sold urban lots.

Zhang freely admitted that his project had faced many obstacles, and that he had not expected the strong local opposition, despite the fact that before he acquired the site it had been used as a sports recreation area and included a stadium for the neighborhood club's soccer matches. In the event, residents of the neighborhood, Rebeuss, rose up in protest. Then the soccer club that called the field home began to agitate, and the Senegalese Football Association joined in the protest. All demanded that the site be saved and the developer abandon his project or build his fancy towers elsewhere.

Senegal has long had one of the freest media climates in Africa, along with one of the best-developed civil societies on the continent, and as the brouhaha about the site in Rebeuss became the talk of the town, it quickly became evident that there was a lot of suspicion of the mysterious Chinese businessman, along with a fair number of hints of ambient anti-Chinese sentiment in the country. People complained that the project was a kind of Trojan horse, a beachhead for a second wave of Chinese who would soon be coming as the country's new conquerors, armed not with guns but with plentiful cheap finance and powerful commercial networks linking them back to China. Few Senegalese would be able to afford luxury apartment housing of this type, the critics said.

Wary of the mounting popular backlash, Wade called in the opponents of the project and implied that it would not proceed as planned. A few weeks later, though, Wade held another meeting, this one with Zhang, the Chinese ambassador, and the head of the Football Association, clearing the way for the deal to go forward. Wade's previous position had been the result of a misunderstanding, a senior presidential aide told the Senegalese media. There had since been a promise by Zhang to build a new stadium for the football team on another site, as well as a few other inducements in the form of projects to be built here and there around the city. A few residents of the neighborhood were even trotted out to complete the picture of harmony and concord.

When I asked Zhang how he had turned the situation around he said, "I settled it."

It seemed clear that lots of money was spread around, though Zhang wouldn't confirm it.

Zhang attributed his success to the luck of impeccable timing, along with tireless work. But just as I couldn't help suspecting organized crime and human trafficking lay behind the story of Chen Rui's travel here from Henan, I felt that only murky forces could explain Zhang's extraordinary rise. Was he a stand-in for bigger interests in China? That might account for how he had amassed the funds necessary for a project this size, or indeed the solicitude of the Chinese ambassador at a critical juncture in his struggle to retain the Senegalese government's approval. But I couldn't prove it.

To be fair, I knew that even allowing for copious *pots-de-vin* (bribes) there was an inherent and attractive logic to the project, one that all by itself might have been sufficient to push it through in a more transparent system.

"They need work," he said, referring to the Senegalese. "The government believes that if you take that site and turn it into a CBD, it will improve the appearance of the city, it will promote their economic development. It could be very important for their economy, and so the government supports what I'm doing."

A few months later, though, Wade was trounced by angry voters as he mounted a constitutionally dubious bid for a third term, and just like that, the tide turned. One of the new government's first acts was to cancel his project outright.

PART TWO

The Devil and the Deep Blue Sea

CHAPTER FOUR

Liberia

Small Fates

Our takeoff from Nairobi was delayed by confusion over seating. The hostess insisted that passengers sitting in the exit rows be English speakers so that they could respond to instructions in the case of an emergency. Two Chinese sitting there spoke not a word of English. I had observed them as we lined up before boarding in a terminal that was full of Chinese travelers to an extent I had never seen before. The two Chinese looked to be in their early twenties, and were Cantonese. The woman was decidedly plump, and the man was reed thin.

Because I was sitting in the next row, the hostess asked me if I could change places with them, and as we all shifted our belongings awkwardly, we chatted briefly. They were heading for Liberia, midway down the west coast of Africa, as was I.

The woman said the quiet fellow at her side was her younger brother. They were from Hong Kong, which seemed strange, given that they showed no hint of the high-polish affluence that one associates nowadays with the city. Her name was Jin Hui, and she was on her way to rejoin her boyfriend, who had a retail business in Monrovia, which she had visited once before, a year earlier. This time, she was returning to be with him, she said, more or less for good.

I told her I had also been to Liberia, first as a college student, later as a young journalist, and that I had returned often to cover the long civil war in the 1990s. I recounted how I had been evacuated from Monrovia aboard a United States Marines helicopter that took off from the lawn of the American embassy after the last of the more or less safe zones in the city had been overrun by fighters during an all-out offensive by the rebel leader Charles Taylor to seize control of the capital.

Jin knew there had been fighting, but it was clear it meant little to her. She was seized, instead, with her own cultural observations about the place, a litany of condescending views involving sloth and filth and laziness on the part of its inhabitants. After sharing them she asked a revealing question: "There is one thing that I have seen there that has shocked me that I must ask you about," she said. "How is it that in a country full of poor people, everything is closed on Sundays? In China people are trying to make money on Sunday, too. Here, everyone goes to church!"

Gently, I tried to explain that spiritual practices were an important part of life pretty much all over Africa. She wasn't buying it. "In China there are people who worship, too, but you have to have your priorities right. If there's no food at home for your children, how can you justify going to church?"

I was traveling to revisit a three-country subregion that had been as ravaged by violence and misrule as any part of the continent. To think of these countries as a unit was no act of abstraction. The fates of Liberia, Sierra Leone, and Guinea had been tightly linked since the Atlantic slave trade, and black returnees from nineteenth-century America and Britain founded the first two of them. Most recently, they had been bound together by the wars that had devastated Liberia and Sierra Leone, and in which Guinea had been both an important player and recipient of collateral damage throughout.

The dirty wars fought here in the 1990s and early 2000s had wiped out people in huge numbers relative to the size of these countries. In Liberia, the toll has been estimated as a quarter of a million people, a figure approaching 10 percent of the population. In each country, in addition, huge numbers of people were displaced, already feeble infrastructure was destroyed, and shattered cities were overrun with squatting refugees.

Even by the standards of a continent full of economies driven by natural resources, each of these three societies was unusually rich in mineral wealth, albeit still largely untapped. Now that they were recovering, and drawing intense interest from foreign investors, not least from China, how would they manage things? How would the Chinese newcomers who were flooding in, people like Jin, operate in these largely unstructured environments? To what extent would the poor citizens of the subregion benefit from all of the new wealth to be extracted? These were the questions that brought me here.

Africa, I believe, is embarking upon an era of sharp divergences in which China will play a huge role in specific national outcomes—for better and for worse, perhaps even dramatically, depending on the country. Places endowed with stable governments, with elites that are accountable and responsive to the needs of their fellow citizens, and with relatively healthy institutions, will put themselves in a position to thrive on the strength of robust Chinese demand for their exports and fast-growing investment from China and from a range of other emerging economic powers, including Brazil, Turkey, India, and Vietnam. Inevitably, most of these African countries will be democracies. Other nations, whether venal dictatorships, states rendered dysfunctional by war, and even some fragile democracies—places where institutions remain too weak or corrupted—will sell off their mineral resources to China and other bidders, and squander what is in effect a one-time chance to convert underground riches into aboveground wealth by investing in their own citizens and creating new kinds of economic activity beyond today's simple extraction.

The proposition at work here couldn't be more straightforward. The timeline for resource depletion in many African countries is running in tandem with the timeline for the continent's unprecedented demographic explosion. At current rates, in the next forty years, most African states will have twice the number of people they count now. By that same time, their presently known reserves of minerals like iron, bauxite, copper, cobalt, uranium, gold, and more, will be largely depleted. Those who have diversified their economies and invested in their citizens, particularly in education and health, will have a shot at prosperity. Those that haven't, stand to become hellish places, barely viable, if viable at all. Liberia, Sierra Leone, and Guinea were all recent democracies, but each was exceedingly fragile, too, with the feeblest of institutions. Where will they fall on this scale?

As my airplane began its descent toward Monrovia, Jin tapped me on the shoulder to ask if I could help her with their immigration forms. She couldn't read English. I couldn't imagine how terms like "Name" and "Date of Birth" could cause much difficulty for anyone who had traveled even slightly before. "I can't read Chinese either," she said, her head bowed. Apparently, neither could her brother.

As I opened their passports, the fiction of their Hong Kong origins vaporized. The documents confirmed that the two were indeed siblings, but they came from a rural part of Guangdong province. I filled out the forms, remembering countless flights in the past when Africans, usually old women wearing traditional cloth-wrap clothing, had importuned me to help them with this little act of magic—reading and writing.

Inside the airport, brother and sister disappeared without so much as a good-bye. There was a long wait for checked bags and it turned out that mine had been lost. I hitched a ride into town with two other people I'd met on my flight, Kenyans who worked for an international nongovernmental organization (NGO). From their car they called ahead to a Lebanese-run hotel where they were staying, and luckily there was a room available.

The two-lane road to the city wended its way past villages that looked like they might not have changed in fifty years. We drove by swamps and passed through a forested landscape that opened up here and there to make way for little villages—settlements really—with bare, earthen clearings and thatched-roof huts sandwiched between the ribbon of tar and a backdrop of thick vegetation. The scene reminded me powerfully of how Africa had customarily been written about in Western literature, forever the place of primordial or menacing "bush."

The nature of the settlements changed dramatically as we edged into Monrovia. The most common dwellings were hulking steel shipping containers that had been converted, occasionally with great flair, into living quarters. Most had cutout windows; some boasted screen doors and awnings; some, little appendage-like terraces. Others were painted in vivid colors.

As we proceeded into Sinkor, which was the heart of the city, though, these touches of charm fell away. The population density rose steeply, and the prevailing feeling became one of squalor. Many of the better buildings and houses bore the names of foreign groups, especially Western NGOs and American missionary organizations, big and small. They were out to save this country; others, surely, were there to profit in it.

Graham Greene, who spent years traveling in this subregion, had written trenchantly of Liberia in 1936, "There seemed to be a seediness about the place you couldn't get to the same extent elsewhere." This seediness had by now given way to wretchedness, the signs of which were multiplying before my eyes as we proceeded. This country was a nineteenth-century creation of the United States, the closest thing America had ever had to an African colony. It was meant to serve as an example to the continent of a modern, Christian, and democratic state, and Liberians had always believed they had a special relationship with America, or at least the right to one. Why had there been so little progress? Liberians were not the only ones asking. There was now a sizable and fast-growing community of recent Chinese migrants here who were wondering about it, too.

The Royal, my hotel, was $150 a night—a lot for ugly and cheaply furnished rooms, with old, poorly fitted fixtures and a floppy bed. Having been cooped up for so long on airplanes, I was desperate to walk, and set out in the glowing late afternoon to change some money and look for an item of clothing or two so that I could shower and change. The shops along my path were almost all in the hands of foreigners. This meant Lebanese, of course, but also Hindus and Muslims from South Asia, Israelis, and now, here and there, Chinese newcomers.

In other parts of the world, petty commerce and small business were usually regarded as essential lower rungs on the socioeconomic ladder. They were one of the first and best options for upward mobility for the poor and scarcely educated. But in Africa, in a great many countries this sector had been taken over by migrants from afar who had the benefit of capital and developed trading networks and often more schooling. Still, it was hard to imagine that Chinese of this class, even with all of their famous energy and enterprise, their connection to what was set to become the world's largest economy, would bring anything different.

After dark, I hailed a cab to the old downtown. Only then did I begin to realize what had improved since my last visits here. There was electricity, lights all about, where years before there would have only been darkness. We were well into March, but garlanded high above Broad Street were long strings of Christmas lights that were still blinking red and green in a kind of prolonged celebration of what a big deal the return of electricity was for the people of this city.

I recalled how during the war, Liberians stewed in their homes without power under curfews that began as early as 6 p.m. Nightclubs became dayclubs, opening their doors by early afternoon.

We drove around the hilly circumference of Mamba Point, past the cavernous old Masonic Temple, which for decades had been the exclusive club of the Americo-Liberian elite. These were descendants of returned American slaves, whose lock on power Graham Greene said had resulted in a kind of African Tammany Hall.

As we approached the little strip on the Point where the hotel I had often stayed in was located, I told my driver about some of the battles I had seen waged here, about the accordion-like block-by-block advance and retreat of militias in the close quarters of these cratered streets. The fighters, most of them boys, were led by reckless commanders with names like General Butt-Naked, and they fired rocket-propelled grenades and sprayed their machine guns without bothering to aim. I also described the archipelago of strewn corpses one would find in the mornings, after the conclusion of big firefights. These scenes had taken place less than fifteen years earlier, but to the driver they had no resonance at all. I might as well have been speaking about another country.

It was Saturday night. I felt like drinking a beer. The driver, William, took me to one place after another, but they were deserted, or too noisy, dense with smoke and prostitutes. When he pulled up to a place with a bright sign that read Metropolitan Disco, I resolved to have my beer no matter what. Just as I approached the entrance, a Chinese man and woman emerged, suggesting I had made an auspicious choice. They paid me no mind as we passed each other, but their air told me that they ran the place.

I sat inside on a high stool in a dark recess. Local dance music was blaring from what may have been the worst sound system I had ever heard. Within moments, I was approached by a prostitute named Lisa.

She wore ropy black braids and a skimpy white cocktail dress that was badly stained. Even in the dimness, she looked like she had been through an awful lot, and despite being given no encouragement, she persisted with her pitch. A second woman soon joined in, and was just as annoying.

I swiveled away from them and began to cast my eyes around the club. To my surprise as I did so, I noted a Chinese TV program playing a military day parade in a long, endless loop. The scene was Beijing—Tiananmen Square, to be precise. It was the big, annual military parade held each October 1, for the anniversary of the founding of the People's Republic, and the large projection screen filled with huge numbers of Chinese soldiers goose-stepping, gesturing severely with their peculiar sideward and upward glancing salutes as antiaircraft guns and tanks and missiles rolled past.

When at last I broke my gaze I discovered someone even more mes-merized than me. At the nearest table, a Liberian man watched, leaning forward in rapt concentration for the entire time it took me to empty my drink and go.

After my second night, I decided to leave my Lebanese hotel. I couldn't justify the expense, and among the names of contacts I had prepared for the visit were a few Chinese in the hotel business. On Monday morning, I called one of them, Li Jiong, who told me his rooms were $100 a night, all inclusive, which meant three meals and laundry, too. I still didn't have any clothes, but it sounded like a deal that would be hard to beat, especially when he said there was free wireless Internet. Li came to pick me up straightaway in a late-model Mercedes van, and as we drove down Tubman Boulevard, I came to understand why he was so excited to have me.

"You're the first *lao wai* I've ever had as a guest," he told me, using words that literally meant "old outsider," or foreigner. It was an every-day expression in China, but we were equally foreign in this place, giv-ing the formulation a peculiar ring.

As we pulled off the road into Li's driveway, passing under a crudely painted sign in Chinese that announced the name of his place as "Nin Hao Zhongguo" (Hello China), I explained to him what had happened to my still unrecovered baggage with Kenya Airways, and that I was in desperate need of clothes.

"No problem," he exclaimed cheerily. "We'll drop your things off here and I'll take you downtown to do some shopping." It was the kind of response I would grow accustomed to from him, almost regardless of the challenge I raised.

Li's building was situated on a steep hillside that sloped downward from the road. He called it a hotel, but in fact it was little more than a sprawling and charmless concrete villa. My basement room was dark and hot, and the air conditioner didn't work. Located between the phone-booth-sized shower and the small, ill-painted bedroom was a filthy storage space that was strewn with junk. As I shut the flimsy door and contended briefly with its cheap and jiggly lock, I consoled myself with the thought that I stood to get to know some more Chinese people here, which was all to the good.

Li summoned his driver, a placid-looking older man, and together the three of us set off on the short ride downtown. We followed the same route I'd taken in the taxi on my first night, tracing the circumference of Mamba Point, where we passed the white walls of a compound that I'd missed in the dark. Its red lettering indicated a Chinese medical clinic, and when I asked Li if he knew the people who ran it, I was surprised to hear him disparage the owner as a flimflam man from Hebei province.

The early afternoon air fairly suffocated, and as we edged forward through the narrow downtown streets, Li grew impatient with the driver and began barking instructions to him in a language that one might charitably call broken English. "Turn here!" It was a one-way street going the opposite direction. "No. Stop! Go, go!" We parked in front of a literal hole in the wall, a shop that belonged to squatters in a building that looked like it had been shelled during the war. While the boss played chess in the shadows with a friend, young men drifted in and out inspecting the fashions, which were draped over barrels and strung from cords that ran overhead.

After Li coaxed me into accepting the shop owner's offer to try some things on, employees held up a bedsheet for me to stand behind while I peeled off my sticky old clothes. I quickly settled on a couple of shirts and pants, and we headed back to the hotel.

Along the way, we passed in front of the grand, 1960s-vintage presidential residence, which I'd been told stood empty, awaiting badly needed repairs. "The Liberians would like China to renovate it, but they haven't said so directly," Li told me. "There is a difference of psychology at play in this. China knows they want it fixed, but it is waiting for some kind of expression—a request. It's a matter of face. Liberians haven't yet understood the workings of face."

With little forewarning, Li began to riff on politics.

"Liberia is a country that is controlled by the United States," he told me. Perhaps that was true sometime in the past, I replied.

"No, it is still the case," he said. "There are Americans in every section of government here. At least one. You could say that Liberians are your cousins," he said between laughs. "The Americans give a lot of money to this country, but it just gets wasted. It never reaches the people. China has learned from that. We don't give away money. We build things. That way, the people can see some impact. This government is very close to the Americans, but the people don't like your country very much. They feel that in all of these years you have never achieved much of anything here."

That afternoon I made some rounds in town. As I set off, Li told me that dinner would be served around 6:30. There were ten Chinese lodgers at the hotel and the routine called for everyone to take their meals together. Some were teachers from the local Confucius Institute, China's ambitious project to create Chinese-language schools in countries all over the world, and others, he said, were construction workers.

When I got back to the hotel, arriving just moments before mealtime, Li was standing in front of the gate, waiting for me. I went to my room to drop off my things and wash up, but found there was no towel there. When I told Li this, he summoned a young Chinese man who worked for him and told him to fetch me one. "We don't usually give them out because most Chinese bring their own," he said. "They wouldn't want to use one that a black person might have used."

A dozen of us took seats around a large, round table in a barely appointed room by the driveway, and a shy young Liberian woman served us large heapings of Chinese dishes: crab, fish, pork, glass noodles, eggplant, and a variety of greens. After Li's fulsome introduction, the conversation around the table turned stilted. It was the first time that many of those present had eaten with a non-Chinese person, and this produced embarrassed silences between awkward observations, along the lines of how well I used chopsticks.

One by one, the Chinese boarders got up the moment they finished their food. Most of them repaired to the recreation room, in the basement next to where I slept, to watch TV shows from China for an hour or so before turning in. I left the table, retrieved my computer from my room, and sat on the terrace where Li had invited me to join him. When I got there, he was already playing cards loudly with three of his tenants, so I ordered a beer and began using the Internet.

When his card game ended, Li served me another beer, declining to drink one himself, then launched into what I had begun to regard as the standard pitch of the self-made Chinese man. He stopped just short of boasting about his self-reliance as a jack-of-all-trades who built this "hotel," with its ten bedrooms, saying he'd even made the door frames and windows by himself. I held my tongue about the crude finish to much of the work, or about the filth in the basement, or about the dead cockroach I found in the flimsy shower stall when I checked in.

"We are all born equal for the most part," he said. "What we become depends on our own self-application, our *nuli*." The word means hard work, and it is one of the words I encountered most among people of his type.

In our brief ride together when he had first picked me up, Li had declared that it was his personal destiny, his *yuan fen,* to get rich in Africa. Now he was rejecting that.

"I have a *yuan fen* because I work hard. That's why I have a house like this and a car and other businesses. Without hard work, destiny is meaningless."

In that earlier conversation he had spoken almost glibly about this country needing ten more years to develop, but now on this, too, he presented a different view.

"The people in charge here have no idea what they're doing," he said. "How else could you have 80 percent unemployment? How else could they be unable to feed themselves well? Three-quarters of the people here eat just one meal a day."

I asked him where the fault lay, expecting him to invoke "laziness," as I'd heard from countless others, but he never mentioned the word, sounding instead a bit like a Reagan-era Republican baiting an audience with talk about welfare queens.

"They go around begging for money, asking America for $20 million here, the Europeans for $15 million there, and when they fail to get a project completed, they go to the World Bank and ask for more. What they should be doing is inviting people to come in here and produce things. They don't let foreigners own land! They should be saying to investors, 'You want land? Take it!' As long as you are going to hire Liberians, and produce something, it's a good thing. We'll come back in three years and see what you're doing, and if you are making money, maybe then we will ask for something from you."

Li's advice seemed heedless of the fact that one of the most common grievances Africans have about Chinese, as we've seen, is that their companies rely heavily on imported Chinese labor. At Li's own hotel, as best I could reckon, he had only three Liberians working for him—the house girl who had served dinner; the elderly, disrespected driver, who was part-time; and a night watchman. Most assuredly they were earning very little.

It also seemed not to have occurred to him that Liberia had already been down the road of leasing out large tracts of land to foreigners. The terms were usually exceedingly generous, but this had never led to the development of anything more than little enclave economies and miniature company towns. The Firestone Rubber Company, which for decades had controlled vast stretches of the Liberian countryside, was the best example. Li had built up a head of steam, though, and I didn't want to dissipate it with my objections. "The Liberians have all of this wealth, all of this good land that they cannot use, all of this forest, these big trees, redwood trees," he specified, laughing as if in wonderment. "Chinese people would die for this wood. What [the Liberians] need to do is hitch their fate to people who know how to exploit these things, and that will pull this country out of poverty."

This region's forests, when you see them from the air, appear to be as thick on the ground as heads of broccoli.

"Do you realize that if you cut down all the trees here there will be no more rain?" I asked him. "Did you know that the countries to the north of Liberia are all arid?"

"But it would take twenty years to deplete these forests," he said. "By that time they will have oil. You've got to use your resources to create some basic wealth."

With that, he stood up and excused himself, saying he would be right back. His optimistic projections seemed far-fetched given that he had disparaged the government just minutes earlier. "There are villagers in China who have more talent for government than the people who are running this country," he had told me. "You couldn't find ten competent people here."

A minute later, he returned, beaming, as he thrust forward a sample of the redwood that he had spoken of. It was a segment about thirty inches in diameter and maybe ten inches thick, which he hoisted like a trophy—and for cause. It was iroko, which sells for tens of thousands of dollars per mature tree. The species was already all but extinct in Côte d'Ivoire and Ghana, both of which still had intact forests when I first arrived in the region thirty-five years earlier.

As we spoke, Li's wife, whom I had seen little of, hovered in the background, visible, but only just. She had a pleasant face composed of soft features but I never saw her smile. She looked to be in her early thirties, with a nice figure but one that was always concealed in long, drably colored skirts and cotton tops. Li, by contrast, took in the warm evening air in shorts and shirtless. When his wife was out of earshot, I asked him if she liked it here. A dark, conspiratorial smile flashed on his face. "She has no choice," he answered.

I had heard him and so many others vaunt the Chinese tolerance for hard work and "eating bitter," but this comment revealed something else that was just as common: material advancement was the goal; there was almost no stopping to smell the roses.

Li told me that he had only recently gotten into the timber business, which he called the "resource trade." At first he had sold whatever timber he could get his hands on, but he quickly discovered that general logging in a country as undeveloped as Liberia required huge investments.

"It's not something a small operator can do well here. You need heavy equipment. You even have to build your own roads. So I gave up that idea and got into logging redwood."

Li spoke with evident pride as he explained how he had begun deploying two or three work teams at a time, each run by Chinese, who essentially roamed the deep forest on both sides of the border with Guinea for ten days to two weeks in search of their special quarry. "There are only a few other Chinese who are doing this kind of work at the moment. But I bet within a year, there will be many more."

I asked my host what had drawn him to Africa in the beginning. "Back home, I had a lot of friends who had already been to Africa," he told me. "I didn't know which countries were good, or where you could make money. I just knew that China was already pretty much developed."

Li had arrived in Liberia alone in 2006, with modest savings from a variety of small businesses in his native Zhejiang province, not far from Shanghai.

"They had just chosen their new president. The country had just come out of the war, and I sensed there were lots of things that I could do. I knew the market was wide open. I knew the resources were plentiful. At that time, there was no electricity. There were no good roads, or even streets. One couldn't drink the water. It was far from comfortable here, but I started investing anyway. I spent a lot of money renting a house. I had to deal with lots of theft and lots of robberies, but the idea was to eat bitter and to understand the country.

"I used Chinese-style expectations at first, thinking [the country's] development could go fast, but as I got to know the place better, I became more realistic, more patient. By the third year, they started repairing the streets with World Bank and U.N. money. The lights started coming on. We figured it would take another two or three years before business really picked up, but this is a slow process. It involves government, laws, and lots of other things, not just money. The country had been at war for too long, and the people with money and education had all left. All that remained was poor people, and we had not understood how difficult it would be. You could say that we came early."

He started out by selling air conditioners and household electronics that he imported from China, but found that the market was too small and too poor for him to make real money that way. The idea to build a hotel came from watching the rise in the number of official Chinese projects in the country. He figured that if he could capture a regular share of the traffic of Chinese cycling through the country on short-term contracts and missions, he would do well, and the Chinese

embassy encouraged him. (Now I understood why he had never bothered to translate the name of the hotel on the sign that hung above its
entrance gate.)

The conversation circled back to his wife. He told me their marriage had been arranged. They had a single child back in China, a son,
who was approaching high school age. His wife had arrived just a year
earlier, once they felt the son was mature enough to be left in the care
of extended family.

I asked if it had been difficult to live separately, to be here so long
without her.

"If that had been tough, we would never have made it," he said. "My
wife is just like an employee, a worker. I must rely on my own personal
strength. I must choose my own path. If I succeed, people will praise
me. If I fail, it's no big deal. I'm the one who decided that we would
come here, and I committed to the long run even before I arrived."

Did he think he had achieved success?

"No one will tell you they've finished succeeding," Li replied. "But
when I think about what I've started here, with no language, with no
experience here, and now I have this wood business, I feel like I've done
well."

The next morning, Li overheard me complaining loudly on the
telephone to Kenya Airways about my lost bags.

"Black people are not good at getting things done," he said, when
I had hung up. "Their customs were formed back when there was no
telephone and no highway. It's very easy for them to put anything that's
not immediate out of mind."

Li had given in to the age-old expat's game of armchair diagnosti-
cian of whatever ails Africa. To change the subject, I asked him what he
thought of the country's rival communities of Lebanese and Indians.
Were they as hardworking as Chinese? Would they lose their grip to the
newcomers?

Li said that Chinese merchants had certain advantages in sourcing
the manufactured goods they sold in China. "We don't need to buy
a ticket to go to China to do business. We have our people there. We
know the scene best. We will get the best prices."

Then he said something that surprised me, and took some of the edge off his earlier race talk. "I don't believe in the idea that some nationalities automatically work harder than others. It's all about making money work for you, and everyone is different. What I can say is that if you pay them well, even blacks can eat bitter just as much as any Chinese. If you don't give a Chinese enough food to eat and you give him no incentive, there's no way he'll work hard. That's what makes any country develop."

Because I have grown so accustomed to a certain strain of Chinese discourse that emphasizes how distinct from others they are, and usually by clear inference this means how superior they feel, this struck me as a rare response.

"I reject this," Li said, commenting about Chinese notions of superiority. "I know that lots of Chinese people feel this way, but that's because they haven't experienced anything. Being outside of the country, coming in contact with different people all the time has allowed me to understand."

Moments later, Li plied me for my schedule. My plan was to go visit the Chinese medical clinic in town, and if my bags were recovered later in the day, as promised, I would set off the following day for Gbarnga, an important city in the north. I had been there under dramatic circumstances during the war, when it had been Charles Taylor's rebel capital. Now I was to meet with a team of official Chinese agricultural trainers who worked at a school there.

"What the hell do you want to visit those people in Gbarnga for?" he asked. "You realize they're different from people like us, don't you? They are government people. They haven't come here on their own. The reason they are willing to meet you and show you around their school is to make propaganda. That's one of our government's bad points, you know, propaganda; it's always trying to put a good face on everything."

Many Chinese have grumbled to me about the unbearable stresses and tensions of daily life back home, and about the lack of rights, the deficiencies in the rule of law, and injustices of every kind. A few even spoke to me with deep skepticism about the soundness of China's booming economy and its implicit promise of future prosperity. But very few questioned China's actions in geopolitical terms, easily buying into the state's line about the country being a new kind of nonheg-emonic power, unlike the West; a genuine and sincere partner of the "developing world."

As I prepared to set out for the private medical clinic, Li offered a dismissive word on all such Chinese clinics. "These people have all chosen to come to a poor place to make their money. Even if you are not sick, they will try to sell you medicine, and all kinds of treatments. They are not trustworthy." Despite this, Li offered to take me to the clinic since he had to go to town anyway. I was beginning to feel like his captive, and didn't tell him that I had already briefly met the doctor, and his female companion and partner, the day before at a coffee shop near the hotel.

Li Jiong's driver tapped the horn gently when we reached the white-walled clinic, and the gates quickly opened. When I climbed out of the van, I found Dr. Dai, its codirector, sitting on a low wooden chair, drinking Chinese tea in the shade of a large mango tree off to the side of his blue-roofed clinic. I approached him smiling, with Li Jiong fol-lowing a step or two behind, fully expecting that we would both be invited to join him for a drink. Dai gestured for me to sit in the one available chair; he barely acknowledged his countryman, limiting him-self to a simple grunt and nod of the head.

Slighted, Li spun on his heels and walked away, not saying a word. I tried to imagine the loss of face suffered by this self-described for-mer peasant, a man who could now afford to drive around in a late-model Mercedes he'd paid for with cash. Before I could even inquire, Dai launched into a quick explanation. "Chinese here have made a bad reputation for themselves by selling crappy goods," he said, clearly associating Li with the trade in junk. "You can get away with that once or twice, but afterward, people understand what is going on and then your reputation is finished. *Our* reputation is finished."

In the space of a few minutes, the two had denounced each other on the basis of pure prejudice, and there was a remarkable symmetry to their charges, of seeking one's fortune amid poverty, and of peddling shoddy goods and services.

Dai was a swarthy man in his early fifties. He was dressed in white pants and a pink shirt made from expensive-looking cotton, and he mopped sweat from his brow constantly there in the courtyard. His face was unusually expressive, even theatrical, as were many of his gestures, whether he was mugging or mimicking a procedure. The more I watched him, in fact, the more he reminded me of the late American comedian Jonathan Winters.

With the air cleared of one kind of unpleasantness, Dai tried to clear it of yet another. He recalled our conversation the previous day about Liberian employees, when he had told me that he didn't hire locals, because they were dirty and lazy and prone to stealing.

"Actually, there's something else," he said. "The patients don't like them. I've had white people—a German diplomat, for example—tell me directly: 'I trust your work and your hygiene, but if there were blacks here I couldn't use your clinic.' This is not something I can do anything about. I can't change the thinking of white people." This was a reasonably clever, if unconvincing, formulation, a bid to launder his image a bit by projecting his prejudices upon others.

The day before, with his partner, a severe, much younger gynecologist named Zhai Yu, looking on, Dai had spoken to me of the appalling state of need this country was in. He said the five-story John F. Kennedy Medical Center, a gift of American aid from the 1970s that was very much in the mode of the gigantic central hospitals that China was now building around the continent, had no more than twelve doctors. For lack of means and of training, he said, IV lines were live-swapped between patients.

Dai then spoke of his admiration for Western NGOs, and of his similar desire to do good in Africa.

"The diseases in this country are all diseases of the poor world, malaria, yellow fever, dysentery. There is no way that people should have to live with these things. That's why I really respect NGO work," he said. "Those people come to Africa to improve the quality of life of the people here. I have a deep admiration for this sort of thing. The people here need a lot of help. Many of them have no idea even that malaria is caused by mosquitoes. They don't know the consequences of high blood pressure. They don't know there's a relationship between sugar and diabetes."

Both Dai and Li had expressed scorn for their countrymen's obsession in Africa with making money, and yet each of them had so clearly come with that purpose in mind themselves. This was reflected most clearly in Dai's choice of a location for his clinic, the Mamba Point neighborhood, which is tucked away on a tiny spit of seaward-projecting land, and separated from the rest of the oppressive downtown by Monrovia's tallest hill. Foreign embassies, the United Nations, aid agencies, and yes, NGOs, had long kept their offices or housed their staffs here, giving the area the feel of a foreign enclave.

How many Liberians was he serving, I asked?

"It's pretty embarrassing, but most of my patients are international people—NGOs, the U.N., Lebanese. Maybe 20 percent of the people I see are Liberians, but the main reason for that is financial." I took this to mean that most natives could not pay his high fees.

Dai told me that he had been drawn to Liberia initially by an older sister, who was doing business here years earlier. He came from Shijia-zhuang, a medium-sized city not far to the south of Beijing, where he said he had been a senior supervising internist at a large hospital. The further along he got into his story, though, the more I had the impression he had been driven to Africa by a midlife crisis. Dai had abandoned a solid career and left a wife behind to start a clinic in a poor and all but unknown place like this on what must have seemed for him like the very edge of the global frontier. And he did so in collaboration with an attractive, albeit strikingly austere female doctor who was young enough to have once been his student.

"I was fifty years old, and normally I would have just kept working until sixty and retired. But I didn't want to live my life that way. I was weary of the routines, I was tired, and I wanted change. What did my friends think? They thought I was crazy." No one in his circles had ever heard of taking time off, or dropping out, much less setting off for a ravaged little country in West Africa that was still early in postwar recovery.

Dai said nothing about his wife, and was vague about his son, who he said was studying—he couldn't say exactly where—in Arizona. The fact that his son had made it to an American college made him proud, but he seemed worried about it nonetheless. "All he does is use the computer and play games."

I asked Dai if he could give me a little tour of the clinic, and after some mumbling about how modest a place it was, he agreed. There was only one patient in the treatment room, a Liberian man, as it happened. He was moaning softly when we entered, and lay on a cot by the wall, which he seemed to want to hug for its coolness. While Dai explained that the man was recovering from malaria, two uniformed young Chinese nurses stood smiling at attention. The older of the two had been here for two years, while the younger nurse had just arrived.

I asked Dai what he made of Liberia's prospects.

"I want to stay on here. Liberia is a very rich place," he said, now smiling. "So much forest. So many resources. Of course they can develop—eventually."

When I replied that many resource-rich countries in Africa had remained poor, he turned almost downcast. "Well, yes. I just think that a lot of these countries need more help. Africa needs help."

Li was waiting in his car when I took leave of the doctor, and he was still in a bad mood when we pulled out of the compound. I apologized for Dai's rudeness, which set off an outburst by Li about the man's arrogance and lack of manners and breeding. I had other business downtown, and asked the driver to drop me off so that I could make my way on my own.

I was soon talking at a restaurant with Tiawan Gongloe, a man I had known as a human rights advocate during the worst of the war years. He had recently served in the government of President Ellen Johnson Sirleaf as labor minister. He told me that governance in Liberia was better now than it had been for four decades. For the first time in memory, he said, people felt safe to voice their opinions, and to publish virtually whatever they wished to. Ordinary people were hopeful for the first time in a generation.

I expressed a more pessimistic view. Others had told me the new government had settled into many of the bad old habits of the past, doling out spoils among the small and insular old elite, most of whom traced their ancestry to the freed American slaves. People spoke of rampant corruption, and about the government's ponderousness in administrative matters.

Gongloe would have none of that, so I changed the subject to the Chinese.

"When I was minister, the Lebanese told us to watch out for the Chinese, and the Americans told us this, too," he said. "But I told the Chinese if they bring their own investment and they give our people jobs, they'll be welcome here."

Gongloe said that the price of work permits for foreigners had been fixed at $450 for thirty years, and that one of the first things he did was raise it to $1,000. "People have been taking advantage of our generosity for a long time," he said. "Since the beginning of time, the Lebanese have been bringing in their own people to work as ordinary store clerks, and we have to put a stop to that—not just by the Lebanese, but for everyone."

Gongloe's theory was that what scared other foreigners about the Chinese wasn't their numbers, or that they had lots of money or exclusive networks, but that they got things done. It was an argument I had often heard from Chinese themselves. "People appreciate them here because they move at a faster pace than anyone else," he said. "On January 15 they promised us farming tools, and by February, the tools were here. The others, for instance, the Europeans or the Americans, will say they are going to help you, but first they must send an assessment team. It becomes very bureaucratic."

Gongloe cited a new university campus the Chinese had recently completed on the northern edge of the city. "They didn't do a lot of feasibility studies. They just went and got the job done."

I asked about complaints I'd heard here, as elsewhere, that big Chinese companies used all kinds of tricks to get work visas for their nationals, pretending they would occupy highly skilled jobs, when in fact many of them were ordinary laborers.

"There are no exemptions for unskilled workers from other countries, except for government projects, bilateral projects, or things like teaching jobs," he said, which sounded to me like a rather wide-open door. "Maybe you can find some people let in to cook Chinese food, because we don't have people who know how to do that, and maybe some of these people end up pushing wheelbarrows in the off-hours. But this is the way the Chinese organize things. If you go to the rebuilt national stadium, you'll find Chinese workers doing agricultural production for themselves there. They are also making rattan furniture. These are all construction workers."

———

I set off for Gbarnga with a hired taxi and a driver named Diabaté. The last time I had been there was to interview the warlord Charles Taylor, in what he fancied as his rebel capital. Liberia had been divided in two by the war, and the writ of the internationally recognized government in Monrovia scarcely extended beyond the city.

We left just late enough to hit the afternoon rush hour. The streets were choked with cars and with sidewalk vendors. These included freshly killed animals of all kinds being sold for their meat, from massive, meaty sea bass, held aloft by the tail, to "grass cutter," a large bush rat that was a delicacy in much of West Africa. One man hoisted something I had never seen sold this way before: a pygmy deer, or duiker, whose grayish coat glinted with accents in different colors like a hologram. A few yards away, another man held up a civet cat.

The traffic quickly dissipated when we pulled off the coastal road and turned inland. On the outskirts of the capital, Diabaté alerted me to look up as we sped past a newly built university campus that was China's gift to the country, and its single biggest aid project to date. From there, we wound our way through hill country, passing turnoffs here and there for vast Firestone rubber plantations. Until nightfall, we left almost all signs of development behind, pushing through little villages with mud-walled huts that were decorated in stenciled charcoal patterns, where women sat under trees in the early evening air, pounding ingredients of their dinner meals with large, wooden mortars.

The people at the Chinese-built agricultural school in Gbarnga I was to visit had initially declined to receive me. Then they said that if the Chinese embassy approved my visit, they would organize a tour for me. Their reluctance was puzzling. I was well aware of feelings among many Chinese that Westerners held unfriendly attitudes toward their country, and that the Western press was hostile. Attitudes like these were most pronounced among Chinese people who worked for state-funded projects, although in a few instances I had had people hang up on me when I'd identified myself as a writer and had scarcely begun to ask about the possibility of a meeting.

When we pulled up to the entrance of their large, fenced compound with a towering sign that read "China Aid," it was about 8 p.m. The Central Agricultural Research Institute, or CARI, consisted of a cluster of brand-new buildings, including a long dormitory wing with mosquito-netted beds, where I was led to drop off my belongings and wash up. While I was doing so, I overheard a contretemps involving Diabaté in the parking lot below. When I descended, I learned that the Chinese staff had refused to allow him to spend the night on the grounds of the high-walled complex, even if he slept in his car. Diabaté was angry, and there was shouting back and forth. I was surprised by the inflexibility of the Chinese, who seemed embarrassed but held their ground. The rules were the rules, a man named Rong, who was in his early twenties, kept repeating.

I felt bad for Diabaté. I gave him some money and told him to find a hotel in town, and to return in the morning. And with that, nine of us, all men, gathered around a dinner table in a large cafeteria and a simple but delicious dinner was served from a lazy Susan—rice, chicken, and steamed vegetables—all grown right there, I was told proudly.

After the customary small talk, we got into a discussion about Liberia and about their project. The leader, Li Jinjun, a short, plain-looking man from Hunan province, led the conversation, announcing flatly at the outset that what they could accomplish was limited because "Liberians don't understand much." Li was not only the boss, but he had been there the longest, and yet he still seemed surprised as he told me matter-of-factly that Liberians had very different ways of thinking from Chinese.

"Yes, but people are different everywhere," I said, to which he shook his head.

Li revisited the theme of Liberian religiosity, exhibiting the same incredulity I had heard from the young Chinese woman I'd met on my flight into Monrovia. "No Chinese person would worry about God if he didn't have food first. I've visited a church in the United States and I've seen churches here, and they are not at all the same! Here, they are simply dancing, two by two. They are crying and throwing themselves onto the ground and fainting the whole time. I couldn't believe it!"

This prompted Rong to note that Jesus had lived more than two thousand years ago. "A Chinese person would have a hard time believing that someone who lived that long ago could be relevant today," he said, once more shaking his head. "We have Confucius, who we recognize as a wise figure, but we haven't gone so far as to make him into a god!"

"These people expect the government to do everything for them," Li said. "They expect help from the U.N. They wait around for help rather than working."

How then do "they" eat? I asked. Don't "they" farm their own land?

"Very little," Li replied. "I don't get it. If these were Chinese people, they would be struggling to solve their own problems. They wouldn't be waiting on the state."

I didn't want to argue with my hosts. I wanted them to talk. But I felt like reminding Li that perhaps forty million Chinese people had died of starvation a half century earlier because they followed their government's orders. It was the largest famine in history. A snapshot taken then would have given a very different picture of the supposedly essential character of Chinese people, and it would have entirely missed the point. Governments matter. Markets matter. History matters. International circumstances matter.

"This project is going to be different," he said. "The Liberian state has been required to put up the land for us here, and the Chinese subventions will only last for a limited time, say for three years. After that, this center will have to pay for itself, and China will only continue to provide experts to train people. This way, they won't get in the habit of depending on others. They'll learn to support themselves."

The others nodded as Li spoke, and when the boss had finished, one of them chimed in, adding, "Little by little, we can change them in this way."

When I asked how many people they imagine "changing," they said that when the project reached full operation, it would be training about three hundred farmers a year. "You'll have Liberians who come here to work, and they'll have food to eat, and you'll have people on the outside, looking in, the ones who have shunned work, and we'll see the impact this has on them," Li said.

With his alert eyes and rapid speech, Li was clearly a quick thinker, and I got the sense he had picked up on my skepticism, even as I tried to mute it.

"Isn't this country closely tied to the U.S.?" he asked, willfully provocative. "How did the Americans fail to change this place? They've spent a lot of money here over the years, haven't they?"

I told him I was not aware of any country coming from afar and transforming another country's culture or economic circumstance through aid programs alone. A grizzled, older man who sat directly across from me nodded in seeming agreement as I spoke. Later, I learned he was a mechanical engineer. "We won't change the entire country, that's for sure," he said. "It's enough that we're able to change a portion of the population."

"If we change even one of them, that'll be a victory," Rong said.

As the meal came to an end, I shared with them the population projections demographers were making for the continent, that there would be twice as many Africans by mid-century as there were today. With two billion Africans, including vastly more people who will have attained middle-class status or better, and over a billion Chinese, whose lives will be much more affluent, much more globalized and deeply involved in every corner of the world, it was possible to imagine the unfolding relationship between China and Africa as one of the most important in the world. How Africa develops, how it harnesses its resource wealth, who helps shepherd it through its many crises and challenges, from war and poverty to institution building and security, will all depend to a much bigger extent than appears to be the case today on China, a still somewhat reticent global actor.

My hosts were in no way prepared to see that far. In fact, the conversation momentarily stopped in its tracks when I made my demographic observation. It was as if the rude barbarian had said a bad word or committed a faux pas. "Wow," Li replied. "That's going to be a huge problem for the whole world."

That night, as I pulled the mosquito net down around my stiff dormitory bed, the dinner conversation played over and over in my head. There were notes of ignorance about Africans and their circumstances, and palpable naïveté. There was also a kind of optimism and self-belief that was striking, if perhaps equally naive. Here they were discovering Africa and setting goals with the idea of having a quick impact while giving no hint that they were aware of how thoroughly trodden the ground they were walking upon was.

My thoughts turned to my father, a public health physician who had worked in this very same district a generation earlier pushing a concept that would sound deeply familiar to them: the training of small cadres of health care workers who would then go forth into their communities and train many others in basic health care techniques. This work was done in the belief that through the power of positive examples, little by little things could change and lives could improve.

We all gathered early the next morning for another communal Chinese meal, this time of porridge, boiled vegetables, and steamed buns, and a few of us, led by Li, were out the door very quickly and bundled into a large four-wheel-drive.

Our first stop, to my surprise, was a hilltop installation of Cuttington University. This was the very institution that my father had worked with in the 1980s to help build a national primary health care system for the country from scratch. Historically, the school had had a strong agricultural mission, and the Chinese team had evidently looked to it both for talent and as a partner in building a training program.

The school's little agricultural station where we stopped was nothing more than a smattering of faded staff villas poised atop a verdant hill. Li climbed down from the wheel and summoned an older local man from one of the villas, whom he introduced simply as a "tree expert." The two of them talked, as best they could, given Li's limited English and the Liberian's heavy patois. No explanation was offered for the visit.

It was not the rainy season, but there had been heavy downpours recently, and this vista, with moist slopes and green valleys all about, made a powerful statement: this was rich land, just waiting to mightily reward whoever could muster the resources and the right strategy for farming it.

From there, we drove down into a valley to inspect an area of flat farmland irrigated by a Chinese-built system of dikes and canals. The narrow, mud-banked channels of the canals seemed well constructed and were clearly doing their job of controlling the flow of water throughout an area as large as several football fields. The muddy land had not been planted yet, though, and although it looked as if it had once been cleared, it was already heavily weeded; the notorious African "bush" was reasserting itself. As we trod through this heavy growth, we came upon three bare-chested Liberian workers who were wielding hoes and machetes against the weeds.

Rong remarked that before their team had arrived in these parts, the locals knew nothing of hoes at all. "Everything was done with machetes, even digging," he said incredulously. "Is all of Africa like this?"

As we moved on, I assured him that the hoe was a common, indigenous instrument in this region, and was widely known as the *daba*. Speculating out loud, I said that it had probably existed locally since the Bronze Age. My attempt at cultural history made little impression.

As with the previous stop, my hosts had never explained where we were going, or why, and it wasn't until we'd reached the far end of the long field, and emerged from the overgrowth, that I could hear the voices of children playing and understand that we were approaching a school. We climbed up a muddy bank and into a thick bamboo grove where we came upon and slightly startled a peasant woman who had just harvested a large African breadfruit, which she set on the ground on top of a bolt of dyed cloth. Just beyond her, at the perimeter of the school, a number of students had noticed our approach and started cheering enthusiastically.

By now, it was nearly 9:30, and the only sign of activity anywhere was the play of the students in the earthen courtyard. There were several dozen of them, and to my surprise, they ranged from near toddler to what looked like eighteen-year-olds.

Li, who was clearly familiar with the place, approached the office, where we found the principal, a smiling, well-fed woman named Lilly, who explained that the school had fifty students and five teachers, but that school was out today. She gave no reason. Lilly obligingly said we were free to walk around, and so I wandered through the three classrooms arrayed all in a line in what was in effect an old shotgun building with dirt floors and no windows. There were few desks and chairs, and there was no light or electricity, either.

In the only classroom that was occupied, I found two eighteen-year-old girls who sat sharing a desk, one of them dutifully copying the notes from the tattered notebook of another. I asked them what they were studying. The girl nearest to me announced that they were in the fifth grade.

"There is no way we can change their ways here," Li said. "There is no education. There is nothing to work with."

Our next stop required us to drive a little ways to the headwaters of the irrigation system. There we found a lake that sat behind a small dam that far predated the arrival of the Chinese here, and the ducks swimming in the still water amid all of the softly lit greenery made for a gorgeous scene.

We walked uphill on the road from there to a spot where a handsome new gray-and-white building sat, its Chinese tile roof a clear giveaway of its origins. From a distance, it looked lovely, if strangely out of place. As we drew closer, the mood of our jaunt changed from casual and ambling to more than faintly angry as my hosts began to tell the building's story. It was intended as a storage facility and rest house for their researchers.

"Three weeks after we finished building this structure, they came and stole everything," Li said. When he unlocked the door and we entered, he minutely detailed the trail of damage: the sinks and the toilet fixtures that had been ripped away, along with the electrical switch boxes that were extruded from the walls, and even the window frames that had somehow been crowbarred out. He took me to the back of the building to show me the kinds of reinforcements they felt forced to install to protect against theft in the future. Crude iron rebar now covered the windows.

"We had fixed this place up pretty nicely," Li said. "It's not so nice anymore, but it is more secure. You really can't blame them. They have no food. They have nothing here. They can only depend on theft to survive."

CHAPTER FIVE

Conakry

Late to the Banquet

My stay in Conakry, Guinea, had begun promisingly enough, with the Internet and electricity and air-conditioning in a cheap downtown hotel all functioning without a hitch that first night. Before bed, I'd watched a bit of TV. Programming on the local channel was suffused with talk about the rule of law and the importance of democracy, which had only just arrived in Guinea, after decades of dictatorship and nightmarish misrule.

I was surprised the satellite package offered stations from Senegal and Zambia, among other places, and many of the programs I'd chanced upon randomly were all about democracy, too. On the Senegalese show, a leading figure from the ruling party faced serious questions by skeptical, well-prepared reporters, and when that was finished, opposition politicians were allowed to weigh in and vigorously contradict what they'd heard.

With morning arrived disappointment like a faithful companion. The electricity switched on and off constantly, and each time it was cut, I lost my Internet connection, requiring me to run the length of my floor and down a flight of stairs to reset the hotel's router manually.

I ventured out for lunch at midday, stopping a taxi and giving the driver the name of an upscale restaurant, Le Damier, that I'd heard about, run by a longtime French resident of the city. His first turn landed us on the main boulevard, plunging us into a colossal traffic jam. There was the normal confusion of cars with impatient drivers contending for space, along with street vendors of every type, and polio victims imploring anyone with an open window for coins. What stood out above all, though, was the fearsome teams of military police, all dressed in black, commando-style uniforms, who worked the scene, going from car to car along whole stretches of the main street demanding bribes.

Little more than a year earlier, Guinea had experienced a military coup by junior officers, and when the population bridled about their plans to retain power, demonstrators were shot, stabbed, bludgeoned, and raped in large numbers during a protest at a sports stadium. Through international pressure, the coup leaders had recently been forced out of office and an elected government replaced them, but this police display in the street suggested to me that the cancer of armed power had not been completely excised.

Halfway through my three-course meal, a Chinese man in late middle age appeared at the top of the wooden stairway, accompanied by a much younger Guinean who was dressed soberly in an olive suit. There was one free table between the wall and me, and they were immediately directed to it, placing the older man barely two feet away.

The man's clothes dated him as surely as the lines on his face: a simple, lightweight shirt in white cotton of a style I associated with the former president Jiang Zemin, along with dark gray trousers and thin white socks. He sat bolt upright and exuded an easy authority. I pegged him for a senior company official, or perhaps a veteran diplomat, although he struggled in English and could speak no French, the official language in Guinea.

After twenty minutes or so, a handsome, younger Chinese man climbed the stairway and appeared in a well-cut suit, fuchsia tie, and very pale matching fuchsia shirt. The younger man greeted the Guinean in polished and culturally attuned French, gracefully inquiring about the well-being of his family, and in its own way the generational contrast was strong evidence of the progress China was making in its global push. I couldn't recall seeing many American diplomats in these parts capable of such finesse.

The two Chinese then talked for more than thirty minutes, leaving the Guinean to fiddle with his phone.

The fancy service at Le Damier involved having a waiter wheel over a large cart with samples of the various dishes: beef, fish, fowl, and a local delicacy, peanut sauce with rice. Amid the abundance, the older

Chinese man appeared to have difficulty choosing, before telling his countryman, "I'll have the Indian dish," pointing to the peanut sauce. The younger man gently corrected him. "That's not Indian cuisine, it's black people's food," he said, and with that, the older man promptly changed his selection to a meaty cut of fish.

With the two continuing to ignore their Guinean counterpart, the conversation turned to matters of money. The younger man wanted details about the price of an unnamed commodity by the ton, perhaps bauxite or iron, the country's biggest exports. Then he made something of a boast. "In Paris, I've just met the son of the president of Senegal," he said. "He wants us to invest, but I don't think we want to go there."

The older man seemed impatient and returned to the subject of buying a shipment of whatever raw mineral product they had been discussing. He was hell-bent on consummating his deal. This drew a note of caution from his colleague. "Whatever you do, don't pay them money until it's loaded onto the ship," he said. "You can tell it to them just like that."

My notebook had sat there on the table, open, while I used my iPad, and now I began to write in it. At that moment, a very prosperous-looking man I took for a local approached the table next to me, saying loudly *"Ni hao, ni hao,"* before continuing jovially in French. "It's been a long time!"

"Yes," the younger of the two Chinese men said. "I went back home to China to see my wife. She just delivered a baby girl."

After a round of congratulations, they all turned their attention to the neglected Guinean man, whom the newcomer also seemed to know. The older Chinese man asked his colleague to explain to him that they would be sending him a ticket soon to travel to China for the first time.

When the Guinean newcomer walked away, they resumed their conversation in Chinese, neglecting their tablemate. After several minutes of this, the Guinean man said he had to go, announcing that he was on his way to the president's protocol office.

I spent the late afternoon at a large, two-story web café called Mouna on Avenue de la République, where drinks and snacks were served. It was teeming with young people who paid by the minute to check their Facebook accounts, chat with relatives or friends in France and elsewhere via Skype, and exchange flirty stares. High on the walls above the central seating area hung prints of classic photographs by Robert Doisneau, interspersed with old black-and-white portraits of Ray Charles, Muhammad Ali, and Miles Davis. Could a Starbucks soundtrack be far off?

The sidewalk outside featured a constant parade of *bana bana*, each with his own little gesture for making a claim on your attention through the plate glass that separated their dusty world from the air-conditioned one of ours. But as darkness fell, the *bana bana* had been replaced by a crowd beginning to form on the sidewalk, hugging strangely to the walls of buildings, as if trying to avoid being hit by something. I could hear a siren, then many sirens, as a motorcade roared past, speeding down the trash-strewn boulevard, lights flashing, guns waving from men piled tightly into the back of vans and pickup trucks.

Things continued like this for at least five minutes as the president made his way home from his office. The frightening men who were deployed to protect him wore the same black uniforms and berets as the police I'd seen that morning, holding people up in the street.

When the crowd dissipated, I gathered my things and picked my way past the potholes in the darkness, walking four blocks on a cratered street lined with shabby walk-up tenements to the restaurant where I had scheduled a dinner meeting. The warm evening air was thick with moisture, and the long blackout, the everyday companion of residents of this city, had forced many people out of their homes, to eat or prepare food in the open air, or simply to stand around and chat.

The little place I was going to boasted unfussy local specialties of grilled fish and chicken. I joined my dinner companion, Amadou Dano Barry, whose caramel-colored skin was common to many among the country's Peul minority group. Barry, a well-connected academic at the University of Conakry, listened with keen, intelligent eyes, laughing often as I related the story of my lunchtime eavesdropping.

Speaking in elegant French, Barry surprised me with his comment. "The Chinese are not in a hurry to go it alone and implant themselves here. Their government doesn't seem to be pushing the big state companies to make huge investments. They don't give one the impression they've given in other places, say, the Congo."

In Congo, one of Africa's richest mineral states, China had recently and controversially negotiated a mammoth resources-for-infrastructure deal valued at $6 billion. In exchange for building new roads and railway lines, along with many other things, including hospitals, housing, and a new university, China would be guaranteed a supply of copper and cobalt over a period of twenty years.

Civil society critics of the package deal said that by agreeing to terms like this, Congo risked vastly underselling its assets. The Western powers and international financial institutions that had traditionally been Congo's leading economic partners were unhappy, too. They complained that China was positioning itself as a "preferential creditor," one that would jump ahead of the country's traditional lenders in the reimbursement queue. Whatever they thought of the Chinese deal, many Africans believed that Western complaints were a demonstration of bad faith, motivated mostly by chagrin over having been shown up by China, the world's new, fast-rising power.

Guinea's vast underground wealth placed it in the same league as Congo. Rather than explaining why China was not committing in Guinea, as I expected, Barry made clear that the Asian power was neither cool nor indifferent to the big opportunities here. He explained that China had already once attempted to score a big coup with a deal similar to the one in Congo. This had come during the brutal rule of Dadis Camara, the leader of the group of junior officers who took over the country after the death of longtime president Lansana Conté.

"Dadis had the idea that if he could supply reliable electricity and water to the population, which is something that no other president here has ever managed to do, he'd be able to stay in power. The Chinese offered him a $5 billion package deal, which they supported with lots of *pots-de-vin* and they would build infrastructure, in exchange for iron ore, bauxite, and oil exploration rights."

From the description, I took this to be a China International Fund (CIF) initiative, which for months had been the subject of an intense media polemic. The package was offered to Guinea's leaders within days of the mass rape of demonstrators protesting against military rule.

Critics in both Africa and the West adopt it as a prime exhibit in the argument that China's approach toward the continent, especially its position of not judging the internal affairs of other countries, is ultimately harmful to the emergence of democratic rule and better human rights and governance. Others rushed to defend China against these charges, saying that however shady, CIF was a private Hong Kong–based holding company, and arguing that it is unfair to judge Beijing by CIF's actions.

Everyone I spoke with in Guinea's small intelligentsia, however, claimed to know that CIF executives enjoyed top-level access to the Chinese leadership, and for them, this was proof enough that CIF's actions were in some meaningful sense an indication of China's modus operandi in Africa.

"The Chinese didn't want to put themselves out there directly," Barry said. "That's why this thing was structured a 'private' investment. Things might not have worked out this time, but these things tend to work for the Chinese in Africa. That's because Africans have not mastered management. Our leaders are lazy, and their attitude is that the detailed stuff is too complicated. Their priority is to be able to say to the population: See what I've managed to get done? This allows the Chinese to win on every front, and they will implant themselves because they understand that Africans aren't up to doing certain things.

"The Chinese come and they want your iron, your bauxite, your petroleum. In return, they'll deliver you turnkey projects, where they supply the materials, the technology, and the labor, with salaries that are mostly not paid in the country and do not contribute to the economy.

"On the African side, no one verifies anything. No one knows the real costs. What we're talking about is, in effect, barter, and the reality is that you'll get your infrastructure, but after five years, if you're lucky, it will be in a deteriorated state. You won't bother to maintain it, and you won't care, because it is like something that fell out of the sky and into your lap."

Barry said that Guinea had experienced the very first example of this model shortly after its stormy declaration of independence from France in 1958, under the country's first leader, the socialist dictator Sékou Touré.

"The Chinese were very quick to establish ties, and right away they offered to build us the Palais du Peuple [National Assembly building].

Ever since then, practically every African leader, whatever his ideological orientation, has gotten a palace of some sort from the Chinese. The problem is, they never taught us how to maintain it. Even now, when the lightbulbs are burned out, we have to call the Chinese to change them."

The next day I went to see the head of an umbrella group of national civil society organizations, Aziz Diop. He is a burly man and he was draped in an ample and well-worn traditional boubou when he met me at a restaurant in a neighborhood of cratered streets near the oceanfront. He began by lamenting how, over the decades, Africa had acquired a reputation as the beggar continent, and he was worried about dependence on China. "From the Guinean point of view, Chinese money is too easy, and that facility allows the government to meet its immediate needs, and to avoid sound decisions," he said. "What is more, China is not at all particular about things like democracy and human rights."

Like most Guineans I spoke with, Diop was having none of the supposed separation between the CIF and the interests of the Chinese state. Whatever its legal basis as a corporation, he believed that CIF was essentially serving Chinese purposes. "The Chinese had no second thoughts about rushing in to do big business with the junta. What we want are partners who respect good values."

Like Barry before him, Diop complained that Chinese projects were negotiated with a total lack of transparency. "If we are paying for big projects we want them to include real transfer of technology and of expertise, but the Chinese bring all their own workers, and the few Guineans are reduced to the role of task boys. In one case we had here, a Chinese company was hired to build a bridge and they did most of their work at night, and they wouldn't let anyone onto their site. Between the groundbreaking and inauguration ceremonies, they give out no information at all, nothing."

Diop said that his group and others in the civil society coalition had repeatedly tried to speak with Chinese contractors and Chinese diplomats to impress upon them the need to reconsider their approach to things in Guinea, but had been either patronized or turned away.

"You go to see them and they say go see your minister, or go see your president, he's the one who approved these arrangements."

I heard very similar language from disgruntled civil society figures virtually everywhere I traveled.

"There is a risk that they should consider, though, that one day the people of Africa will come to see China as an unfriendly country," Diop said. "That could put all of their interests in danger over time. They should think about this a little more."

Rarely, if ever, had I met anyone who could be fairly described as plainly "anti-Chinese." In fact, in countries where China's engagement had deep roots, it was common for people of all descriptions, including well-educated members of the elite and the most ordinary of folks, to recite a history of Chinese aid and solidarity. But as China ramps up on the continent today, as a voracious and increasingly rich and strong market-driving power, the optics surrounding its presence are changing, leaving a common set of adverse images in the minds of people all across Africa. There was mounting resentment over the way China was seen to be exporting its labor, dumping cheap goods, despoiling the environment, dispossessing powerless landholders or flouting local laws, fueling corruption, and most of all, empowering awful governments.

Some of this was merely the expected price of success to be paid along the way to becoming a newly minted global power. In this regard, these criticisms often reminded me of the attitudes of another era, when the United States was newly making its power felt in faraway parts of the world.

Diop's admonition to China, however, amounted to a warning that in an Africa where governments often sit on narrow ethnic or regional bases, and where presidential clans, either literal or figurative, loot and despoil their countries with impunity, China's conception of foreign affairs as an exclusively state-to-state matter would ultimately place its own interests at risk.

The next morning I was hastily summoned to a meeting with the minister of cooperation, Koutoub Moustapha Sano. A confident, youthful man in his mid-forties, he had studied in Malaysia and remained there for sixteen years, eventually teaching comparative law. He nodded approvingly as I told him about my travels in the region, saying of the Chinese, "You are right to conclude that they are everywhere in Africa nowadays."

When it came to detailing Guinea's cooperation with China, Sano seemed light on information, or at least on information that he could freely exchange. Between platitudes, however, he said that in order to jump-start "cooperation" between the countries, Beijing had recently given his country a $39 million grant. The gesture had come during a visit by the Chinese foreign minister, who explained that he had first visited the country as a young man, with Zhou Enlai, Mao's longtime deputy. Beijing had also recently donated a number of buses for Conakry's bare-bones municipal transport system.

"China has an approach, and we understand how it works," Sano said. "They give you a loan and they want you to work with their companies. If you want to build a hotel, for example, they'll arrange the financing for you and ask you to work with their companies. They are looking for markets for their companies."

I asked how the grant and the buses, which were not loans tied to business contracts, should be understood.

"They are very smart. They don't say this is in exchange for anything. But of course when they begin doing business with you, they may expect certain things from you in return. In that light, you might consider these things to constitute a bribe." Sano paused and smiled, before adding, "We understand this."

I knew from a variety of sources about China's purported dealings with the junta that had controlled the country until recently. A senior African official of the World Bank official had told me, for example, of the sudden and secretive acquisition of two thermal generators aimed at restoring power to the capital and thus justifying the continued hold on power of the junior officers who ruled the country at the time. "Everything was paid for by the China International Fund," the official told me. "Nowhere did this deal appear in the government's books." The junta leaders were removed from power before the generators could be hooked up, though, spoiling what was seen almost universally here as a Chinese bid to buy influence with a weak and vulnerable regime.

Sano nodded as I told this story, but would neither confirm nor deny it. His tack changed, though, when I mentioned the name of Mahmood Thiam, a former Guinean official who had been widely seen as the bag man for the Chinese during the junta's desperate deal making. Thiam had reportedly fled Guinea when the junta came apart, and gone on to represent CIF in business deals it was pursuing in other parts of the continent. When I asked Sano for confirmation of these details, he looked uncomfortable for the first time in our conversation, saying he was not in the government at the time.

"We know that Thiam is not in the country, and it is possible that he will never return," he said.

Does this mean he is guilty of something? I asked.

"It means that when there is smoke there is fire."

I asked Sano what he made of the blind eye that China turned to questions of democracy, human rights, and transparency, all under the banner of noninterference.

"For me, keeping quiet about bad things happening in a friendly country is definitely not good," he said. "When you have a friend, you expect them to tell you what is good and what is not good. That only seems normal to me."

CHAPTER SIX

Freetown

Instruments of Magic

Freetown, Sierra Leone, is located twenty minutes by air from Cona-kry, a straight shot to the southeast along the West African coast. My meetings there began with Kelvin Lewis, a local reporter I had met in the 1990s during the long and terrible insurrection commanded by the rebel leader Foday Sankoh. Since then, Kelvin had started his own newspaper, which had quickly become one of the country's best.

Sankoh, a former army photographer, had been sponsored by Charles Taylor, the warlord turned president of next-door Liberia. A favorite tactic of his soldiers involved amputating the hands and feet of villagers in order to spread terror through the countryside, causing peasants to flee and allowing his forces to occupy the land and plunder its diamond fields and other riches.

We rendezvoused on the second-floor terrace of a downtown res-taurant that overlooked the street. Kelvin had with him a couple of cell phones and a calendar-style agenda book, and had the same sleepy eyes and heavily drawling speech that I remembered. As we waited for our food, he regaled me with stories from the final stages of the war, when the rebels had surrounded Freetown and briefly seemed poised for total victory. At great personal risk, he had managed to make his way across the bay to Lungi, where the main Nigerian contingent of a regional peacekeeping force was massing for a counteroffensive. He was fitted with a bulletproof vest and steel helmet and fell in with them as a reporter as they crossed the estuary and routed Sankoh's unsus-pecting forces.

During their siege of Freetown, the rebels had destroyed all of the country's best hotels. One of them, the Bintumani, a stone's throw from where I was lodging now, had been especially hard hit. "They stripped the tiles from the floors and ripped every single cable out from off the walls," he said. The end of the war was still months away, but as soon as the Nigerians had pushed the rebels out of the capital, a group of previously unknown Chinese businessmen arrived in Freetown and successfully negotiated the takeover of the Bintumani at a fire-sale price from a cash-strapped government that had barely escaped being overthrown.

"Nobody had ever seen Chinese businesspeople like this in Freetown before, but as soon as they got their concession they went to work on the place, and before anyone knew it, they had it fixed up, and once the war was over, they were sitting pretty. They had finished their renovations, and they had the only international hotel that was functioning in Freetown."

This, in Kelvin's mind, was the moment that marked the beginning of a new scramble for Sierra Leone. In the modern history of this country, anywhere profits were being made one was likely to find Lebanese, who began arriving here in the 1890s. They dominated the retail scene buzzing below us on the shabby downtown streets. They controlled the lucrative government procurement business. They'd cornered the markets for textbooks used in the country's schools and the cloth used for mandatory student uniforms. To change money, one had to go through them; to buy food from a supermarket, ditto. And nowhere was this truer than for the biggest and dirtiest business of all in Sierra Leone, the diamond trade.

Almost immediately in the wake of the Bintumani's reopening, Kelvin told me, Chinese road-building companies started showing up and landing contracts in the capital, and very quickly afterward began appearing further afield throughout the country. "The people who had traditionally done the roads, especially the Italian and Senegalese companies that had received some good contracts in the past, they were not happy."

According to a narrative that by now was common currency in Freetown, those early Chinese deals were mere preliminaries for a far bigger prize they sought, which was to take control of and revive a collapsed mining industry that sat on immense reserves of iron, rutile, titanium, and many other industrial metals. When its war was ending,

Sierra Leone looked like an open field. After the Bintumani was redone, the Chinese newcomers dangled sweeteners in their bid to win major mining concessions. These offers reportedly came to include building a new "second city" for Sierra Leone entirely from scratch, renovating the antiquated Freetown airport, building a brand-new seaport, and constructing a smelter to process the new iron ore production. To their dismay, however, the Chinese prospectors in Sierra Leone were scooped by the even faster footwork of an obscure and unusually colorful Romanian-born businessman named Frank Timis.

Far more than most, Timis's story reflects the nature of high-stakes business in the corrupt and unstructured environment of poor, postwar African societies like Sierra Leone.

Timis was said to have grown up in Transylvania, left school at twelve, and fled communist Romania at the age of sixteen, by walking forty-two days through the former Yugoslavia until he reached Trieste, Italy. Whether that is true or not, eventually he made his way to Australia, where he was granted political asylum.

In Australia, he began as a simple laborer for a company that mined gold and diamonds, but he steadily rose to become a field assistant, and finally project supervisor. Later, he started a company that leased earthmoving equipment to the booming mining sector of Western Australia. By the early 1990s, now an Australian citizen, he was running a small exploration company of his own. He had also been convicted three times on narcotics charges, two of which involved possession of heroin with the intent to sell.

In 1996, seven years after the fall of communism in the country of his birth, he returned to Romania. There, Timis advised the government on the creation of a new mining code, and in short order conducted a geological survey of Romania. He also won for himself mineral exploration rights for about 5 percent of his homeland's total territory, including what would soon be recognized as some of the most lucrative concessions in the country.

Here was a man who was preternaturally drawn to extractive industries, who was extraordinarily restless, and who through whatever means, legitimate or not, had a knack for working his way into the good graces of people in government. Wherever he went, he would trail controversy, legal troubles, unsavory rumors, and hard-to-shake doubts about his reputation. All of this paled, though, in comparison with his uncanny ability to be in the right place at the right time.

After making good money in Europe in a variety of mining and oil ventures, Timis showed up in Freetown in 2004. Speaking of a devastated country with one of the shortest life expectancies and lowest per capita incomes in the world, in interviews he took to describing Sierra Leone as a "jewelbox," and the "Switzerland of Africa." He quickly invested £6.6 million, which won him a large minority share in an obscure Bermuda-registered company called the Sierra Leone Diamond Corporation. SLDC had been registered since the late 1990s, but had no record of producing diamonds. That didn't deter him.

Timis's new company may have had no cash flow, but it enjoyed the mining rights to 25,000 square kilometers of land—more than a third of the entire country. Six months later, Timis increased his ownership of his new company to about 30 percent. A few weeks later, in September 2005, SLDC announced it had discovered iron deposits at Tonkolili estimated at one billion tons.

By 2008, after the company had changed its name to African Minerals, these estimates had risen to two billion tons, and by the following year to five billion. Indeed, each year brought a new rise in confirmed deposits. In 2011, Timis's company controlled what was considered the world's biggest iron deposit, by a large margin.

Along the way, Timis formed partnerships with two large, state-owned Chinese partners, China Railways Materials, and later the Shandong Iron and Steel Group, whom he allowed to buy into his company. This gave him the means to greatly expand the scope of his operations, and to rebuild the defunct railroad to the mining region and to build a new port at a place called Tagrin Point, both of which were needed to lower production costs and boost export capacity.

The talk of Freetown while I was there was still of how Shandong Iron and Steel had labored for nearly a year behind the scenes, even as it was haggling for a stake of African Minerals, to get the Sierra Leone government to cede it outright control of the huge mother lode of iron, deemed so vital to Chinese industry. The rumored inducements included an under-the-table offer of $150 million to President Ernest Bai Koroma. If this was true, it makes Timis's success in the country even more impressive.

In the end, the Chinese bidders would have to settle for second fiddle in one of the biggest mining deals in recent history. Surely, they learned a lot along the way about making friends and winning influence in murky African backwaters.

The manager of the Bintumani Hotel, a man named Yang, was expecting me on the afternoon I decided to drop in there. When I was ushered into his office off to the side of the front desk, I was a little surprised to find someone so young.

Yang had a broad face and wore thick, frameless glasses under a bristling shock of black hair, and he was possessed of an easy smile, which revealed teeth that carried heavy stains of tea and tobacco. He told me that he had graduated from college in 2002 at the age of twenty-two and worked a series of unremarkable jobs in Beijing for a few years before setting off for Zambia with a classmate in 2006 on what seemed more or less like a whim.

As was true for so many Chinese in Africa, he said he left because of the pressures of life back home. "Surely you must know how great the stress there can be," he said. "You graduate and right away people begin telling you that you have to buy a house, you have to buy a car, you must get married, you must help your family."

His classmate's family's connections led the two to a rural part of Zambia, where he landed his first job, working with no prior experience in the construction sector as a supervisor for a private Chinese company that was building a water reservoir. "I was the only Chinese on the site. I worked a full day, every day. I cooked my own food, and I had to supervise the blacks. On top of that, I spoke almost no English, and had to use a computer all the time to look things up and translate. The good thing is that I learned a lot."

From Zambia, Yang made his way to Sierra Leone, parlaying his construction experience in a couple of projects in southern Africa into a much better job running and overseeing the expansion of the Bintumani, which as I said earlier, belonged now to a big, state-owned Chinese building company.

"When I was in Zambia, I used to think to myself, how could a country be so disorderly? Coming here made me understand that

Zambia is a relatively advanced country. In Sierra Leone, everything was either broken or run-down."

Yang confessed a longing to go back to China. He cited professional restlessness and ambition as the reasons.

"We are expanding here and we are in talks with the government about housing developments, but these are pretty small projects. It's only in China that I'd have a chance to do something really big."

The Lebanese owners of the place where I was staying were putting up a big, modern structure right there on the elbow of the peninsula, a stone's throw from where we sat, and it was clearly a response to the big Chinese push in the surrounding beach district. It seemed like a clear, if belated attempt to draw the line and prevent the newcomers from taking over a domain they once had to themselves. Yang laughed at the idea that the Lebanese could measure up as competitors.

"For a very long time, this was an easy country to make money in," he said. "Now it is getting more competitive. I've had many Chinese friends come here on business, and they tell me that whenever they encounter Lebanese in business, the Lebanese try to take advantage of them. They are always snooping around, trying to understand your prices and costs and looking for ways to undercut you. If they control a market, they'll always try to get you on price, but that's changing now, as other people enter business."

The Lebanese control of markets had been extremely costly for Sierra Leoneans, he said. Yang used building supplies as an example, saying they sold here for five or six times what they would cost in an open market.

I had dinner that night in a hard-to-find Chinese restaurant; a faintly lit building that sat on a high embankment on the opposite side of an unfinished divided highway. If not for my driver, I would never have found it. No name was to be seen.

When I arrived, two fetchingly dressed young Chinese women were emerging from the building, which aroused my curiosity. I could just now make out Chinese lanterns dangling by the door. I climbed the steep steps and was greeted languidly by a local girl who stood in the doorway, all but blocking the entrance. "Is there food here" I asked.

"Yes, but only Chinese food," she said uninvitingly. Her remark nonplussed me.

I distinctly heard Chinese state television, CCTV, playing loudly beyond the threshold as I made my way in. A chubby, disheveled Chinese man was standing alone in the open, white-tiled dining space, where there were a handful of empty tables. He, too, seemed slightly confused by my presence, so I said *"Ni hao!"* He nodded silently, looking like he wished I would go away.

"Does this place have a name?" I asked.

"Beijing Fandian," he said, meaning Beijing Restaurant, warming a bit to the idea of my presence.

I said I had been told the place had been advertised as the best food in town. With that, another man emerged from a room back behind a high, bamboo bar. "He's the owner," the first man said. "The real Beijing guy." We exchanged greetings, and it was clear from the heavy northern burr I heard in his first few syllables that this fiftyish man of medium height was indeed an authentic Beijinger.

He circled back after I had been seated to take my order. We then began to exchange small talk. He asked me whether I was just traveling through the region or if I was working. I told him I was working. He issued a typically Chinese exclamation, *"Waa,"* then asked, "Why would someone come from such a developed country to such an undeveloped one to work?"

I turned it back on him. "I've been here since '93," he said. "When I left China, it, too, was an undeveloped country. We had barely begun our reform and opening." There was something about the spontaneous-sounding way he said this that suggested he had given this history little prior thought, at least recently, and was faintly surprised or at least impressed by his own observation.

I told him that I was a writer and that I had lived in China recently, and in Africa for years in the past, and that I was interested in the new Chinese communities in the countries I was visiting.

At that moment, an attractive Chinese woman in her late twenties entered the scene and our conversation broke off. She was dressed in cutoffs and an oversized T-shirt, and she seemed very familiar with the setting. After the restaurant owner returned to the kitchen, someone came and served her what must have been a previously ordered dish, and she finished it quickly. She then got up and plopped herself the-atrically in a chair directly in front of me. Next to it, an oscillating fan circulated the warm night air in her direction.

Sensing that she had been monitoring me closely from the moment of her entry, I addressed her with a common greeting used with young women, *"Mei nu, ni hao,"* meaning something approximating, Hello, lovely. She was duly flattered, but as protocol would demand, she turned down the compliment. "I'm no *mei nu,"* she said.

I asked the woman what she did in Sierra Leone, and her odd reply took me aback. "Nothing at all," she answered.

"Have you been here long?"

"Yes." She nodded. "Eight years."

"Eight years of doing nothing?"

She told me she was from Hubei province and asked me if I knew it. I told her yes. She named her hometown as Wuhan, a deeply grimy provincial capital a few hundred miles southwest of Shanghai. "That's where kung pao chicken comes from," I said. She hadn't known this. "The food is very hot in Wuhan, isn't it?" I asked.

This brought a grin to her face and she said she had just eaten a very hot dish. Eventually the young woman told me that she lives "off of a friend." When he was busy, which I assumed to mean in the coun-tryside on mining or logging business, she said she lodged in a little boardinghouse attached to the restaurant. "And when he's not busy, I stay at his place."

She was twenty-nine years old. She said she had worked in "enter-tainment," and in restaurants, before striking up the relationship with the man who kept her. This all suggested to me she had come here, at least initially, to work in what's known in parts of East Asia as the "water trade," meaning prostitution.

When a short, middle-aged man emerged from the kitchen in the back and beckoned the young woman to join him at another table for a game of mah-jongg, I took my leave. I shared a taxi with a disheveled-looking older Chinese man who was also going to Aberdeen, the beach-front neighborhood where I was staying. I asked the Chinese how long he had been in Sierra Leone.

"Seven years," he answered in a choked voice. His Mandarin was not filtered through some regional dialect, just very rough; a familiar kind of Lost Generation diction, the speech of a person of a certain age from the inland provinces whose schooling had been aborted by the Cultural Revolution.

He gave his name as Jin Guoshen, and put his age at "fifty-something," which was unusual not just for its vagueness, but because he looked so worn that I assumed he was at least fifteen years older. When I asked what he did for a living, he replied with one word, *"Xiuli,"* which is about the most general way possible of saying repairman. "I fix appliances, refrigerators, microwaves," he said, adding with a chuckle, "cars, too. Basically I can fix anything."

Late one afternoon, I set out from the muggy low city near the port to the hilly residential part of town that hugged the gentle slopes up above and beyond an old downtown landmark, the Paramount Hotel. It would be dark in an hour or so, and the light just then was as full and delicious as I could remember seeing it anywhere in Africa, with its thick, tactile reds, electric greens, and deep, aquatic blues. I was on my way to meet Joseph Rahall, the head of an indigenous NGO named Green Scenery, a leading member of Sierra Leone's small but intensely vibrant civil society.

We met in a small, stifling room on the second floor of his villa as the sun set. There was no electricity in the neighborhood, and Rahall sat beside the room's lone wood-framed window as we spoke. He wore an elaborately patterned, wax-dyed African shirt, and had a gaunt face brought to life by intense eyes, a husky voice, and busy, expressive hands.

He gave me a quick history of NGOs in the country, which got their start in earnest in the mid-1990s, during the war, when civic-minded people like him were preoccupied with the horrors that had plagued Sierra Leone—things like summary executions, forced conscription of children into militias, rape, mass amputations, and slave labor.

"Immediately once the conflict ended, though," Rahall said, "people began pushing into other areas. Almost overnight, democracy and rule of law became big themes. After the space was created, things just took off. People's consciousness was already there, and after so much suffering, we had this powerful surge of civic involvement."

The bright optimism of those early days had since faded into a tougher, less hopeful realism. People had come to terms with the fact that building a viable, prosperous democracy in a country this poor would be a difficult long-term struggle, and as he spoke, Rahall continually tacked between notes of darkness and light.

For now, he said, there was a formal democracy. "Many things are rubber-stamped. As a matter of fact, I can't say that they are doing things any better than the past governments. What has changed is the fact that people can talk freely now, and this has begun to push back the frontiers of fear.

"What we are crying for in Sierra Leone is transparency. We have gotten the government to agree to review all the old contracts. We've gotten them to rewrite the mining laws. We are engaging with the government, pushing to educate people. But on the revenue side, we are doing very poorly. The money they are getting from mining concessions is very small, and either [the government] doesn't have the resources to deal with the companies, or they are benefiting from corruption and allowing people not to respect the rules.

"The Chinese work in a very peculiar manner. They prefer to deal directly with the president and to make a spectacular gesture, and that is that. They don't go for any public discussion, and they won't give importance to many international norms, or to civil society, or to principles like democracy. That is the backdrop to some of their big deals in this country—not just iron, but also for oil and for timber."

Despite these misgivings, Rahall said that the arrival of Chinese money had given countries like his new options, and hence more breathing space, meaning unaccustomed freedom for once from the West.

"People have welcomed the Chinese because they were an alternative, because there are times when you can find yourself with no investors, and the West just wags its finger at you and calls you corrupt. When our countries weren't able to get money from the World Bank, or from their traditional donors because of the EITI [Extractive Industries Transparency Initiative] process rules, or environmental concerns, or because of financial transparency issues, the Chinese were there, and many people welcomed this, and not only the folks in government. The promising idea of this Chinese alternative has begun to show its real face, though. Nowadays, it feels more like being stuck between the devil and the deep blue sea."

The familiar West was clearly the devil, in Rahall's construct, and the Chinese, still a novel presence, were the deep blue sea, with their seductive packages and all too neat and simple terms which risked leaving countries like his loaded up on debt and their supply of minerals exhausted.

"They come these days with big investments and with big projects, but it is important for us to recognize that what they are really doing is looking out for their own best interests . . . [and] that what is good for them may not be good for us. The natural resources we have are depletable, and we need to find a way to invest productively, to devise new kinds of wealth creation, so that when the resources are all gone, which will happen sooner than people realize, there will be something left. We've already seen this process play out with our diamonds, which have never benefited the people of Sierra Leone, and that is because the people in government have always been so busy figuring out ways to steal."

We are accustomed to thinking of democracy, which has become the norm in thirty or so African countries, as an unalloyed good, but Rahall had put his finger on an inherent problem. In the continent's early phase of ongoing democratization, electoral politics often had little to do with nation building. Instead, the four or eight or ten years in power allotted to many leaders were devoted to feeding at the trough, or in the colorful political idiom of Nigeria, enjoying one's "turn to chop." In country after country, this problem came on top of an older, even more fundamental obstacle to the pursuit of any effective national development strategy: the sheer scarcity of experienced and competent people to fill out the civil service.

"We lack capacity," Rahall said. "The government is so weak in policy formulation. It is so weak in negotiating. It is so weak in monitoring things. It is just as weak in implementation. It is basically weak at everything, and that is because we don't have the human capacity."

By the time I walked out of the meeting with Rahall, night had resolutely fallen. The cars that had choked the little byways were gone now for the most part, leaving the streets clotted with pedestrians, who made their way in the dark in the middle of the road. As my driver

nudged his wreck of a taxi slowly through the foot traffic, our headlights were the most powerful source of illumination for as far as the
eye could see. They cut channels through a blackness thick enough to
feel tangible and they revealed the people they landed on with the brilliance of a paparazzi's flash: youth clustered playing games in wooden-
framed doorways, couples in affectionate embrace, young women
freshly washed and dressed up stepping with a lively bounce out into
the night. Others similarly refreshed by their evening bucket showers were content to loiter not far from the entrance to their shacklike
dwellings in their pajamas and baby powder.

The dark meant cool, at least relatively speaking, and for Freetown's
slum denizens it made this the witching hour for enjoying the parade
of life and the company of others. While I reveled in the exquisiteness
of the humanity captured in this scene, there was no pretending this
was a fitting way for people to live in the capital city of any country on
earth in the early twenty-first century.

Rahall had mentioned that in a good year, the entire national grid
of Sierra Leone produced 10 megawatts of electricity for its 6.3 million inhabitants, less than a modest-sized American city. In per capita
terms, the Sierra Leoneans who appeared in the beams of our headlights enjoyed roughly one one-thousandth the wattage of your average American.

Joseph F. Kamara, the head of the country's Anti-Corruption Commis-
sion, received me in his upper-floor suite in a tumbledown building
on a ragged downtown side street. He sat erect behind a black desk,
appearing serene, almost as if in meditation, when his secretary led me
in. He was a large man, tall and heavily set, and he was dressed soberly
in a dark, pinstriped suit, red-striped tie, and frameless glasses. Altogether, he dominated his small and uncluttered office, which showed
little obvious sign of bustle or even busyness.

Outside of his building, I'd walked past a crowd of people milling
on the broken sidewalk, waiting to get in to recount their tales of corruption. Many others, I knew, sent him anonymous tips. But the reality
was that there were very few people to follow up on the complaints,
and virtually no one of comparable competence to the commissioner

to prosecute and make any charges stick. His first sentence certainly did nothing to disabuse me of this impression of being overwhelmed. "Sierra Leone has not had a good experience with natural resources," he pronounced, mantralike.

Kamara was the second occupant of the commissioner's chair, whose creation was one of the little victories of civil society that Rahall had pointed to. Kamara's job was to try to bring the proceeds from the country's sale of minerals into the public coffers for the first time and reduce the incidence of major fraud, bribery, and graft.

Kamara said he had increased the number of prosecutions five-fold in his two years in the job, but he would be the first to admit that his office was fighting a steep uphill battle against powerful, moneyed forces that operated in the shadows. These included old-line Lebanese barons, eager Chinese newcomers, big multinationals, as well as murky, out-of-left-field entrants like Frank Timis and his African Minerals company, whose interests in Sierra Leone he said had become so big that the country now risked something he called "state capture."

"The economy used to be in the hands of the Lebanese, but what you are seeing is the emergence of new players. My challenge is to make sure that no deal is bigger than the law."

From the vantage point of his modest office, it was hard to imagine how this man could possibly stay ahead of the forces of corruption arrayed all around him, and they certainly didn't stop with foreigners. Friends of Kamara had told me about the scarcely concealed hostility toward his efforts shown by people in the president's office and in the legislature. And it was easy to see why. Instruments of law were no match against an older kind of government magic, patronage networks and corruption.

He had investigated and convicted the minister of marine resources for trafficking offshore fishing permits, many of which went to the industrialized Chinese vessels that overfished the scarcely policed waters off West Africa's Atlantic bulge. Under his predecessor, a minister of health had also been convicted in a major procurement fraud scheme. But these were decidedly small potatoes compared to the larger challenges the country faced, challenges involving mineral extraction and land. Kamara made no effort to prettify the African Minerals deal that had given Timis control over so much of Sierra Leone's territory and turned his hitherto little company into a global giant in the realm of iron production.

"We have not even lifted the veil on African Minerals. It took place before I was in office, and I did not want to start out appearing to have an agenda. It seems like some things have happened that were not right, and the government has made various promises about doing something to correct this, but it is not clear they will have the muscle."

CHAPTER SEVEN

Why Mali?

The draw some African countries exert on China because of their natural resources is so obvious it feeds our stereotypes of the country as the aggressive new manufacturing superpower willing to do anything to lock up global mineral supplies. But apart from a medium-sized gold industry, Mali, a large expanse in the northwest of Africa, boasts little of the resource wealth that so many assume is China's one true preoccupation. For years, Mali has been a proud and stable democracy even though it perennially ranked as one of the poorest countries on earth. Despite this, when China revealed its infatuation with the continent, Mali was anything but overlooked.

Beijing built a conspicuously large embassy in the capital, Bamako, where its companies big and small can be seen everywhere, hustling for business. Chinese migrants are numerous, particularly active in sectors like small hotels and commerce, both retail and wholesale. China has been showering aid and new lending on the country at an impressive clip. At the time of my last visit, Bamako was just a few months away from inaugurating one of the biggest projects China had carried out anywhere in the region: the gift of a giant third bridge spanning the Niger River, at one end of which would be a large and conspicuous new municipal hospital complex.

With scant means of its own, over the years Mali, an overwhelmingly Muslim country, had astutely developed a foreign policy of ingratiation to outside powers. Saudi Arabia had paid for an earlier big bridge named for King Fahd, as a gesture of Islamic solidarity. Muammar Gaddafi showered gifts on the country to buy influence, like the brand new Cité Administrative, a large complex of government offices that hugged the downtown riverbanks. The United States had become a generous donor because of Mali's exemplary democracy, and because of its willingness to cooperate in American military schemes that aimed to bar the spread of Islamic terrorism. Meanwhile, as the old colonial power here, France was jealous of its influence and sustained economic assistance of its own if only to keep up with the others.

All of these cards have recently been scrambled. First, Gaddafi was overthrown before the Malian government could inaugurate his gift of a new headquarters. Then, Malian rebel groups began an insurrection in the country's far north, imposing harsh Islamic rule. Next, the country's elected government in Bamako was overthrown by junior officers, just weeks before national elections were to be held. France intervened in January 2013 to defeat the Islamists and restore the country's territorial integrity. But all of that took place after I left.

The poky, old Bamako that I'd known for years had become the fastest growing city in Africa and the sixth fastest growing city in the world. There were now immense new boulevards, monumental traffic circles, and active building sites all about. Nearly all of this was the work of Chinese companies, who now completely dominated the construction sector.

As almost everywhere else in Africa, they had gotten their start with big Chinese-funded projects, whether they involved lending or outright gifts. After the initial contracts were won and the jobs completed, many companies had stayed on, taking advantage of the amortized costs of shipping their heavy equipment into the country (and often benefiting from preferential import duties in the process). This allowed them to milk the steady market in multilaterally financed development projects, where they typically entered the lowest bids to build things financed by the World Bank or the African Development Bank.

In Bamako, though, I discovered there was a new wrinkle to this pattern. Right next door to the airport terminal where I had landed stood a construction site for a brand-new terminal. A placard bearing a red, white, and blue emblem announced that it was financed with American aid, under the aegis of the Millennium Challenge Corporation, a vehicle created under George W. Bush. At the very bottom, in smaller print, I read that the actual contractors were Chinese.

Mali's population was growing even faster than the continental average. Together with Burkina Faso and Niger, all among the world's ten poorest countries, it formed a cluster of nations in the Sahel, the band that crosses Africa with the Sahara to the north and savanna to the south, where the United Nations expects the population to increase at astounding rates of 500 percent or more by 2100. For Mali, that would mean going from fifteen million people today to about eighty million at century's end, according to the median projection. High-end projections forecast half again as many more people. In all likelihood, this will mean plentiful new misery in a region whose prospects are constrained by fragile soils, sparse rainfalls, and literacy rates as low as 30 percent. But because of this extraordinary growth, Mali was also urbanizing like crazy, and like so many other parts of the continent, it was even sprouting a substantial middle class for the first time. Where others were put off, Chinese builders had no trouble figuring out that this all spelled big business and moved in to exploit it. Against this backdrop, Western diplomats say, in recent years Chinese lending to Mali was being disbursed at an annual clip that ranged somewhere between $200 and $500 million, suggesting interests that went far beyond construction.

I first met Tiébilé Dramé in Haiti in the early 1990s, following the military coup that overthrew Jean-Bertrand Aristide. He had been serving there as deputy director of the United Nations human rights monitoring group. Dramé had led an interesting and intensely purposeful life, and it was a story that was closely intertwined with the birth of democracy in Mali in 1991. He had gone from being a leader of the student movement that overthrew the country's military leaders that year, to senior official in Amnesty International, to publisher of an independent newspaper, to foreign minister, to leader of a small opposition party and two-time unsuccessful presidential candidate. Throughout, he had impressed me as one of the most sophisticated and deeply informed people I knew in West Africa.

Over lunch, Dramé lamented the haphazard way his country's affairs were being run. "We have no policy toward the Arab world, even though we sit at the very door of the Arab world. We have no policy toward the Far East, even though those countries are favorably disposed toward us. I'm not sure whether in all his years in office, ATT [the widely used moniker for the country's president, Amadou Toumani Touré, whose second and final term was winding down] has even held a one-hour meeting on relations with China."

Dramé said that under Touré, relations between Mali and China had been conducted on an informal basis, at the personal level, and were handled by the president himself and a small number of close associates. The stories about the shadowy, abruptly acquired fortunes of people believed to be close to him were persistent, and many of them involved ties with Beijing.

Like others in the know in Bamako, Dramé did not believe China's primary interest in Mali was construction. The real prize, he insisted, was Malian farmland, something that powerful outsiders had long coveted.

Dramé invoked the saga of the Office du Niger, a French scheme to dam the Niger River, in the middle of the Delta region that lay hundreds of miles upstream from Bamako. A dam was completed in the 1940s, but the French scheme of irrigating 1.2 million hectares, mostly to grow cotton, never came to fruition. Land was cultivated by the French, but never on anything like that scale, and the Malian state, which inherited what many have regarded as an albatross, today farms on less than one-tenth that amount.

In the early 2000s, shortly after President Touré took office, the Malian government became seized with the idea of attracting foreign investors in land, especially to the fertile and easily irrigated Niger River Delta. "The Chinese started coming first, then the Libyans, then others, like Lonrho [a large British conglomerate with roots in colonial Africa], which came to grow sugar," Dramé told me. "The Saudis came, too. What started as a trickle quickly became a rush, and the Libyans were the most enthusiastic. They won control of 100,000 hectares and built an immense canal, with an expensive tarred road."

The Libyan investment became a lightning rod, though, sparking a controversy about foreign control of land in Mali that has never let up. "The contract with Libya was signed in such a haste that they forgot to put a date on it," Dramé said. "We denounced it right away as illegal, because it was little better than a rummage sale of our national assets. We asked the government to publish the names of the beneficiaries and the acreage of the land, making clear that we were not systematically opposed to the sale of land, but rather to the opacity of these sorts of deals. We were also opposed because people live on these lands, and they are being displaced by force." Dramé said that gendarmes had repeatedly been employed to forcibly expel peasants. "When the foreign party buys the land they come and ask you to pay for the cost of displacement. You pay for their services, their vehicles, their gas, and in exchange they take care of everything."

Over time, public opposition to these practices forced the government to put on the brakes. In the last year or so before my visit, Dramé said, the state had stopped issuing new titles, and then took the additional measure of suspending 300,000 hectares' worth of recent deals.

This was all eerily reminiscent of corruption-laden transactions in China, where local governments customarily negotiated deals behind closed doors with contractors who submitted secret bids for coveted blocks of land. The lack of transparency naturally favored all kinds of sweetheart arrangements, and the making of easy fortunes by builders and officials alike. To top things off, local officials often used their own municipal police to chase off recalcitrant original residents, rendering protest and dissent futile.

Many critics had sounded alarms about a Chinese takeover of African land, often failing to note that China thus far cannot be said to place in the first rank of foreign investors in this sector, including in Mali. This doesn't mean, of course, that China doesn't need African farmland, or indeed that it doesn't aim to eventually obtain control of as much of it as it can. China has 20 percent of the world's population, and only 9 percent of its farmland. There were only two large developing countries with less arable land per capita: Egypt and Bangladesh, and massive construction, pollution, and erosion were whittling away at China's farmlands all the time. Vaclav Smil, a prominent environmental scientist who studies China's land use and food security, has said that as the country's living standards rise, by 2025 its food needs will far surpass what is available on today's open market.

Africa alone has 60 percent of the world's uncultivated arable land, and whatever Beijing declares, it stands to reason that China will come to see its food security as increasingly bound up in bringing that land into intensive production. By any calculation, Mali, with its sparse rural population and vast inland Delta, would be one of the greatest prizes. But as Chinese interests accumulated titles, Dramé said, they had usually abstained from farming the land themselves. Rather, unexplainably, they were renting their newly acquired farmland back to Malians.

"We want to know what is the point in operating this way, and why the government allows it."

I was curious to know what American diplomats thought of China's interest in Mali. The embassy arranged for a roundtable conversation. The diplomats present spoke of Beijing's deftness in milking the market in contracts let by multilateral lenders, like the World Bank and African Development Bank, but they seemed to share the sense on the street that this was insufficient to explain the extent of China's involvement in Mali.

One of the embassy officers said he had been to the presidential office complex, atop Mount Koulouba, and seen a large plaque, which noted that the Chinese had built it. "Wow, that's like having a plaque on the Old Executive Office Building," he remarked. "Our concern is that if Mali ever disagrees with China at some point on an issue, they [China] can say, What about that $100 million that we've just loaned you?"

But wasn't that the way big foreign powers had always treated small, weak countries? I asked.

The diplomat ignored my question and said that official Malian government contacts of his had expressed concern to him about the growing ties with China. "There is a group that says that this relationship is getting too big, too fast, and that the Malians might not be able to control things in the end," he said. "There is a concern about Malian reactions to this once people perceive that the Chinese are eating their lunch."

I inquired how it had happened that the State Department's Millennium Challenge Corporation had been used to fund the expansion of the Bamako airport by Sinohydro, a leading Chinese construction company. The question went unanswered.

The diplomats seated around the table stared at their shoes while the conversation marked a pause. Eventually, someone spoke up. "Congress [recently] passed a law saying that foreign, state-owned companies could not bid on MCC contracts. That was done last year specifically with the Chinese in mind."

The airport contract was worth $71.6 million. It wasn't only the Malians who were having their lunch eaten. In fact, until the law changed, China had been winning a huge share of the work on MCC-funded American projects—not just in Mali, but all over the continent. Most of the time, diplomats here and there had told me, American companies were not bidding for the work.

At the simplest level, this seemed to reveal the disinterest of American construction and service industries in competing for business in Africa, even when it involved relatively large projects with safe, U.S. government–guaranteed financing. Just as significantly, it highlights a completely different ethos of engagement by Washington and Beijing. Like most rich countries, the United States began moving away from tied development assistance decades ago, allowing its aid money to be spent anywhere, so long as the technical conditions of its projects were met.

As a newer player on this scene, China was much more mercenary. Its funding in Africa was strongly tied, meaning that borrowers were obliged to employ Chinese contractors, materials, and labor, an arrangement that meant capital it loaned flowed back to the motherland. At the same time, Chinese companies were eagerly competing for work funded by richer countries or by multilateral lenders like the World Bank.

Almost every Chinese I contacted on this visit said he would need clearance from his embassy before speaking with me. This led me to Liu Qi, the economics officer of the Chinese diplomatic mission to Mali. For two days he never answered his phone, and my messages were not returned. On the morning of the third day, Liu answered and then immediately asked me gruffly, "Who gave you this telephone number?" He then abrasively instructed me to be at his office the next morning at ten. "It's not at the embassy. It's the commercial office. We're on the other side of the river."

The next morning, I arrived at the large complex of the Chinese commercial mission, which sat behind high walls and a heavy iron gate.

We parked across the way from a very large swimming pool. There was no sign of anyone around, but I was urged to go inside, and so I entered the large, newly minted structure, with its marble floors and high ceilings. A second later, a slightly built man in his early forties appeared, descending a grand, twisting staircase. He identified himself as Liu, and walked me briskly to a capacious but sparsely furnished office for our discussion.

By way of introduction, Liu said he had spent almost all of his professional life working in French-speaking countries, including Guinea, Haiti, and Togo. He seemed pleased when I addressed him in French, and his response demonstrated a real flair for the language.

Liu began our interview proper with characteristic bluntness: "What do you think of Chinese neocolonialism?" he challenged, with an unconcealed sneer. I didn't take the bait. "I hope that you will inject a new realism into the discussion about China and Africa," he said, continuing in his lecturing tone. "Because the international community is still controlled by the Europeans and Americans, and they are having a lot of difficulty adjusting to the new realities of globalization.

"In China we want to establish win-win relations with African countries. We want to help them develop. We have no other ambitions. We do not seek to become colonizers. We respect their sovereignty and we do not interfere in their internal affairs."

Liu was a handsome man with a tidy, unlined face. He had come to the office this Saturday morning dressed in jeans, a black polo shirt, and loafers. But despite the informal getup, he was full of himself.

His style contrasted sharply with the legions of American diplomats I'd encountered over the years, with their overweening preoccupation with rules of attribution followed by endless boilerplate. Here was a diplomat who spoke his mind and didn't bother with minute rituals over the rules. They never even came up.

Liu deployed all of the Chinese diplomatic lingo I was used to—the wooden stock phrases about win-win, about noninterference, and all-weather friends that reminded me of so much machine language. But he didn't stop there, never concealing his view that a real contest was on, one that he fashioned as being between East and West.

He began ticking off China's big projects here: the third big bridge over the Niger; a major new hospital; a National Assembly headquarters; a new stadium; two sugar factories in the north; a textile factory in Ségou; new highway construction. "All this is about is development assistance."

If it was somehow refreshing to see someone be so forthright and at ease with language, after the charm wore off what lingered was not the feeling of being convinced through supple or elegant reasoning, or even for that matter the feeling of having been respected. As he gained momentum, he became more and more tendentious, making woolly claims, for instance, about how the Chinese were naturally peaceful and nonconfrontational because theirs was an ancient rice-farming culture.

I thought about our encounter for days afterward—Liu's brittleness and self-indulgence, the apparent absence of critical self-examination, the flattering view he held of his own country and its history—and the more I did so, the more it reminded me of what I had learned about American arrogance, vintage, say, late 1950s or early 1960s. This was a time when the United States was becoming a big mover in broad new swaths of the Third World, including Africa. Its men, too, had arrived with their own shallow certainties and with a highly flattering view of themselves.

I was put in mind of a story I'd read about Richard Nixon's visit to Ghana as vice president to represent the United States at that country's independence ceremonies in 1957. In his book *The Fate of Africa: A History of Fifty Years of Independence,* Martin Meredith describes Nixon as "the most enthusiastic" of the visiting dignitaries: "From the moment he touched down in Accra, he rushed about shaking hands, hugging paramount chiefs, fondling black babies and posing for photographs. It was not always to good effect. Surrounded by a crowd of Ghanaians at an official ceremony, he slapped one man on the shoulder and asked him how it felt to be free. 'I wouldn't know, sir,' replied the man. 'I'm from Alabama.'"

At the end of our discussion, Liu was gracious enough to escort me downstairs and out to the parking lot. I wasn't sure how to decipher the little wincing expression he made when he got a glimpse of my taxi, a badly beaten-up pink Mercedes 190, but I'm pretty certain it wasn't admiration.

I asked him if he used the swimming pool much, and he grunted no. He got most of his exercise on the tennis court, which he said was on the other side of the building.

As I puttered off, I thought of the Americans I'd met with the day before. One of them had complained that the U.S. commercial attaché positions that were once a fixture in almost every embassy in Africa had mostly been eliminated. His entire region was now down to one. Marble floors, tennis courts, and swimming pools, those were the stuff of dreams.

I met the head of the American aid mission to Mali early that afternoon at a charming little restaurant on a rocky side street in central Bamako. The area was full of grimy auto repair shops and parts dealers. In pitifully small pools of shade here and there, way down-market food vendors scooped out servings of meat and rice onto well-worn metal plates for their clientele.

A sprinkling of foreigners were seated at the Café du Fleuve when I arrived, but it wasn't hard to recognize Jon Anderson. Wearing a sport coat, he was dressed more formally than anyone else. He was seated toward the rear, amid large potted plants, with his back to the wall.

Anderson, in his fifties, a veteran of American overseas aid programs, struck a glumly serious pose, and began our discussion much as his counterparts at the embassy had the other day, impatiently asking a series of questions. He wanted to understand Chinese policy: What was Beijing's role in encouraging emigration and in supporting its people on the ground in Africa? Who are all these migrants? Where are they from, and why are they coming?

"It would really be useful for us to know what the Chinese are up to," he said. "What they really think about their work here. Who they are. What are their long-term interests? So far, we've been limited to speaking with them through translators. We've got very little idea about any of this."

Anderson listened intently, though, as I recounted the story of Hao Shengli, how he had set off alone for Mozambique, having no prior knowledge of the country, and then, later, after acquiring land, sent for his young sons to establish a brood in his new home. This was a more colorful case than most, I explained, but I had met many Chinese people who broadly resembled Hao. They had ventured forth to build new lives in Africa without the least hand of their government. Indeed that seemed to be the general pattern. I also acknowledged that I had met others who, in ways small and large, had received help or encouragement from their government, which in its own well-known general manner was keen to see Chinese go forth and settle in or do business in every corner of the globe. I don't think Anderson disagreed, which I interpreted as progress on the part of American diplomats.

Five years earlier, the U.S. ambassador to Chad, to cite a memorable example, had sat ramrod in his large office and made light of China's mounting profile in Africa, his air alternating between dismissive and patronizing. "It is ridiculous to think of China challenging the United States," he said, exasperated with my questions. "China is just one country among many that are represented here, and there is plenty of room for everyone. This is not a contest."

He had been right, of course, on the last point, although not necessarily in the meaning he intended. Already, that far back, across Africa, there was a widespread and growing sense that China, at least in economic terms, was on its way to becoming the indispensable partner, the country that mattered. It was seen in the eyes of so many already as an expeditious new power that could change the direction of nations or even whole regions of the continent in ways that the West with its countless rules and procedural demands, its frequent if inconsistent insistence on good form in areas like democracy and human rights and corruption, had promised but never seemed to get around to.

Countless conversations with Africans suggested to me that they saw the United States as the epitome of all of these disappointments. The idealism of its rhetoric far surpassed that of the worldly and knowing Europeans, who had colonized Africa and never completely extracted themselves. But this only contributed to the African sense of being let down by the United States. Americans made beautiful, principled speeches and imposed countless conditions on all manner of things. But in the end, in Africa they seemed to move the ball very slowly. They regarded Africa not as a terrain of opportunity, or even as a morally compelling challenge to humanity, but as a burden, and largely as one to be evaded as much as possible. Since the Battle of Mogadishu and the ensuing Black Hawk Down debacle in Somalia in 1993, and the genocide in Rwanda the following year, Washington's abiding concern in Africa was avoiding being left holding the bag. Outside of energy markets, even business in Africa usually left the country cold. America managed to convey the smug message that it would always have far bigger fish to fry.

In the time since that conversation in Chad there had been enormous change on the ground in Africa, with China figuring ever more prominently as the economic driver. And Washington's belated recognition of this oozed forth in the worried conversation of Jon Anderson, accompanied by something most unaccustomed to me in this part of the world: signs of American self-doubt.

Anderson began in a nuanced and cautious way, not speaking of what he knew, but of what he had heard. "Everyone in the aid community says that the Chinese are doing a lot of highly visible things, parachuting hardware [by this he meant major, very visible projects like bridges and stadiums], but not really involving themselves in the hard work of institutional development and of capacity building." In passing, he acknowledged that 90 percent of the requests made to his Millennium Challenge Corporation were also for construction projects.

"I personally think that infrastructure is incredibly important, but I'm also not willing to say that [it] is the answer to all the big questions here. Infrastructure reflects the priorities of the governments. This does not necessarily mean that a bias for hardware equates with the best development choices. In many cases, it may reflect nothing more than the fact that because construction projects are visible and tend to be big, that they leave something behind that is tangible, that leaders can point to and take credit for. It becomes their argument for staying in power."

The darling of Anderson's aid mission was a program in the Delta meant to help small-scale farmers obtain titles for land they had long worked under traditional tenure arrangements. The initiative seemed to embody many of America's most cherished ideals: notions like private property, the rule of law, and the entrepreneurial potential that ownership unlocks for the individual. In its spirit, it was similar to many other American initiatives on this poorest of continents. In the lingo of the Beltway aid establishment, it was called "capacity building," and it was looked upon fondly, so much so that it had taken on the weight of ideology, becoming an article of faith.

Time and again, during our conversation, Anderson spoke of creating the right "software" for Africa, which for him represented the opposite of China's "hardware" approach.

The most immediate problem with the American program in Mali was that it wasn't working very well, especially when measured by the progress of Anderson's cherished land title program, which had a five-year congressional mandate. The Malian government had been dragging its feet in implementing the program, and had sometimes actively impeded it. European donors, too, were pushing countervailing priorities.

"A lot of people in the Office du Niger, and even in the broader donor community, are opposed to issuing titles to peasants, because they are opposed to allowing what they see as suboptimal usage of acreage like this which has such a huge potential," he said.

While the Americans fought bureaucratic battles to advance their agenda of granting deeds to peasants on about five thousand hectares of land, China's Sinohydro was busy building a $230 million waterworks that would connect the farmland to the region's huge irrigation grid. It was the same company that was building the big airport expansion in the capital, and here again it was the Americans who were paying.

Anderson said American builders routinely showed no interest in work like this in Africa. They feared high operating costs and complicated bureaucratic regulations, and they were unfamiliar with the African terrain. Africa occupied a relatively blank space in the minds of most Americans, and when they stopped to think about it, aided by old and deeply ingrained habits of press coverage, all they could imagine was violence, corruption, disease, and horror.

Before we had met, Anderson had been encouraging when I told him by telephone of my interest in visiting his Delta project; he all but promised to arrange something for me. Now, though, he was strangely hesitant. If it was simply an American project I wanted to see, he said I could do this more easily by visiting the airport expansion site. I waved that idea off, saying I had come to Mali because of an interest in land issues. This interest had only grown during our lunch, when he had spoken almost rapturously about the agricultural importance of the Delta.

"Technically, biophysically, its potential is incredible. The whole

Delta region is a huge, flat expanse of land that can be irrigated by gravity," he had said. "You just open the canals and water flows down-hill from the river, with no pumping. Someone will have to get the soft-ware right, but what is certain is that one day, when world food prices start to go up, this area will come to be seen as one of a select few places in the world with big, untapped potential. It will be hugely attractive."

The Malian government certainly understood this. That much was clear from an extraordinary letter to investors to be found on the web-site of the Office du Niger:

> Did you know that the Republic of Mali has a gravity-fed irriga-tion potential that is unique in the world? In fact, thanks to its natural course, the Niger River waters a plain of nearly a million hectares that are suitable for rice cultivation.
>
> Unfortunately, only 60,000 hectares are developed.
>
> Since the advent of democracy in our country in 1991, the government of the Republic of Mali has assured much greater land tenure security in the Office du Niger, with security being assured by ordinary and emphyteutic leases [a type of contract that obliges lessees to improve a property via construction] of 30 and 50 years respectively, renewable as many times as the two parties agree to.
>
> Already, Malian and foreign investors have obtained, by emphyteutic lease, many hundreds, even thousands of hect-ares. You too can do like them and invest in the Office du Niger. Thanks to the contract that links you with the Office du Niger you have the opportunity to exploit the land for 50 years and pass the [land] rights on to your heirs.
>
> It's a safe place to invest your money when one thinks that in other countries, nearly 10 million francs [$20,913] are neces-sary to make one hectare productive. But in the Office du Niger, it will cost you only 3 million [$6,274].

When I asked again about visiting Anderson's project, he told me that I would have to find my own transportation. Furthermore, it was Fourth of July weekend, and he wasn't sure he could find anyone to receive me in the field.

I pressed my case, and he said he would see what he could do. He promised to get back to me that afternoon. With that, he plunked a 10,000 franc note on the table and excused himself. He never called. I emailed him later in the day, but my message went unanswered. The following morning, I texted him, and there was no reply to that, either. When I called his cell phone, there was no response. Indeed, I never heard from him again.

Shuai Yuhua, a longtime resident in Mali who worked as the administrative aide to the director of a major Chinese construction company, was waiting for me by the tiny swimming pool of my hotel, drinking a beer when I arrived. A stubby built man in his forties who seemed tightly wound at first blush, he peppered me with lots of questions about my intentions before announcing that his boss would like to meet me for dinner. We drove off in his late-model Toyota 4x4. Riding through the city at dusk, with its instant pedestrian markets now at their peak in the rush hour's cooling air, Shuai told me dinner was to be at his boss's residence, inside the company compound, on the other side of the river. From experience, I figured it was going to be a long night.

Shuai received a diploma from Wuhan University in the 1980s and had been among the first generation of young Chinese to do graduate study overseas, early in the reform era. In the state's wisdom, he was seen as suited to become a translator and sent to Paris to study French. Rather than return home, he had worked a series of jobs in France for many years, including company man and restaurant owner. He'd married a Chinese woman there, eventually raising a family of two sons, who were not quite teenagers yet. They spoke little Chinese, Shuai said, calling them *lao faguo*, a colloquialism that meant authentic French people. Shuai said he loved France, where he returns once a year. "It's free there," he said by way of explanation.

Years after his arrival in France, Shuai received an unexpected phone call from a college classmate, Liu Zhonghua, who had become an executive for China Geo-Engineering Corporation, a big, state-owned civil engineering company that was now making a push into

French-speaking West Africa. Liu, who spoke no French at the time, persuaded his old friend that he needed him in Africa, and Shuai has been his right-hand man ever since. Shuai had proven himself indispensable. In a company steeped in Chinese culture and habits, with few who spoke French, Shuai had become their ambassador to Mali in effect. It was clear that he knew the country well.

His cell phone rang as he drove. As we crept pass vendors of telephone cards, washcloths, towels, gewgaws of all kinds, he engaged with someone in French in what could not have been a more typically Malian conversation. There was much inquiring about the caller's family members, until Shuai focused on the man's wife, asking more and more detailed questions about her health. Finally, he repeated a diagnosis of parasites, and asked, deadpan, "She's not going to die, is she?" He was joking. "I hope everything goes well," he concluded. "But listen, don't put everything on God. You have to do your part, too!"

When the call concluded, Shuai laughed out loud. Then he turned to me, deadly serious. "The first thing you need to know here is that Malians are always making excuses, and the biggest trump card of all is God. Invoke God, and you are without blame."

On the heels of this criticism, he proclaimed that Malians were among the happiest people in the world. "Happier than Americans, and certainly happier than Chinese. If everyone around you is the same," he said, "you don't have to worry about being poor." I thought of China when he left as a young man, when a statement like this might well have applied. "What counts is fairness," he continued. "If things become unfair, then the situation can become explosive."

We were now talking politics, if only briefly. "The most important thing for a developing country is stability," Shuai said. "If things are unstable, there's no development. Nonetheless, there is a contradiction. If there's no democracy, things can't really be stable. So how do you get democracy? What I've seen in the African context isn't really democracy. Yes, they are voting, but everything is determined through money. People control who votes through money.

"Chinese people are just about everywhere," he said, again erupting with manic laughter. "You should never go anywhere where there are no Chinese."

"Is that because such places are too dangerous?" I asked.

"Wrong. It's because those are places where it is impossible to make money."

In gathering twilight, the sky had taken on hues of cool, deep blue, with a burnt orange fringe at the horizon. We passed the turnoff road to the airport, with "Bienvenue" signs emblazoned on its archway built of molded stucco in the Sudanese style. I asked Shuai if there had been much new construction on the north side of the river, where the city has always petered out. He misunderstood me, thinking I was talking about the desertified north of the country, where war would break out a little more than a year hence.

"All the people running the country come from the north, including the president, who is from there," he said. "They are constantly wasting money, investing in places like Timbuktu and Gao—so far away, with so few people. The problem is that the government doesn't have the money to just move everybody to the south. All the good land and all the water is here. If they built housing for everyone, don't you think all the northerners would come?"

This was an utterly Chinese viewpoint. Social engineering on a vast scale—whether moving millions of people to build the Three Gorges Dam, or implementing the One Child Policy, or bulldozing old neighborhoods in Shanghai to make way for skyscrapers—was expected of government. Even those who resisted it doubted that Beijing would ever abandon this top-down approach.

We pulled off the main road and onto a smoothly paved feeder road built by his company and leading to its headquarters. After another mile or so came the horn-tapping ritual, and the opening of a heavy metal gate by a Malian watchman. We drove through a large parking lot filled with more than a score of heavy Chinese trucks, and a similar number of other big pieces of equipment—earthmovers, tractors, and the like. Shuai parked at the edge of what appeared to be the compound's residential zone, with a large dormitory-like building off to one side, and a bunch of modern Chinese knockoffs of traditional African dwellings—round, earthen-colored, and covered with thatched roofs.

As we descended from the Toyota, we were met by the boss, Liu Zhonghua, dressed in slacks and a crisply pressed shirt, along with his wife, a tall, attractive woman several years younger than he who wore a gauzy blouse. *Fantasy Island,* I thought to myself, as we strolled through lanes bordered by sculpted hedges, past sunken fish ponds, through exotic flower gardens, and then into a large, enclosed kennel, where the Lius kept more than a score of animals. Most of their pet-rearing efforts were concentrated on purebred Great Danes, Labradors, German shepherds, and huskies.

As night fell, we were ushered into one of the bungalows, the boss's executive dining area. It was dominated by a large, round table, which had been formally set. Djénéba, a tall, young Malian woman, appeared on the scene to serve us. She was dressed fetchingly in a tight outfit that vaguely brought to mind *I Dream of Jeannie.* I asked for wine, and she brought a bottle of good Bordeaux.

Liu was surprisingly reticent in the early stages of the meal. His wife and I spoke mostly pleasantries. They seemed content to let Shuai carry the early conversation, which he did between gleeful jaunts around the circular room with an electronic flyswatter in the form of a plastic ten-nis racket. With it, he zapped the insects, which had somehow found their way into our fancy hut through openings in the thatched roofing.

I learned that my hosts' teenage son was attending a preparatory academy in New Jersey. They were concerned about his performance there, and about how it might affect his getting into a top American college.

A large-screen television that hung on the wall across from me played China's nightly state news broadcast on channel CCTV 4. The program was little changed from my years in China, including the stiff, otherworldly anchors who were led by a silly-looking, pudgy-faced man who was the main presenter. We had finished the elaborate early courses, and had begun eating Chinese hotpot, when a current affairs program began about regional tensions in the South China Sea. The moderators wasted little time in saying that to the extent that China had a problem with its neighbors, it was all due to American provocation.

In the midst of the TV discussion, a map of the region played on the screen and it traced a gigantic loop that dangled southward from China's shores and hugged the coastlines of a dozen or so countries in Southeast Asia, including mainland nations, Indonesia, and the Philip-pines. Within this loop, known in China as the "cow's tongue," Beijing was in effect claiming all of this sea for itself. No effort had been made on the program to represent the points of view of Vietnam, the Philippines, Indonesia, or Brunei, just to name a few of the countries directly concerned. My hosts asked me what I thought about the matter.

I told them I wasn't an expert in maritime law, but that intuitively, the Chinese map seemed rather unfair. Why should China's rights extend so far afield from its shores, while the rights of its smaller neighbors were tightly circumscribed?

Shuai and Liu listened to me unabashed, but Liu's wife looked embarrassed. "It's better not to discuss politics," she said, using a phrase I'd heard a thousand times in China. "It surpasses our understanding." Shuai brushed this off and debated sportingly for a few minutes, until Liu was drawn out for the first time. "This crisis is really about the character of the Vietnamese people," he announced, rather sternly. "We supported them against the Americans for many years during the war, giving them all kinds of help, including all kinds of weapons. They were poor and needy and we helped them like brothers at a time when we had little to eat ourselves."

There was little to dispute about this sentiment, even if it seemed only tenuously related to the maritime dispute we had been discussing. Liu's comment reminded me of what the diplomats had said at the American embassy about countries like Mali becoming indebted to China, not just financially, but morally as well, and how at least a few Malians worried about loss of sovereignty, or at a minimum, loss of maneuvering room.

The Lius' conversation looped back again to their son and college. There was then an exchange of glances with his wife that signaled a decision to speak frankly. He announced that they wanted to buy a place in the French countryside where they would finish their years. "You work all of your life like this," Liu said, "and you don't want to return somewhere where you can't breathe the air. You want to relax and enjoy life in a place that's clean and stable, without constant turmoil. Without worries."

This opened the way to a longer, more intimate discussion about his homeland.

"China has too many problems," Liu said, shaking his head, pausing a beat before explaining that the Cultural Revolution of his youth had "exploded the ethical and moral basis of our civilization. Foreigners come to study the genius of our culture, but we ourselves have lost sight of it. Deference, honesty, hard work, sacrifice, they have all suffered. The young people today, they're pretty useless. You can't even talk to them about these things. They don't understand. On top of that, we've got 800 million peasants who are culturally handicapped." For this, he used the words *wen mang*, which meant illiterate, but in his usage had the ring of uncouth.

"Freedom is a very important idea," he continued, "but in China, it is misunderstood. You render people free and to them it simply means everyone can do whatever they want, without responsibility, without regard for others, without respect for the law. What kind of future do you think China will have?"

I worked my way through the country's many contemporary challenges: the rich-poor gap, rampant corruption, the aging population, the lack of great industrial companies that can innovate and wield brand power, the despoiled environment, exorbitant housing, inadequate education.

Mrs. Liu now urged us again to stop talking "politics," and stop we did, and soon I was on my way, in Liu's car, with his driver, Coulibaly, whom he insisted I use for my trip upcountry.

The highway that took us north out of town, in the direction of the Delta, rose and fell over loping, hilly countryside, taking us through cluttered and unsightly townships that consisted mostly of half-realized industrial zones and new migrant quarters before Bamako finished petering out.

From my earliest days on the continent, my fascination with Africa was bound up with maps, and none more so than the red-covered foldable ones produced by Michelin. The story they told, via a sparse assortment of colored or dotted lines representing Africa's transportation infrastructure, was not just how to get from one place to another, but how the continent was tied together—or not. The scarcity of the lines, sketched against a backdrop of immense yellow deserts, vast, green bands of forest that extended north from the coast in West Africa, or in the case of the region I was driving through, the endless, dry scrublands of the Sahel—color-coded in white—spoke of much more than the mere hugeness of the terrain.

The important roads were drawn like veins, in bold crimson with black borders, and what was most striking about them was their paucity. Most of them had been laid down under European rule. Studying them, one quickly understood Europe's goal was extracting as much value as possible from Africa's lands and from its peoples, and especially of making imperialism self-financing. There was little variation on direct mine-to-port routing for almost all the terrestrial infrastructure.

Expressions of narrow, national self-interest on the part of the colonizers were evident in lots of other small details, too, like the narrow gauge of the railways. But nothing jumps out at the map reader more than the disinterest shown by the empire builders in connecting African peoples across the borders imposed upon them, especially when the country next door "belonged" to a European rival.

Our route was one of the three most important roads in the country, connecting Bamako with Timbuktu and the vast northeastern desert hinterland beyond, and it stood out on the Michelin map, all fat and red. After ATT-Bougou, a township consisting of grids of planned communities and subsidized housing, named after President Amadou Toumani Touré, who was later deposed, what appeared on the map as the highest quality road in the country abruptly narrowed to two lanes, with macadam that was riven with giant potholes or rippled and buckling from heat toward the center, and shoulders that were crumbling. Fela Kuti, the late Nigerian Afrobeat star and bard of outrage against misrule and corruption, had sung eloquently about outcomes like these, whereby government neglect had "turned electric into candle."

China was building most of the new highways in Africa nowadays, and it was busy in Mali. Liu's company was even in on the game. But Mali either didn't have the wherewithal to properly maintain this fragile ribbon or simply couldn't be bothered. As the road wended through giant rock formations that looked like huge, stacked pancakes, there seemed little hope for transformation of the continent in the costly new roads being laid down in black tar here and there by a new group of foreigners.

For the next several hours, there was little to see. Now and then, the car would pull through a big village or a small town. They usually announced themselves by the appearance of clusters of women sitting in the shade of gnarled baobab trees amid neat piles of succulent mangoes freshly harvested for sale. The countryside itself was a kind of corrugated bleakness, marked by cultivated areas that hugged to the road, and huge expanses of open land under a big, punishing sky.

It was mid-afternoon by the time we approached Ségou, a legendary old river town and gateway to the Delta. On the outskirts, we were greeted by an extraordinary proliferation of billboards and placards trumpeting this or that foreign aid project, almost all of them employing the de rigueur French euphemism for such things: *"coopération."* It was a festival of Western generosity; even Luxembourg had a sign advertising its largesse.

The most conspicuous sign of all was not Western at all, though, nor was it Chinese (by design, they weren't big players in the aid game). It belonged instead to a Libyan venture named Malibya that controlled 100,000 hectares of prime, irrigated farmland in the Niger River Delta managed by the Office du Niger, and it was the first hint of the growing foreign competition over land in the Delta.

Ségou was prime tourism territory, famed for its mud-dyed cloths and for its pottery, as well as its old Sudanic architecture. I wanted to stay right on the river, and after turning off the main road we eventually found a place, the Auberge, that sat across the street from the Niger's concrete floodwalls.

It was too late in the afternoon to begin exploring the Delta, so I set out on a long walk, following the Niger's floodwalls upstream, in the direction of Bamako, and savoring the sights in the softening light. Clusters of boys played at the water's edge. In other spots, women and girls bathed on the riverbank, pouring river water from buckets to rinse suds off their bodies, and paying little mind as I walked past. On the river, a mile or so wide here, fishermen from the Bozo ethnic group cast nets from a standing position in their spindly pirogues, somehow managing to keep their balance.

I had first come this way over thirty years earlier, as a college student traveling by train and bush taxi from Côte d'Ivoire with my younger brother, Jamie, and as I doubled back walking the dusty, unpaved streets through the heart of the old city, memories of that trip and of two subsequent visits came flooding back: the buildings—old, earthen

African structures or the functional Cartesian French colonial ones; the fat, buzzing flies that follow obsessively as one walks, eager for a sip of one's sweat; the sweet smell of mangoes from trees that hung pregnant and heavy with the fruit.

The one thing that was different now was that there were no people. The streets were all but abandoned. I tried to imagine why this was, and could only figure that it was a late Sunday afternoon, that people were at home, perhaps readying for early family dinners. But the picture changed instantly as I rounded a corner and came across a large open space in the midst of a residential quarter and discovered a soccer game under way played by barefoot young men amid clouds of dust on an uneven, earthen pitch.

Early the next morning, I set off with Coulibaly into the vast zone controlled by the Office du Niger. I was seeking out a Chinese man with whom I had been in contact. He worked at the construction site of a new sugar complex his company was building. I also wanted to visit the place where the Americans were said to have employed Chinese contractors to build the waterworks for a Millennium Challenge Corporation–funded project. Somewhere in this area there also lived a man named Faliry Boly, the head of an independent Malian rice growers' syndicate, who had lots to say about the presence of Chinese, Americans, and others on this land.

Just north of Ségou, the service road that leads into the Office du Niger ran straight and true for miles through land that was largely unworked, even though at regular intervals one could see the extensive waterworks of canals, channels, levies, and bulwarks, all meant to govern a steady flow of water and keep a land of black soil green with cash crops like sugarcane, cotton, and rice. The Office was created in 1932, the result in equal parts of French colonial ambition and envy. Its main proponent, an obsessive French civil engineer named Émile Bélime, had studied British irrigation schemes in India and sold Paris on the idea that by creating dams and waterworks in the Niger Delta, France could cultivate cotton on a scale to rival Britain's immense Gezira project in Sudan.

At Markala, we stopped to pay a road toll and then entered into a natty little town. It was an old French administrative center, and the markings were all still there—neatly laid-out streets, big, café-style restaurants with outdoor seating, and giant shade trees everywhere. Soon we would cross a major bridge over the main dam on the river. The crossing would mark our formal entry into the Office.

Over the crest of a hill the waterworks came into view. There was an immense truss bridge, over 2,600 meters long, that was built by the French using forced labor between 1934 and 1947. When we reached its foot, I found a plaque that read, "In memory of all those who lost their life in the completion of this project." It was here for the first time that I got a true sense of the stakes involved in the Office. The dam was the very heart of the French empire builders' ambitions, raising the water on the river high enough to feed two major canals, with raised dikes, and irrigate a huge expanse of land that would otherwise have been far too dry to farm.

Below the bridge and off in the distance, women bathed in the spray of the river. On the flat land that stretched to the horizon on the near shore, huge flocks of cattle grazed. And to my amazement, perched acrobatically along the very lip of the dam's sluiceways, fishermen cast nets to capture fish swept along by the powerful stream, their technique reminding me of the way grizzlies await salmon swimming upstream. As we descended from the bridge onto the far bank, I noticed signs of a large Chinese presence. The construction company that had subcontracted with the Americans had a big work site just off the road, and there were placards and billboards for other Chinese companies.

Gao Yi, my acquaintance at the sugar plant project we were looking for, had told me that it wasn't far from the bridge crossing, so we drove on, entering an immense, highly ordered domain, with crisscrossing networks of canals, and fields planted tall with sugarcane, interrupted now and again by stands of eucalyptus trees that blew wispy in the hot breeze. The road was impeccable but eerily empty, save for teams of Malian workers pedaling to or from their jobs on cheap bicycles.

We now saw Gao driving toward us to guide us to his place of work. Just then, a Malian motorcyclist appeared out of nowhere and glanced Gao's vehicle. The motorcyclist was not injured, but he was furious, and he lit into Gao, whose French was rudimentary. I gradually found myself pulled into the dispute. The Malian man was threatening to get the police. I told him I had seen the whole thing and that Gao had done nothing wrong. The motorcyclist cursed me and then turned to Coulibaly for support, banking on national solidarity. I told Gao we should just leave. We jumped in our 4x4s and drove off.

No sooner had we left the main road than Coulibaly turned to me with an unhappy look playing on his face. "We don't like the Chinese," he said flatly, presuming to speak for Malians in general. "That man is lucky the police didn't come, because they would have ruled it was the Chinese man's fault. We are Malians. We've already been forced to learn French. We don't want to be speaking Chinese someday."

The new plant's perimeter was sealed off by a high, white wall. At various points along the wall grew gigantic baobab trees, which were revered in many Sahelian cultures. As we parked near a line of trailers like those used by Hollywood stars on movie sets, I imagined myself being asked to don a hard hat any minute for a routine tour of the plant, which rose in the near distance and appeared nearly completed. I'd been on enough of those tours over the years to know they usually were a waste of time. Gao, a wiry thirty-year-old of medium height, spoke very fast, constantly smiled, and seemed genial. He ushered me into one of the trailers, which turned out to be a construction company office. A male colleague of similar age sat at a desk smoking a cigarette and staring at his laptop. At another desk sat a Chinese woman in her mid-twenties who followed our conversation closely.

Gao launched into a routine explanation of the project. He told me when the work on the plant had begun and when it would be completed. There were three hundred Chinese workers involved. Some thirty Chinese would stay behind to run it once it was finished. Gao, who was an engineer, specified that this would not include him. "I get to go home!" he said, and was clearly very happy about this. A moldering older plant, which we had seen along the way, was built by China in the mid-1960s, he said, but the new plant would far outstrip it, producing 100,000 tons of sugar per year.

Gao wasn't an immigrant per se, but he'd been in Mali for some time, out here in the middle of nowhere. His family was from Tangshan, a city near Beijing that had suffered the twentieth century's deadliest earthquake in 1976, the same year that Mao Zedong died. His parents were farmers, but he'd been born at a lucky time, when China's economic reforms were kicking into high gear, unleashing unimagined opportunity for people of his generation.

Gao had done well in school, studying English, and this had won him his first overseas job with a construction company in Guyana, where he had worked for four years as a human resources manager. A girlfriend had left him during that time, losing patience with the wait for him to come home, even if he did have good career prospects. A second girlfriend had left him in the two years he'd been on this project, he said, with a wince that suggested this one was harder to take. "If I were a thirty-year-old woman, this would be a really bad situation for me, but I'm a man," he said. "I can still recover."

His recreation and socializing here were terribly limited. "Basically nothing," he said. There were very few women, and after hours most people sat around drinking heavily, or lost themselves surfing the Internet.

I turned to the young woman in the trailer, and said I imagined she was very popular here. I'd made a clumsy mistake, though. The word that I used for "popular" was meant for things, not people, and she corrected me graciously. Her boyfriend was in China, which meant he was waiting for her. She, too, was an English-Chinese translator, such a common career path.

Gao took me to lunch in the company canteen in another trailer. From behind a booth a Chinese cook prepared Chinese food for an all-Chinese crew of workers. There was small talk among a handful of workers who were seated nearby, older, rough-hewn men who were clearly of a lower pay grade.

Gao continued his complaints. "I get no vacations. We get very few guests. All the time we see the same people. It's unchanging. Every day is just like the last.

"Do you know why Chinese are out here doing this kind of work? It's because the Europeans and Americans can't."

"Why not?" I asked. "The French did the original work here." Actually, the French used forced labor here and in other African colonies, as I indicated earlier.

"Yes, but the French can't work like that anymore. The Americans are a little bit better, but the French, definitely not. But it's not because we can eat bitter; it's because we have no choice. Of course we would like to live like Westerners. Of course we'd like to take vacations and to go home frequently, but we can't. The Americans are smart. They take jobs that win them big profits. But we are a poor society and we're struggling to rise higher. We're stuck with work that doesn't make much money."

I said the Chinese companies wouldn't be out this far off the beaten path if there wasn't decent money to be made. "The problem is that there are too many of our companies chasing after this kind of work," he said. "China is screwed. We have so many people that we have no choice but to go overseas to look for whatever work we can find."

Narrowly speaking, he was absolutely right. But there was so much more to what had drawn China to a place like Mali. Rising powers throughout history have forever faced a simple but fateful choice: whether to take on the established players in their backyards, in places where their interests are greatest and most deeply entrenched, or try to expand into relatively uncontested zones of the world. In the course of the last century, Japan had been the lone non-Western power to challenge the established global order and it had tried both approaches. It had moved into decadent, Qing-ruled China, which was contended over but not firmly controlled by Western nations a hundred years ago. And then, feeling its oats, it had challenged France and Britain directly in Southeast Asia and then Hong Kong, while also frontally, and ultimately disastrously, challenging the United States in the Pacific.

China's big push into Africa was a textbook case of the first type of expansion. Western interest in Africa waned after the fall of the Berlin Wall. Western Europe was drawn instead toward its immediate backyard to the east. These were countries with which it had deep historic and cultural ties, whose populations were literate and easy to train but starved for capital. The United States, meanwhile, tied itself up in a series of wars in the Middle East and South Asia. By the turn of the millennium, China, which was fast growing and increasingly ambitious, had surveyed the global scene and grasped that little attention was being paid to Africa. The continent offered minerals and other natural resources, fast-growing markets already primed for patient, deep-pocketed investors, and land to help secure China's food supply needs well into the future.

Ever since, companies like Gao's had been pouring into the continent and winning market share from the complacent European contractors who had long dominated road building and other public works on the basis of political backing from their governments and corruption. The Chinese newcomers were able to capture market share easily from the established players via an unbeatable triple play: cheaper financing from Chinese state banks, cheaper Chinese materials, and cheaper Chinese labor. In stark contrast to their Western counterparts, even the Chinese managers on big projects tended to live modestly, often in the same compound with their staff. And if need be, they were even willing to take losses on projects to break into new markets and to keep the country's colossal, state-owned construction sector at full employment.

This new reality was proclaimed bluntly at a 2011 meeting in Paris between a delegation from the China Development Bank, one of China's most important overseas lenders, and a group of major French construction companies. The French complained that the Chinese were winning all the business in Africa because of their big price advantage, and asked their guests what could be done about it. The response is described in *China's Superbank: Debt, Oil and Influence—How China Development Bank Is Rewriting the Rules of Finance*, by Henry Sanderson and Michael Forsythe:

> "You can never beat China; you can only turn yourselves into the IBM of construction," a Chinese executive lectured his French hosts. By that he meant that the French couldn't compete against Chinese companies in building railways and power grids. IBM doesn't make hardware anymore. The French have 80 years of experience in West Africa, but the Chinese have just arrived. He admitted that the Chinese don't understand the local society, the politics and the environment. "Why don't you provide a consulting report about the political, social, and environmental impact of the project?" he suggested. The Chinese side would pay the French a consulting fee.

As a result of this passing of the guard, Chinese workers on big construction projects were coming to Africa by the tens of thousands and many found to their surprise that they liked it. They discovered that Africa was a continent of wide-open opportunity, and in many countries they felt welcome enough to want to take their chances and stay on. These pioneering new settlers were the founders of burgeoning new communities here and there, growing Chinese foodstuffs, selling Chinese necessities to one another, opening Chinese clinics and schools and restaurants, and even brothels. They took advantage of financial and trading networks via relatives and acquaintances back home. And as word of their comfort and success spread in China, as we have seen, they had in turn drawn many fresh newcomers in their wake.

In 2011, tens of thousands of Chinese were evacuated from Libya by their government amid the conflict that overthrew Muammar Gaddafi. One day, perhaps soon, China would no longer be content to send ships to mount emergency evacuations like this. In places where its interests had taken root deeply, it would impose its demands on the local government for the respect of its citizens, and of their property and investments. And perhaps not too much further down the road, it would find itself in the position of wanting or needing to actually intervene.

In this way, for all of China's denials that its overseas ambitions could be compared to those of Europeans or Americans, for all of its insistence that its actions are driven by fraternal solidarity with Africans, its fellow victims of colonization, its fellow travelers on the path to development, what I was witnessing in Africa is the higgledy-piggledy cobbling together of a new Chinese realm of interest. Here were the beginnings of a new empire, a haphazard empire perhaps, but an empire nonetheless.

I found some of this spirit captured in a 2012 interview with Zhong Jianhua, former ambassador to South Africa, who described the continent's allure for China this way:

Africa has a population of more than one billion and huge market potential. Africa's latent demand in terms of population size and room for expansion is much higher than in Southeast Asia or Latin America.

When you start from a lower starting point, there is more room to move up. In Latin America, per capita GDP has reached $6,000 to $7,000. It's even higher in Southeast Asia. This is a lot different than the room for growth in per capita GDP in Africa, which is between $300 and $3,000. This is the significance of Africa.

"China is a bit freer now," Gao said as I prepared to leave, "but still not altogether free. You can't compare it with Western countries. But at the same time, most Western people probably have the wrong idea about life in China. They think that whatever you do, the CCP [Chinese Communist Party] is following you around, ready to arrest you. It's like our ideas about America. We think everybody has a gun in their pocket, and there's danger everywhere.

"Back home, ideas about Africa are way off, too. I get lots of questions from friends asking about animals and telling me to send pictures of them. People think it's a big mess here and that it's really dangerous, that there's nothing but crises all the time. That's because the news just focuses on the negative. It's the same with the way Americans think about China. It's also the way Chinese people think about Americans. Our news always accentuates the negative."

We were now on our way to Alatona, a tiny town where I hoped to find that American project. Heading north we sped past wispy stands of acacia and men on bicycles. The land was flooded from abundant overnight rains, and at this hour, with the peak heat past, people were out in the fields cultivating rice. Children played or bathed nude in the canals, and, here and there, farmers used simple, kerosene-fueled threshers that spit the rice out into mounting piles and blew the chaff into the breeze. It reminded me of harvest time in rural Sichuan province.

We drove on for some time through an unchanging environment, making our way through the staggering vastness of the Office. To carve out this domain, France had dismembered its neighboring colony, Upper Volta (now Burkina Faso), lopping off 23,000 square miles, and had organized the forced resettlement of tens of thousands of peasants to work the clay-heavy soils of the Delta, planting it with long-staple cotton, which for all their pains would eventually prove to be a poorly adapted crop. The African mortality rates, meanwhile, were staggering.

Mali (then known as Le Soudan français, or French Sudan) was but one of France's many African possessions, and far from the richest or most important in the eyes of the *métropole*. In the end, there was no way that a medium-sized power like France, with its modest population and limited means, was going to be able to see its ambitions through. As in other places, France's dreams here withered with the end of colonization. At Mali's independence in 1960, Paris touted the Office as the "prototype of disinterested aid to a developing country." But the reality was far less positive. France had never managed to cultivate more than 150,000 hectares in the Office, a paltry 5 percent of the irrigation zone, and even maintaining this properly quickly proved to be beyond the means of the impecunious new Malian state.

Still, foreign powers regularly came sniffing—notably the Americans, the Dutch, and, of course, most recently the Chinese, and the interest of other outsiders like these is certain to grow. Where else on earth does one find 3.6 million acres of sparsely inhabited, irrigated farmland?

On the other side of the continent, in Ethiopia, India was eagerly grabbing up rich farmland, driven both by the old-fashioned profit motive and the need to secure future food needs. So far, Beijing had been more tentative, but given the Chinese presence here, it was tempting to project speculatively on this score. Indeed, ongoing Chinese political discussions encouraged one to do so. In 2011, for example, delegates to the annual session of China's parliament debated a proposal to seek employment for as many as 100 million Chinese on the African continent. One champion of this idea, Zhao Zhihai, a delegate and researcher at the Zhangjiakou Academy of Agricultural Sciences in Hebei province, said: "In the current economic climate, with so many of our people unemployed, China can benefit from finding jobs for them and Africa can benefit from our expertise in developing any type of land and crop."

China saw an urgent need to secure its food supply into the future. It had a nearly endless supply of people, eager for a better life. Before long, it will have the world's largest economy. And it has a deep civilizational patience, a belief in planning and in engineering on the largest of scales. What else would it take?

———

The dirt road delivered us to Alatona just before 3 p.m. It was more a spot than a town. The only thing visible was a *poste de contrôle* guarding a passage over the levee. Some policemen lounged in the near distance under a lone, large shade tree. A clutch of vehicles, which had stopped as bribes were solicited, sat immobilized nearby.

Once over the crest of the levee, I saw the work crew. In the waning heat, a half dozen Malians were loading reinforced concrete buttresses into the bed of a large truck. From fifteen yards away, two Chinese watched from the inside of a Toyota pickup.

I climbed out of Coulibaly's vehicle and approached the Toyota, stopping by the driver's window, where a Chinese man sat wearing ordinary street clothes. This was the boss, I thought; his countryman in the backseat was dressed in a laborer's coveralls. An awkward moment ensued as the boss glanced at me dartingly and then proceeded to gaze straight ahead, almost as if he was willing me to disappear. I tapped on his window, which he lowered halfway electronically, producing a blast of intense air-conditioning.

"*Ni hao*," I said, and introduced myself.

The boss, who had been nodding as I spoke, turned to the man in the backseat and exclaimed, in Chinese, "How strange!" The man in the back grunted the word "strange" in agreement, and the window slid back up. I gestured for him to open it again, and he did, albeit wearing an uncomfortable look on his face. He asked if I had been a student in China. I told him no, but that I'd lived in Shanghai, which produced a look of dreamy approval from him. "Shanghai. Great place!"

The boss said they'd been working on this project for just under a year, and would be finished in another month. They were lodging right out here in the middle of nowhere, in a cluster of trailers not unlike the ones I'd visited in the morning.

"Are you going back to China?" I asked. In unison came an exuberant "Yes."

These were the kind of Chinese Gao had spoken of who were doing work that the French, and in this case Americans, were unwilling to do. There were nine of them here altogether, and the brunt of their work seemed to consist of overseeing seventy Malians with whom they had no common medium of communication, except through a lone translator.

The man in coveralls eventually got out of their 4x4, donned a broad-brimmed hat, and walked over to the truck-loading scene, which he halfheartedly supervised. He told me he was from Wuhan, but was unwilling to engage otherwise.

When I asked him how the Malian workers performed, he replied, "They work hard, as long as you watch them."

In the late afternoon we found the town of Molodo at the end of a flooded dirt road about a third of the way into our drive back to Ségou. With its rutted, red clay streets and big, stagnant puddles the place was a throwback to another age. Ancient tractors and other vintage mechanized farm gear sat idled in the margins of pathways, some with their wheels sunken into the dried mud. The traffic, such as it was, consisted of carts drawn by braying donkeys.

We turned a corner and fell upon an exquisite old mosque, a creditable replica of the Great Mosque at Djenné, a huge earthen structure that is one of the world's architectural wonders, dating back to the thirteenth century. With its stenciled form and smooth, sculpted skin, the Molodo mosque wasn't nearly as imposing as Djenné's, but it was sublime in execution, and all the more delightful for being totally unexpected.

We found Faliry Boly at his two-story home a few minutes later. His long driveway had been repurposed as a kind of narrow courtyard that afforded shade in the late afternoon. He was stretched out and propped up on an elbow on a thin foam mattress placed atop a tatami-like mat.

In Bamako, a certain legend clung to this man. People spoke with a mixture of admiration and puzzlement over the direction his life had taken. He had been a gifted and popular student, one with a social conscience and a precocious political bent. He had reached adulthood during the eve of the downfall of Mali's long socialist dictatorship and the establishment of one of the first democratic governments in the region.

While peers became activists in Bamako or set off for exile in Paris or elsewhere, Boly left school a year before finishing his studies. "If I had gotten my degree, I would have been required to teach, and I didn't want to do that." He went to the countryside instead, marking a total break with convention. Since independence, the dream of nearly every

African youth lucky enough to get a higher education was to live well in the capital or to go abroad.

"I am a rice farmer here," Boly announced to me flatly, with fifteen acres to his name. "I came here in 1986. At the time, people said I was crazy, but I love the land, and I stayed. From 1986 to 1997, I didn't read a newspaper. I did crossword puzzles and I read novels. When I return home from my fields each day, I have my foam mattress and my mat. There is no great luxury here, but I have my freedom, and I like it that way."

Boly had a thick salt-and-pepper mustache and kept his head shaved bald. He was dressed nattily for a farmer, in a checkered pink poplin shirt and neatly pressed khakis, and he smoked Dunhill cigarettes, whose distinctive flat, red box with golden trim seemed to signal a minor indulgence amid the manifest simplicity of his surroundings.

As we spoke, his teenage daughter appeared from another part of the courtyard and began preparing a sweet and powerful traditional tea over a small charcoal furnace, whose fire she stoked carefully with a straw fan. One quickly sensed Boly's deep affection and pride in her, and after a few rounds of the viscous drink, my notions about what kind of place a girl occupied in a family like his were proved wrong when he announced she had just passed her baccalaureate examination and would be leaving soon to attend university in the capital.

In the end, Boly made his way into politics, like so many of his peers, but his arena was out here, where in 1997 he became the head of the Union of Agricultural Workers of the Office of Niger. The union, known by its French acronym, SEXAGON, was formed that year amid a drive by the Office to expel small landholders who failed to pay water usage fees. The Malian government had recently begun trying to attract private investors to the Office to reverse the steady decline of agricultural production, and Chinese companies were among the first to come knocking.

"I went to see some Chinese investors who won a lease to produce seeds, but they refused to receive me," Boly said. Other Chinese investors, leery of his union background, had taken the same stance with him ever since.

In the late 1990s, a representative of the French Communist Party on a visit to Mali came to meet with Boly, who still laughs over their encounter. "He said the Chinese are coming, and they are very enterprising, so you must be careful. I told him that the Chinese were predators in the same way that the French were. The only difference is that Chinese theft is the theft of an office clerk. A long time will go by before you understand what has befallen you."

Boly said he had become accustomed to people asking him to proclaim himself pro- or anti-Chinese. "I don't like them or dislike them, save for one thing, which I really admire: they know how to remain themselves, which is a dream that any African can understand and respect."

He also gave the Chinese credit for patience. China was playing for the long term, and not always for a quick score or for short-term profits, and he cited old Chinese investments in Mali in textiles, sugar, and tobacco, most of which hadn't panned out terribly well, or had even lost money outright. "China has a means of advancing which is different from that of the West. They are like a boa: it observes its prey quietly, taking its time. In the same way, the Chinese are waiting for a long-term return. They're waiting for a maximal result."

Boly's wife had appeared and joined us, taking a seat in the shade next to him on a low wooden chair. She was dark-skinned, and was dressed in a three-piece indigo wax cloth outfit of vibrant green. Like him, she worked in the labor movement.

Boly recounted a story of a small Chinese project whose significance he regarded as much greater than its acreage, a mere 1,000 hectares, 2,200 acres. A few years earlier the operators had secured a lease for the stated purpose of producing seed rice. "They said it was to test products, but that's not true. What they've done is rent the land back to Malian farmers, which amounts to pure speculation and is legally forbidden. What it shows above all is the lack of seriousness of the authorities. They auction off the land and even chase away the small farmers, and then stand by while foreigners lease the land out again."

The Chinese were quietly building a position in the Delta and biding their time for the right moment to begin exploiting it, he claimed. This would be determined by world food supply and pricing.

"I have a hard time imagining a Chinese leader deciding to invest in grain production here in Mali for sale in China," Boly said. "We are a thousand kilometers from the nearest port, and with the transportation costs to get rice to China, it wouldn't make sense. But I can easily imagine them producing rice to sell to us here in this region, which frees up grain from elsewhere for their consumption. And if they become really big players here, that gives China a lot of influence over our [African] governments."

With that, Boly related a recent conversation he had with a senior government official.

"The places around the world where there is gravity-fed irrigation of arable land on a large scale are very few," the official had told him. "We are sitting on top of a jewel; something comparable to the Nile River Valley."

"If it is a jewel, then you shouldn't be selling it off to just anyone who comes knocking," Boly said to the official. "A jewel is something that you hold on to and protect jealously. But this is Mali, so we don't think that way."

When we pulled into the parking lot of Comatex, the Chinese textile factory that had been built in the late 1970s, a large sign out front in faded red with mustard-colored lettering read "*Qualité, Efficacité, Discipline*," reminding me of *kouhao*, the propaganda banners meant to motivate or indoctrinate the public that are still hung everywhere in China.

Jia Jinwen, the chief engineer, greeted me in the parking lot and ushered me inside the plant, which consisted of a series of squat industrial buildings that were neatly laid out but looked their age. Jia was short, dressed in coveralls, and wore his hair in a crew cut. He couldn't understand how I could be interested in his factory, or for that matter in him.

The dimly lit interior of the plant was incredibly hot, but it was a different kind of heat from what one felt outside. Here, no merciless sun pulsed down on you, rather it was the motionless one hundred degree air, filled with the smell of cotton, which in one form or another was visible everywhere. The factory floor was as dense as a circuit board. Spindly machines took mountains of raw cotton and drew strands of fiber that were twisted into thread. Then the threads were woven row by row into sheets of new cloth.

After Chinese largesse in areas like stadium construction and new statehouses left many Africans favorably impressed, fragile domestic industries were then ravaged by the waves of cheaply priced Chinese imports washing over them. Around the continent, textiles had been the biggest victim, and the import trade in Chinese cloth, which often duplicated popular African designs, was carried out by Chinese themselves, typically migrants. Given the plant's location in one of the world's great cotton-growing zones, and the presumably low wages of Malian workers, if any place could compete with textiles produced in China, I imagined it would be here.

"No way," said Jia. "Here the cost of electricity is more than twice as high as it is in China. The labor costs are about the same. The cost of cotton is determined internationally, so they don't have an advantage with the raw materials. So, as you can see, it is the power that makes them uncompetitive. They don't have coal in Mali, and they must draw their electricity from Côte d'Ivoire and from Ghana."

What remained for the factory in terms of a market, he said, was time-sensitive work. This meant specialty orders that couldn't be shipped from China by sea in time to fulfill the buyers' needs. This was a small niche, such as the inauguration cloth that was rolling out of the big printing machines we saw in the second building we visited. It bore the effigy of Côte d'Ivoire's leader, Alassane Ouattara, who had recently been installed as president there at the conclusion of a civil war. Other machines in that big room were printing cloth for an anti-AIDS campaign, and for small orders, like weddings and anniversaries.

Despite these limitations, Jia, who was forty-six, spoke proudly of the factory, where he had worked for five years. He'd gone back home to Handan once a year for forty-five days each time. His hometown was an ancient city of 1.3 million people in southwestern Hebei province, about four hours' drive from Beijing.

"I've only been to Bamako once and to Mopti once," he told me, exhausting his personal account of tourism in Mali in a single phrase. "There's no real opportunity for leisure here. Everything is the same, and it's too hot to do anything."

Jia said he spent the weekends playing cards with the ten other Chinese who ran the plant, or surfing the Internet.

"All Chinese live like this in Africa," he said, "alone with their work."

I asked Jia if anything had been done to prepare Malians to run the plant. "It's not possible," he said. "They'd have lots of problems—management problems, technical problems—in short, lots of things would go wrong." He would not elaborate.

In many places, Africans complained that Chinese occupied construction, industrial management, even general maintenance of projects, and precious few of those skills were passed along to locals. With scant transfer of knowledge and technology, there was little chance of creating a new, native Malian industrial culture. What one was left with instead, critics feared, was a culture of dependency. A dead end like this did not require organized evil conspiracies or even ill will. It represented opportunities seized. Nonetheless, it was a problem as old as colonialism itself, and one in which China, convinced of its own "win-win" rhetoric, had demonstrated little new thinking.

I was returning to the construction company headquarters in Bamako the borrowed vehicle that Liu had so generously lent me. Shuai Yuhua, the affable aide to the director, met me in the compound parking lot and immediately began lavishing me with hospitality. Minutes later, I was back in the paillote where we had had our banquet a few nights earlier, being served a half dozen Chinese dishes and good tea by the tall Djénéba, who was again dressed in one of her formfitting outfits, this one accentuated by a single bare shoulder.

As before, the television was set to a Chinese satellite channel, which was playing a drama set in Yanan, from the early days of the communist revolution. These were a staple of the state-owned TV networks. A thick-haired Mao character, tall and handsome, strode impressively back and forth amid his comrades, who weighed his every word. A fiery, opinionated female beauty commanded deference from the other leaders, including Mao himself.

Shuai was curious to know what I made of the show. I said it seemed pretty generic; I'd seen lots of these during my time in China. "I don't pay attention to them myself," he announced. "From start to end, it's all euphemism, and that's the problem with the state. It's full of bullshit. Everyone knows that if there had been none of this revolutionary nonsense, if the Nationalists had won the war, China would have been rich at least thirty years earlier. Instead, we got leaders who were obsessed with revolution. Human beings want to make money. Men want to enjoy beautiful women, all the time. The perpetual revolution crap we had to endure was anti-social, un-human. You look at countries like France and the United States, their leaders are ordinary people, not supposed heroes. They don't behave like Chinese leaders, each of whom feels he needs to invent his own school of thought. Utter nonsense."

When Shuai got called away, I was thinking of a different kind of criticism the company boss, Liu, had offered of his government. It's common for grand assumptions to be made about Beijing's hand in anything Chinese one finds in Africa. Beijing is generally thought to be actively supporting the entire gamut of Chinese companies as they set up overseas. Many believe that Beijing is minutely organizing the migration of its citizens to the continent. Liu had a revealingly different view of the role of his government. For him and his company, it was an impediment. He wasn't more involved in road construction in Mali because "it's Beijing that decides what we can do, what we can bid on," he said. "We could be doing a lot more construction work but they want us to stick to environmental work. They won't let us bid on the big road projects."

One could draw many inferences from his remark. One is that Beijing is choosing winners among its state companies at work in Africa. One assumes there are rational policy reasons behind these sorts of decisions, but Chinese businesspeople and senior African officials told me that corruption played a big part. The firms that were most favored by Beijing were paying kickbacks in China for their privileges. Corruption like this is, of course, a mirror of patterns of industrial corruption in China, in much the same way that Chinese labor abuses in Africa reflected the poor labor environment and lack of independent unions back home.

Shuai told me I was welcome to use the vehicle again, so the next morning Coulibaly and I set out for the city. There was a village to the west of the capital named Yékélébougou that I wanted to visit. It was on a plain just beyond Djôliba, the mountain that casts its shadow over the old, central city. A Chinese construction company in Yékélébougou was said to have expropriated land there for a gravel factory.

The drive took us through Kati, the terminus point of the east–west highway that linked landlocked Mali with Senegal, the country's neighbor to the west. It was the last of dozens of customs stops on this road, one final fleecing point by corrupt inspectors and police of truck and bus drivers and passengers before reaching Bamako, or alternately, the first of many for those heading toward Dakar.

Everything came to a halt near that last barricade as all manner of vehicle and pedestrian traffic converged: passengers getting on and off conveyances of every description, goods being loaded and unloaded, food and water for travelers being sold, emergency repairs being carried out, sex being negotiated.

The scene of law enforcement agents in a variety of uniforms extorting money, which is reproduced daily across most of the continent, was a sad and vivid reminder of how badly Africa's leaders have failed their people, of the failure of institutions and above all of how governments have never learned that the best thing they can do for African prosperity is to get out of the way. There was irony in the fact that the major army barracks in Kati would be the launching point of a coup d'état that would upend twenty years of Malian democracy.

Once through the bottleneck, it only took a few minutes more to reach Yékélébougou, a village of traditional earthen huts scattered in the shade of old baobab trees. The settlement was divided by a two-lane trunk road that ran parallel to the mountains. Yacouba Coulibaly (a common name in Mali), the former mayor, greeted me by the roadside, and we walked into the heart of the village together, taking a seat in a neatly swept clearing of bare earth, while small children played nearby. There, Coulibaly, a tall and gaunt forty-five-year-old who spoke precise French in a deep voice, explained the gravel story in detail.

While he was mayor, Coulibaly said, he had been in a dispute with one of the largest Chinese construction companies in the country, which he said had taken over part of the nearby mountain to mine rock for gravel and refused to pay local taxes or compensate people who were forced to move. The law called for any potential investor to submit a proposal to the local authorities, allowing the matter to be submitted to a vote by the village assembly. The corporation had instead tried to settle the matter informally, he said, lavishing gifts on some of the local traditional leaders. (All over the continent similar techniques were being used by foreign companies of many nationalities to bypass the law and gain control of large tracts of land or valuable resources.)

In 2006, Coulibaly said he had prevailed upon the region's prefect to force the Chinese operators to comply with the law, resulting in a payment of 7 million CFA francs in taxes. Shortly afterward, though, he lost an election, and since then the corporation had supposedly resumed making informal payments via the new mayor himself and not through the coffers of the local government.

"I know that some of the funds have been used to pay teachers and for school repairs and supplies, but because the payments go straight to the mayor, there is no accounting for the money," he said. "We have no idea what is really happening with the funds, and if things continue this way, we will go to the [state] tax department and file a complaint. One way or another, the truth will come out."

Coulibaly offered to accompany us to the site where the gravel was being ground from rock blasted out of the mountainside. Back on the trunk road, even through heavy rain, I could make out columns of dust rising from the flank of the mountain. We followed in the wake of a huge earthmoving truck, which was barreling toward the mountain, ostensibly to collect another load of gravel. When we reached the site, there was no gate to bar our access, so we drove in and approached the giant hill of stone forming beneath a conveyor belt that steadily dumped freshly chipped gravel from a towering, ramshackle contraption.

A truck pulled up alongside us with a pair of Chinese men aboard, and when they asked what we were doing, I explained that I had heard about their operation and asked if they could speak with me for a few minutes. The two turned toward each other in quick consultation and then the driver waved me off. "Talk about what?" he said. "We don't wish to speak."

Given that dead end, I asked Coulibaly, the driver, to show me the new Chinese-built bridge over the Niger. He snaked his way for some time through disheveled neighborhoods where industries and shanties sat cheek to jowl, and then, in the distance, with the rain letting up, I could make out the bridge construction site, and then the bridge itself.

I had somehow formed an image in my mind of a suspension bridge with soaring, modernistic towers, but there was no glitter or exhibitionism in this structure.

China had instead built something clean and conservative: an assemblage of stolid concrete pillars that made their way across the wide river and lifted the bridge bed skyward, before winding off sideward in the distance. The bridge was not yet open to traffic, but Chinese construction crews and their pickups were driving on it. We got as close as we could, stopped by the barricaded entrance, where protest graffiti commemorated the communities that had been forcibly removed from the area near the base of the new structure.

A Malian man we found sitting there told us there was a way across the river that did not require using the bridge at all. We followed an elevated pathway of old, weathered concrete, and sure enough, it led us across the Niger, though we had to ford in spots where the water was high. These were the remains of the first modern roadway crossing.

We came out on the other side to find a canal that ran perpendicular to the bridge's on-ramp. There, young neighborhood girls were bathing and swimming under the nonchalant gaze of three Chinese workers who sat perched on a rail overhead, smoking cigarettes. There was no way for us to get onto the main road from here—access on this side had been barricaded—forcing us to make a long, uncertain detour through wooded areas into a low-income neighborhood with rocky, uneven streets. As we descended an incline, we came upon a compound with long, high, whitewashed walls. Beyond them one could make out clusters of new pale yellow buildings.

"This is the new China hospital," Coulibaly said. "The Chinese, they built it for us for free."

We rounded a corner and followed the perimeter of the big new hospital that I'd heard so much about during my first few days in Bamako. Then, Coulibaly, the driver, who had told me two days before that Malians don't like Chinese, repeated the phrase: "They built this for us for free." His satisfied look belied his generalization.

In 1970, at the height of the Cold War, the Americans had built their big bridge over this river, several hundred miles downstream, in Niamey, the capital of Niger, and named it after John F. Kennedy. Twenty-two years later, the Saudis had built their bridge, which I had been crossing over often during my stay. As I said, they named it for King Fahd.

In the last few years, Gaddafi's Libya had built an administrative city and two large hotels at the northern foot of the Fahd Bridge, naming it after their dictator and signaling their big push for influence in the Sahel. In the end, Gaddafi was killed before the new government complex could be occupied. Malian friends later told me his name was ripped down that very day.

Here was China's bid for soft power. There were no huge billboards or ostentatious language or grand names. It was simply called the Friendship Bridge, and it would soon be carrying perhaps a third of the people who crossed the river each day, taking them past the biggest and newest hospital in the country. And if people remembered one thing about it, for now, it would be that it was free.

CHAPTER EIGHT

Ghana

Habits of Democracy

Ghana is a medium-sized country in West Africa, but it has always cut an outsized figure in both continental history and politics. In 1957, under Kwame Nkrumah, it became the first sub-Saharan country to win independence, from Britain. Restlessly ambitious, Nkrumah ruled as a left-leaning nationalist and pioneered Pan-Africanism, a political creed premised on breaking down colonial boundaries and forging a unified government for the continent.

Hoping to rapidly industrialize his country, in 1961 he began construction of one of the biggest public works projects ever undertaken in Africa, a massive dam over the Volta River designed to supply cheap and reliable electricity for the nascent local industrial sector. The Akosombo Dam was widely criticized as being far too big and costly, but it was completed ahead of schedule, and even today it still provides the lion's share of Ghana's electricity.

With Nkrumah's economy reeling from debt and people chafing at his increasingly authoritarian and personalized power, he was overthrown in 1966, opening a chapter of rule by a succession of conservative civilians and ruinously corrupt and incompetent army officers under whose leadership average incomes shrank by over a third. They were followed in the 1980s by Jerry Rawlings, a young flight lieutenant who seized power and twice made big waves in Africa—initially with his strong socialist leanings, and then a decade later with an economic about-face and turn to the West. Crucially, Rawlings belatedly allowed a transition to democratic rule, a tradition that by now runs as deeply in Ghana as anywhere in Africa. And during its democratic era, since

1992, Ghana's GDP has grown at a more than handsome average rate of 5 percent.

Here was a country with one of Africa's strongest and most active civil societies embarking on an economic embrace of China that might condition its future for decades to come. A booming natural resources exporter, with large exports of gold, cocoa, and now oil, Ghana was one of a rapidly growing number of African countries where China had recently structured a huge package deal of loans and investments in order to gain a seat at the banquet. Early in their discussions, it appeared likely that Ghana would agree to a resource-for-infrastructure swap, similar to big financing packages that had been pioneered a few years earlier by Angola and Congo, both large African countries that were immensely rich in oil or minerals, and, significantly, lacking in any meaningful practice of democracy. In Ghana's much more vibrant political system, though, public debate helped nudge things in a different and arguably more prudent direction. The country's recently tapped commercial oil production would not be used as direct collateral but paid into an escrow account, as had been the case in Angola. Ghana would remain free to sell its oil on the international market, even if under the contract terms China legally reserved the right to pocket income from its production if Ghana fell behind in its payments.

This might sound like a distinction without a difference, but it was quite significant. Arrangements to pay for a poor country's development in kind, through the supply of oil or some other natural resource, dramatically raise the likelihood of being underpaid for one's products over the long term, especially, as with many minerals, if they involve dwindling, nonrenewable supplies. This is because purchasers lock in discounts that protect them from long-term price rises.

In recent years, China's development financing practices have drawn intense scrutiny from the West, where they have sparked lively debate about Africa's future under what some foresee as Beijing's coming dominion. The lines have most often been drawn over whether China's ongoing thrust represents a step toward the rearrangement of the international system along terms that are more favorable to developing countries, as Beijing's "win-win" rhetoric promises, or whether it is setting the stage for a new era of massive African indebtedness or even, as some intone ominously, of Chinese imperialism.

From the very outset, neither ardent defenders of China nor knee-jerk skeptics in the West have typically shown much interest in seriously weighing African points of view or even in sampling the range of existing opinion. As has often been the case during its history, the continent, in effect, is reduced to a mere stage or backdrop for the rivalries and ambitions of others.

Ghana, where so much is going on with China, and where debate and open conversation are deeply ingrained in the national character, gives great voice to an African perspective.

Edward Brown works at the African Center for Economic Transformation (ACET), a development and economics think tank founded by K. Y. Amoakan, a former secretary general of the African Union, a continent-wide political organization. A bluff, thickset man in his fifties, Brown spent most of his career at the World Bank, notably serving as a representative in Rwanda shortly after that country's genocide. He had joined Amoakan to offer his expertise to African countries on matters of economic policy and development, and when I was last in Ghana he had recently spent much of his time working as a consultant to the government of Liberia.

Brown made a claim about Ghana I had heard often in several variations. He said that of all the countries in Africa, Ghana was among the best positioned to take advantage of its booming natural resource wealth, and of the eagerness of its new Chinese partners to drive a sound development policy. This was because of Ghana's increasingly robust democracy, its relative openness and transparency, and the existence of a substantial and fast-growing middle class, including swelling ranks of technocrats and highly educated professionals.

And yet for all of these advantages, Brown did not sound especially hopeful or optimistic about the impact that engagement with China would have on his country. This was despite the fact that at the time we spoke, Ghana's president, John Atta Mills, had only recently returned from Beijing, where he had concluded a memorandum of understanding for a $13 billion Chinese loan package that he said would "transform our country's economy and the lives of the people of Ghana."

The first tranche of this package, formalized some months later, was valued at $3 billion, surpassing any loan Ghana had received in more than fifty years of independence. By comparison, the International Finance Corporation, an arm of the World Bank that has traditionally been one of the largest lenders to the continent, loaned a total of $2.2 billion to all of sub-Saharan Africa in 2011. In an ebullient interview after the signing ceremony in Beijing, Ghana's vice president, John Dramani Mahama, told reporters from Bloomberg, "The process for accessing World Bank and IMF credit unfortunately has been quite tiresome. They come with a lot of strings, and the procedure for accessing the credit goes through quite a bit of rigmarole, and so it's not easy. . . . With the current financial crisis, it's very difficult to go anywhere in this world and get $3 billion."

Mahama, who would become Ghana's president the following year, had perfectly summed up the appeal of the freewheeling alternative that China represents in the eyes of African governments compared to the traditional leaders of the global financial system.

Throughout the negotiations, Brown remained skeptical about the soundness of the deal, though, and his attitude had nothing to do with being soured on China, much less being somehow anti-Chinese, or perhaps so denatured by his twenty years at the World Bank he could only conceive operating in conformance with Western orthodoxies.

China's recently unveiled investment package for Ghana was wide-ranging, including transmission pipelines that would bring natural gas online from newly exploited offshore fields in the west, hydroelectric dams, and water supply and rural electrification projects. There was to be an aluminum refinery, capable of producing two million tons of the metal per year, using Ghana's own bauxite deposits, bringing to fruition one of Nkrumah's oldest dreams. New roads would be built, and old, decrepit railroad lines in the center and west of the country rehabilitated.

What was there not to like about this? Despite what seemed to be productive Chinese actions, Brown said that questions both large and small hovered over the loan details. He said that packages like these were predominantly drawn up by the Chinese, who survey their own country's firms in advance to see who is interested in bidding for which pieces of the action. "On the African side there is no meaningful input.

The Chinese decide what they want. They arrange the financing. They send their companies. Yes, they consult with the African governments a bit, but in a way it is only to tell them what [the Chinese have] already decided to do.

"I don't know if the finance ministry has the capacity to assess this kind of deal. And in the office of the president, there is one fellow in charge of the China package." He amended himself later, to say one or two. "I am not sure there have been any strong analyses of risk management, of finance, of the cost-benefit, of integration into some strategic vision. We really must reach the stage where we can say, You say you want to help us? Let's talk about what that means, and how *we* want you to help us. The Chinese, meanwhile, are planning everything down to the letter. They will take whatever they can get from you, and if you are not prepared for it, it's too bad for you."

Concerns like these were no mere formalities, he insisted. This was not just a matter of offering face to Africans or preserving their feelings.

"Will investment [like this] lead to growth that is transformative? Will it lift productivity in your country? Will it halt the decline in important industries, like textiles? Will it launch African production in areas where we have true competitive advantage? How will African countries use it to diversify and transform? Unfortunately, this is a serious intellectual challenge that is not being met."

Kwadwo Tutu, a senior economist at the Institute of Economic Affairs, an independent Ghanaian think tank, framed similar concerns in a slightly different way. "Countries are not philanthropists," he said. "They are in business for themselves, and like many businesspeople, they will like to cheat you if you don't enforce your own rules and regulations. For African countries, the only safeguard is to try to negotiate advantageous conditions for oneself. That's the game of life we're in."

Tutu poured scorn on Chinese sloganeering toward Africa, especially about the phrase "win-win," and on China's insistence that it was not a wealthy country, but rather a peer member of the Third World.

"We know that this discourse doesn't have a bit of truth to it," he said. "China is not a developing country; only a fool would believe that. That is why I get angry when they stand up in the climate talks and try to make that argument. It's so self-serving."

Views like this did nothing to sour him on Chinese money, though. "Countries like Ghana need investment, and that has not often been forthcoming from the rich countries."

Tutu had received me in his very chilled office, which was located in an old but immaculate villa set back from central Accra's Ring Road, amid leafy gardens. My cell phone rang at one point, the caller wanting to discuss my plans for visiting a nearly completed Chinese dam project in a northwestern part of the country that had stirred some controversy. Tutu overheard me mention the dam by name and immediately picked up on it to drive his point home. "Bui Dam," he said. "It has been on the books for forty years, and until now, no outsiders have been willing to invest in it. Well, enter the Chinese, who are now doing that."

I asked Tutu if Ghana had been able to, as he put it, "enforce its own rules and regulations," and this prompted a disquisition about the country's past.

"In the 1960s, we had fantastic infrastructure, especially railroads, but they are all run-down now. In the 1980s and 1990s, we ran endlessly after foreign investment; we made the conditions so attractive. That's where all of our efforts went, instead of going into agriculture, which is where they should have gone. We are extracting ten times more minerals than we were before, but we're getting a mere pittance for them. If you factor in all of the social and environmental costs of mining into the equation, then you are left with about a 10 percent return, and they are taking away all of our minerals."

Tutu insisted that he was in no way singling out China; there was no question of exempting the West. Hadn't it been feasting on Ghana's resources for a century? The skepticism he expressed while trying to frame his country's predicament was rather a matter of once bitten, twice shy.

"Are we building a technical and entrepreneurial base that in ten or twenty years [will allow our companies] to go to other countries and exploit their oil?" Whether the partners were Western or Chinese, Ghana remained the passive party. It was still settling for being somebody else's appendage. "If we continue on this way, it is only a matter of time before the new oil discoveries that people are celebrating will be finished, and our children will not have benefited."

Many of the other observations I heard about the growing presence of Chinese and of Chinese money were familiar. Ghanaians
complained that Chinese investors and migrants came to the country
with one declared purpose, but quickly involved themselves in other
pursuits, legal or not so legal. Ghana is Africa's second largest gold
producer, after South Africa, and the stories about illegal mining by
Chinese, who cut down forests and despoiled the land with mercury to
produce their gold, were legion.

Many spoke in broad terms about a Chinese propensity for bribery and corruption, for shoddy goods and for cutting corners. The
Chinese-built National Theater, in particular, came up often. It was a
gorgeously sensuous, modernist structure with a white roof of sweeping curves. The problem, Ghanaians told me, was that only a few years
after being built, it leaked, its tiles were dropping off, and the building
seemed to be falling apart.

Generalizing is always dangerous, but the perception had taken
root, however well founded. After a little more than a half century of
independence, by many conventional indicators, Ghana seemed to be
hitting its stride. New money was flooding into the country thanks
to big oil and gas discoveries. The population was young, signaling
strongly favorable demographics for labor and industry. The country seemed comfortably settled in its democratic ways, experiencing
several handovers of power via the ballot box, and even passing the
test of peacefully making it through an election that was closer than
Bush-Gore without violence or trouble. The country enjoyed a positive image internationally, as witnessed by Barack Obama's decision to
visit Ghana on his first African trip as president. Big new players ready
to invest large amounts of capital, not only China, were clamoring for
business opportunities. One would expect the educated elite would be
boosterish about their country's prospects. Sadly, this was not entirely
the case. Moses Mozart Dzawu, a twenty-nine-year-old newspaper
reporter, conveyed these feelings of uncertainty best when I asked him
what Ghana would be like when he was fifty.

"So far, we haven't had good leaders," he said. "They don't even
know what they are there to do. You have to be asking yourself all the
time, Am I achieving a goal, and if not, why not? Yes, there is hope,

but we have to pray for the right leaders, people who are capable and selfless and who have vision; people who are excited for their country more than they are excited for their party or for themselves."

China's biggest ongoing project in the country was the aforementioned Bui Dam, and I wanted to visit it. Richard Twum, a grassroots activist, had led a campaign against the dam. Early one morning, we took coffee and buffet service in the patio restaurant of my hotel under a thatched roof. Twum, a squat, powerfully built man who kept a stubbly beard and wore a traditional, roughly cut smock made out of a striped, unfinished cotton, worked two mobile phones while he ate.

"As for the Chinese, don't even waste your time trying with them," he said. "They won't cooperate. We've approached them so many times, but they always say, Go speak to our Ghanaian counterparts." He told me that the Chinese dam-building company had settled into a routine with his group, claiming they could not understand English. The contractor in question was Sinohydro, a dam-building specialist, whose more than seventy hydropower projects around Africa made it one of the busiest of China's construction companies on the continent.

Twum was right about Sinohydro's poor communications; in Ghana, the company did not return my calls. "Do we look like colonists? We haven't killed any locals," a senior company official told the *Financial Times* in a gruff and defensive interview. "A dam is a sign of social progress and civilization. You have resources. I have money, technology and management," he said. "We can develop together. The reason we are going abroad is just to make money. In this process, we will protect the environment, assume social responsibilities, help development and help alleviate local poverty."

In lieu of Sinohydro's cooperation, Twum said he would give me an introduction to the traditional king in the locality where the construction was nearing completion.

The Bui Dam was a pet project of the government that had been defeated in the last election. To overcome local resistance, the administration of John Kufuor, now out of power, had described the dam as part of a much bigger scheme of opening up and developing a neglected region of the interior. A modern new city was promised, along with an airport and a brand-new university. The big plans became moot after the election, when a new president pursued new priorities.

The dam was still a year away from being completed, but it was about two weeks away from commencement of operations, when the sluicegates would be closed and water from the valley located in the teeth of a natural gorge from which villagers had just been relocated. The king and his minions would not be moving into the new state-of-the-art city that President Kufuor had talked up. Their concession prize was newly built villages on a hot and dusty plain beyond the gorge.

Twum had said nothing explicit about a bright future for Ghana, but it was clear in listening to his story of activism that people like him were making a positive difference. Civil society works, in part, by demanding more from those who govern: better performance, more accountability and openness, and more fairness. In this way, and not just through the regular exercise of elections, habits of democracy are formed, and this seemed like a vital piece of the puzzle—part of the answer to the question haunting the young reporter Moses Dzawu about how Ghana could eventually assure itself a supply of good leaders.

I had witnessed democracy making a difference in Senegal, where shadowy dealings for some of the most valuable real estate in the country were blocked. I had seen it in Zambia, where the presence of large numbers of Chinese immigrants, and the terms granted to foreign-owned extractive industries, including big Chinese newcomers, had become a major electoral campaign issue, and had led to better pay for miners. Even in a village on the outskirts of Bamako where people had been cheated, I had heard its ex-mayor say he had had enough experience of democracy to believe that justice would prevail in the end. This fed his stubbornness and persistence, giving him the will to petition higher jurisdictions and demand that the authorities look into the matter; demanding, in effect, that they do their job.

Here in Ghana, as in much of Africa, China had conducted its big business with an utter lack of transparency, providing scant public information and keeping the media at arm's length. To the extent the fine print of the huge deals it was concluding was known at all it was a by-product of African democracy: of parliaments, of opposition parties, and of civic groups that had demanded their governments disclose details the Chinese typically would not.

"Initially, the government treated us with hostility, like opponents," Twum said, when I asked him about his organizing efforts, echoing those faraway struggles. "But they have gradually come to understand that dialogue is important, and that groups like ours play a useful role."

Twum said his group had insisted on environmental safeguards, and had pushed to hold the government's feet to the fire on this front. The area to be inundated included a unique river habitat that was home to a number of rare species, including the endangered West African black hippopotamus. "From the beginning we have applied a lot of pressure on this issue," he said. "Partly because of our work, the EPA [Environmental Protection Agency] is aware of the weak environmental reputation of the Chinese contractors. One of the top officials even confessed to me, 'If we leave the builders even a bit of slack, they will flout all the rules.'"

Twum said that Sinohydro had agreed to build the dam under an arrangement known as BOT, or build, operate, transfer. This meant that after completion, the company would remain as operator of the dam until its investment had been recouped. In an echo of some of the big package deals that China was negotiating around the continent, Ghana would repay part of the total cost of the project in kind, handing over a portion of the cocoa crop instead of dollars. For all of his many efforts, Twum said he had not been able to learn many of the details. What he knew was that the project was coming in over cost and would not be finished by the initial deadline, prompting government officials to visit China recently to seek additional financing.

Twum put this down to the successful mobilization of the villagers, which he had helped organize, leading the candidates for relocation on tours to the two other big dams in Ghana, Kpong and Akosombo, Nkrumah's great infrastructure legacy. Learning about the travails of the communities displaced by those projects, their shabby, summary relocation, the lack of integration of their communities into the regional economy, and their trivial compensation primed the Bui Dam area residents to insist on their rights and to push for better treatment. With a look of mischievous self-satisfaction, Twum said, "I think the dam authority needed to seek more financing because they hadn't taken into account the full cost of relocation of these people."

I left Accra for Bonyere to attend the weekend-long funeral of my mother-in-law, who for years had owned and run a popular bakery in the town, earning her the nickname Fine Bread. I then set out from Bonyere toward the dam with the latest of my African drivers, another man named John, who dressed in neatly pressed guayaberas and kept his Corolla spotless, washing it himself every morning.

As we drove eastward through the scrubland out of Bonyere on the smooth, two-lane national highway, we passed Nkrumah's birthplace, the little town of Nkroful. Here and there, little bridges took us over swampy inlets, where billboards in the local language, Nzima, and in English had been erected by the American economic development agency USAID. They read: "Wetlands save us. Let's save the wetlands."

The signs symbolized an undeclared global contest under way over soft power. The Americans were constantly hectoring Africans about their behavior and values—protecting oneself against AIDS, limiting family size, sleeping under mosquito nets. Chinese messaging, as I said earlier, focused on big, tangible things that fairly shouted: This stadium, this hospital, this railroad, this airport, has been built by a people eager to walk hand in hand with you toward economic development. But of course development required more than pouring concrete and building things, just as it demanded more than constant reminding of supposed best practices.

My maps had shown a fairly direct route that would hug the Côte d'Ivoire border. So why was it that we had to drive a hundred miles east to Cape Coast before turning north toward Kumasi and Bui, I asked John.

He muttered something about it being the rainy season, and said that the roads were much better on the route we were taking. Then we suddenly lost velocity on a long straightaway, where John had just passed a truck filled with harvested pineapples. John showed no sign of puzzlement or emotion as he coasted to a stop on the shoulder and pulled the handbrake. He got out and worked under the hood, but to no effect. The car wouldn't start.

In the brutal mid-morning heat we were able to get towed by a 4x4 to the next junction. We found a mechanic's shop that was housed in a little shack off the main road. We were able to set off just before 6 p.m., in the fast gathering darkness. Now John drove much more slowly, which I put down to the nightfall, while playing Ghanaian Christian music on his sound system, switching from one CD to another in what seemed like an endless supply.

It was 8 p.m. by the time we arrived in Cape Coast. We found a darkly lit restaurant nestled amid a beer garden that had gone unused due to the evening rain. Inside, couples sat together chatting across tables in their booths. Melodramatic Nigerian movies played on a large TV that hung by a bracket on a far wall.

When we got under way again, John immediately resumed his religious soundtrack. I felt bad for an instant when I asked him to turn it off, which he did, but not before commenting solemnly, "God is great."

It took us a while to emerge from the center city, which was dominated by a major, gridlocked roundabout, and then we turned onto a road that headed toward Kumasi. I figured we would really be able to fly now, but not two minutes later the sky opened up with what was easily one of the heaviest rains I had seen all summer. John went from sixty miles an hour to forty and then all the way down to fifteen and lastly ten, and even at that speed it was very hard to see. He turned his music back on and resumed singing along with his hymns.

When the rain stopped, the "better" road that had inspired this very long route to Bui was a catastrophe; for long sections the asphalt had disappeared, giving way to flooded, rutted earth. Proceeding slowly, we reached the Pra River, the historic dividing line between the kingdom of the Asante, the central Ghanaian group that had formed one of West Africa's most powerful societies, and the Fante, a smaller, much less centralized coastal group that had long been their foil. The bridge across was of an old truss design, a type often put up by armies a century or so ago, and this one, with its gray, peeling paint and pitted roadbed, felt like it must be approaching that age.

Soon we were entering Kumasi, the country's second city. It was near midnight, and there was no question of continuing. We were able to find a motel that claimed to have air-conditioning, which didn't work. A big bucket next to a low faucet was a stand-in for a working shower.

The next morning we bought boiled eggs, nuts, and juice by the roadside and had breakfast on the fly. The Bui king had agreed to meet me at midday.

Kumasi, like Cape Coast, seemed much, much bigger than in my memory of it from two decades earlier, but the road beyond was all open and green rolling countryside with West African mountains, loping and broken-shouldered, now and again injecting some relief in the distance.

By prior arrangement, at Sunyani, a regional capital, we met a young man from Bui who the king had told us would guide us to the village. The shy teenager was the king's son, who was studying at a boarding school there. The young man knew his way on the dirt roads very well, eventually leading us to a gated archway that he said led into the village. Its signage was in English and Chinese, and although the boy warned that the Chinese guards manning the barrier would stop us to make inquiries about our business, I told John he should merely slow down, allowing me, the foreigner, to give a brisk wave from the passenger's seat, a kind of bluff, which I rightly figured would be enough to get us through.

After a few more minutes of riding up a bumpy incline, the king's freshly built village appeared on the crest of a dusty hill, luminous in its new coats of Crayola paint colors. A dozen goats tugged lustily at the greenery under the incandescent sky, paying us no mind as we emerged from the car.

The king's son led me to the shade of a narrow terrace and offered me a seat there, saying he would announce me to his father and be right back. A few minutes later, a few men appeared, bearing a high-backed ceremonial chair. It was made of solid sections of dark wood that had been joined together with neat joints and bore a studded bronze trim, with two little turrets that looked almost like a sword handle rising from the back. Presently, the king appeared. He wore a welcoming smile but had wide eyes that conveyed a hint of sadness.

Nana Kojo Wuo had dressed in his regal attire for our meeting, a brown-and-gold bolt of hand-woven and -printed cloth that was slung over his left shoulder and hung loosely from his torso. He wore a crown in identical colors. It was shaped like a fez, and affixed around its brim were large, gold *adinkra*—figurines cast in the shapes of animals— which were traditionally used in many Ghanaian cultures both as symbols of royalty and as official weights for gold.

I wasn't sure exactly what protocol called for under the circumstances, so I honored King Wuo by standing as he approached and greeted his outstretched hand with two of mine, instinctively bending slightly at the knee and bowing my head.

Someone spoke up to ask me to wait for a moment after we had been seated, face-to-face on the little tiled terrace. The air was motionless, and after the long, midday ride, it felt incredibly hot. A solid, white metal post buttressed the roof whose overhang furnished our shade. A teenage girl appeared before we got started, bearing a plastic bucket full of bottled soft drinks. To my dismay, they were lukewarm, but I took a Coke nonetheless. Soon arrived the king's court, his three "translators," as one of them said introducing them to me, after they had taken seats in the sun.

The fifty-three-year-old king spoke initially in his language, Mo, and then switched to English, which he spoke impeccably and with polish.

Whether it involved land deals with foreigners or negotiations with governments, traditional rulers in Africa have often played a part in shortchanging the rights of peasants. They typically lacked extensive formal schooling, and were often easily manipulated with money or gifts that reinforced their own privilege and prestige but did little for their constituents. Wuo, though, was clearly cut from a different cloth. He was a graduate of the University of Cape Coast, and he spent most of the week at a job in a city called Nsuta, a couple of hours away, working as a senior district education official. When Richard Twum came knocking, though, to talk about the stakes involved for local communities—farmers of cashews, cassava, and yams—in the building of a dam here, in King Wuo he found a canny and receptive audience.

Leaning forward in his chair, Wuo spoke of the visits he and Twum had made together to the communities displaced long ago by the construction of the much bigger Akosombo Dam. They heard from them how they had had no say in the choice of where they would be resettled, how little money they had received as compensation. The king was determined to win better terms for his people.

"In Akosombo, the villagers were told, 'You pick up your belongings now, because the water is coming,' and they left," he said. "In our case, we chose our site, and we fought for the best terms we could get. In Akosombo, they didn't build new housing for the people like this. We have had a national dialogue to help us know what we should be looking out for and I think some lessons have been learned. We're fortunate because we live in a technological age, where it is easier for people to know their rights. Forty, fifty, sixty years ago, the world was very different."

King Wuo told me that Sinohydro was not involved in the relocation negotiations themselves. (The Chinese had loaned Ghana $622 million to finance the project.) The three affected communities had conducted all of their negotiations directly with the Ghanaian government. But Chinese contractors had built the new replacement villages, which consisted of simple and functional complexes like this one. This conformed to a general pattern in Africa where most of the money China lends ends up in the pockets of Chinese contractors and suppliers. This particular village, one of several that were relocated, was about one square mile, and had four hundred residents.

"The houses are finished, and they've laid the foundation of a new high school," the king said. "We're supposed to get a church, a clinic, a market, a community center, and a police station. The Akosombo people were placed very close to the turbines. We've got a better setting and more land."

But King Wuo was not totally pleased. "Compared to the Akosombo people, it is true that we consider ourselves blessed," he said. "We have not achieved perfection, but there is electricity and potable water and latrines. But if the government were serious, we would have a new city here, which is what they promised. This is what we expected when we made a sacrifice and gave up our land and our sacred burial grounds."

Wuo cited two other major grievances. First, the Chinese had employed six hundred of their own workers to build the dam, housing them in isolated compounds, beyond the humpbacked mountains in the distance. "They have only hired a few of our people, and it is only to do unskilled labor." Second, the government had consented to a more generous payment to his people than had been granted in the past, but it was a one-time affair, he said. "That gorge was our asset, and this dam is forever. As long as it is producing power and they are selling it, the profits should be shared. For sure, we have received something, but what of the people of the future? If they get nothing, they will be cheated."

After we parted, John and I spent a half hour driving around the dam site unmolested, except to make way for huge earthmoving trucks and other machinery that were to-ing and fro-ing, kicking up huge clouds of dust on the grounds. The 354-foot-high dam itself appeared to be already completed, and just waiting for someone's command to close the sluiceway, which still coursed with the waters of the Volta River.

Soon we were on the Kumasi highway, speeding through the countryside as the day fell away. I caught little details amid the blur: hunters with old rifles trekking through the scrub, little teams of farmers winding down their work before nightfall, young men fishing with simple poles from river crossings, people swimming in the gloaming dusk down below.

Signs of urbanization gradually increased, the towns—Bamboi, Subinso, Wenchi, Techiman—growing steadily thicker, with buildings painted in the bright reds, yellows, and greens of the rival cell phone companies. Night had fallen by the time we reached Kumasi, which we bisected quickly to reach the most important road in the country, the 125-mile-long highway to Accra, linking Ghana's two biggest cities. The on-ramp gave way to a sight still rare in sub-Saharan Africa, a four-lane highway.

I had visions of a quick run to the capital and of an early night to bed after the hectic travel. The excitement was such that I fired up my wireless modem and began composing a brief email to friends about how I was looking forward to ending my day.

I never finished the email. Before I could, the traffic slowed, and then stopped. We were surrounded by heavy trucks that belched thick fumes. "This is where the road becomes a problem," said John.

This, it turned out, was an understatement. We crawled along for nearly half an hour, barely advancing a mile while the road transitioned from superhighway to a heavily cratered and thoroughly backed-up two-lane carriageway. A little further on, the bush began to encroach, growing almost up to the very edge of the roadbed, which in the space of a few miles had gone from patchy asphalt to powdery dust.

As I'd seen so many places before in my travels, wherever the traffic slowed down, commerce took over immediately, and the narrow shoulder was filled with rickety merchants' stalls and hawkers perambulating amid some of the thickest dust I'd ever seen.

Things steadily deteriorated from there, with the road opening up into a wide, unmarked corridor of sand and dirt. Heavy trucks and battered taxi vans slalomed left and right, paying no attention to which side of the road they were on as they fought over right-of-way and struggled to avoid getting bogged down. At the outskirts of Accra, after hours of this, another layer of obstruction came to impede our progress during the last ninety minutes or so, when vehicles were forced to stop at roadside police checkpoints that served no other evident purpose but to extort money from the least fortunate.

I later wondered if a vast build-out of roads and other infrastructure by the Chinese could not only get people and goods moving much faster and more cheaply, but might also lead to a change of culture, and of attitudes toward time. Might it at last create an expectation of expedience in African transactions? Ed Brown, the ex–World Bank official, had spoken of the continent's appalling infrastructure as an "element of inertia," as something that until fixed would irrevocably hold Africa back. King Wuo had spoken about it, too, noting that Ghana had had good roads and rails when he was young. I came to learn that where Ghana's roads were concerned, the Chinese had also been part of the problem.

Samuel Inokye, a senior policy officer of the Association of Ghana Industries, took me aback when he said that Ghana's problems with Chinese road builders were nearly identical to problems with Chinese companies and traders that dumped commercial goods. "Our indigenous road builders, just like our textile manufacturers, cannot win contracts against the Chinese, who win everything, but who give us quality that is very low."

The Kumasi road, he explained, was built by the China Railway Corporation. He called it a "good example" of a widespread problem.

"They've been doing that road for five years, and by the time they finish one section, the other section is already spoiled. They are putting in very low bids to get the contracts, and that is part of the problem. They are under constant pressure because of this, and the quality suffers. Even on the latest section, from Apedwa to Anyinam, the margins of the road are already breaking up and disappearing. We have no doubt that they are capable of doing good work, but they are so eager to win the contract that they can only deliver shoddy goods."

I could not be sure of every detail of Inokye's arguments, but I was impressed that he didn't only bash the Chinese or carry water for the Ghanaian companies that build roads.

"The biggest problem is our government," he said. "They will take a long time to disburse funds to a local contractor, and if the government changes in the meantime, the payments will be frozen, sometimes for good. The Chinese, they often bring their own financing, so they don't face these problems as much. You would wonder, though, if there are three or four companies in your country capable of doing this kind of work, why the state wouldn't give them the business? The answer is because of politics. You will fear that these companies are supporters of the opposition.

"The Chinese have to meet standards in place wherever they go around the world," Inokye continued, "but here in Africa the standards are weak, and all of these goods coming in through the back door are impoverishing our countries. The big problem is dumping, which may be hard to prove legally, but one knows it when one sees it. In the market, you see three pairs of socks that cost less than 50 cents. That is unfair to our manufacturers."

I pointed out that the availability of cheap Chinese imports had made many goods more affordable for Ghanaians, especially for the poor.

"This goes beyond consumers making choices," he said. "It goes to the people of this country having jobs, having a future. If you allow people to import these very cheap goods, you are making it impossible for Ghanaian industries to survive. It is killing our economy. It is also destroying our tax base, which is what the government relies on to build the roads that we need."

Inokye proceeded through a common litany of complaints about the Chinese goods allegedly dumped in Africa, dwelling in particular on what he said was the false savings from abysmally poor merchandise.

"You can see the effect in the collapse of the textile sector, which formerly employed thirty thousand people. Now it barely employs five thousand."

The Chinese were not only beating his members badly on price, he said, but they were stealing popular Ghanaian designs, like the country's most distinctive traditional fabric, kente cloth, or textiles bearing the *adinkra* symbols.

"You see a product that costs $20 here that they pirate and then sell for $6. Sometimes they'll go as low as $4. We're not going so far as to say they shouldn't sell things in our markets, but you have to provide your own designs. Copying like that is unfair."

I had Inokye's comments in mind when I met with Zou Manyang, a project manager for the China Railway Wuju Corporation, one of the major road builders in the country. Zou was a handsome forty-two-year-old who carried a black briefcase and was neatly dressed in an olive polo shirt and crisp khakis. He'd been in the country for over eight years, he said, and he started off speaking optimistically about the place.

"Ghana is a good country, a very peaceful country," he said at one point. "In 2008, they had a very close election, but they were able to transfer power very smoothly. In Egypt, Libya, Liberia, Côte d'Ivoire, they had war. This discourages investment. People like Ghana because of this. But you go to some parts of Ghana and people have given up on farming because they have no roads. This is a big waste. If Ghana gets roads, they will be able to farm and earn money and this will allow them to develop.

"They're getting money from the World Bank and from some countries, like the U.S., Europe, Japan, etc., but the money is not sufficient. They need more investment. That's why the roads can't be built quickly. They are also building cheaply, so their roads don't last."

Historically, he was accurate, but things were changing fast. He'd omitted mention of China as a major source of capital for the country. More important, perhaps, companies like his, if not his own, were bidding for—and winning—contracts for work funded by non-Chinese lenders. More of this sort of lending—untied, contrary to China's lending—would mean not just more roads for Ghana, but more business for big Chinese contractors like him.

"I am sure [Ghana] will be in a position to develop this country," Zou said. "But in my opinion, some people in Ghana don't work very hard. Because it is a tropical country, they can get food very easily, so they stay in their houses. They don't want to work hard to make more money. They are satisfied like this.

"It's the same like [minority group members] in western China. They don't want to work hard. They rely on the government to provide support. In my company we have one thousand Ghanaian employees, but it is very hard to change them. They don't work hard. They are very slow. We have problems with turnover. They get paid and then don't show up for work. They are always asking for more money."

I repeated one of the most common complaints against Chinese employers, that Africans are confined to menial work and rarely placed in positions of real responsibility.

"This debate about labor is a false problem," he said. "We can't use African labor [that way] because the capabilities aren't there. All we can do is gradually train people. In our company, the workers are Ghanaian and the managers are Chinese. There's no way to use African managers, because we wouldn't be able to understand each other.

"People want good work from us. Things we make should look perfect. If we just had Africans do the work, it wouldn't be done to that level of quality. The Chinese employee may cost a lot more than hiring an African, but it's worth it, because it improves the quality and the output."

Zou said that Chinese workers had revered Western investors in China and painstakingly studied their ways (many would go a good deal further and say that Chinese companies often stole and copied intellectual property and industrial secrets outright), but Ghanaians showed little interest in learning from Chinese employers.

"I think the government has to do a better job at propaganda," he said. "Work is not easy. You have to love your work; be proud of it. Protect the value of foreign investment.

"Here, the workers are stealing from us all the time and nobody cares. This is a giant problem: stealing oil, stealing parts, stealing tires. You report it to the authorities and they play it down. They don't call it theft. The police come after us if we beat a worker, but if you call the police to report theft, they are worthless. They just release the people, without charges."

We transitioned from talking about the cheap building standards here to discussing the crumbling new roads Inokye and other Ghanaians complained about. Zou acknowledged that his company had had a hand in the Accra–Kumasi highway construction, which they'd worked on nearly five years earlier, but denied any fault.

"The government doesn't know how to make budget projections," he said, attributing the road's problems to frequent stops and starts of the work. "It's not a problem of corruption. They just don't have enough money."

How about lowballing bids in order to win contracts and then cutting corners, which inevitably led to quality issues?

Underbidding wasn't just about beating the competition, Zou said, especially the foreign competition. It was about bigger issues, like amortizing heavy equipment costs, and especially about keeping the pumps of China's enormous public works sector primed.

"Bidding so low sometimes you lose money," he said. "It's true. Other times, you have very small margins."

"Why do it, then?" I asked.

"If you have your equipment and your people in place and there is no business, that is very bad. If you bid low, though, even if you have a tiny margin, you are better off. That's the reason Chinese companies bid low. It's not because we want more market share. The number of companies and people working in this sector [in China] is very large. We need more and more markets to keep people employed. Most of the companies like mine are state-owned, and if you start laying off workers, it will create huge problems for the country."

He acknowledged that "some projects are not done well. If the Chinese government gives a grant to an African country and a Chinese company gets the work, they will often do the project very quickly in order to save money, and this leads to the quality not being good. That is true.

"Sometimes it might be a design problem. Or the original amount might be budgeted for a kilometer of road and the government asks you to build one and a half kilometers. The contractor will use less asphalt, and in these parts the road will go bad very quickly.

"My company pays more attention to quality, though. And that is why we get more projects."

Kofi Bentil and Franklin Cudjoe, both in their thirties, were the young founders of a new Ghanaian think tank called IMANI. I met with them in one of the new luxury hotels that had recently begun proliferating in Accra.

"We are trying to get the government to sit up and take notice, because we are simply stumbling through this relationship with China," Bentil told me. "If you look at the elite, they think that China is the key to the future—a country that will provide lots of money without asking a lot of questions. In fact, we are the ones who are not asking questions. I am not pro- or anti-Chinese, but I want us to get a good deal out of this relationship, and you won't get that by accident. China has a strategy, and we don't, and they will take advantage of us, not because they are bad people, but because we haven't been smart."

As an example, he mentioned the Bui Dam. "In the 1960s, we built Akosombo ourselves. Why should we be having the Chinese build Bui for us?" (In fact, an American company, Kaiser Engineers and Construction, had been the main contractor for the dam project, but the level of Ghanaian participation was high.)

Both men were highly educated and avowed fans of conservative economists like Milton Friedman. They were new at what they were doing and still getting the hang of serving as an ideas shop.

Bentil cautioned about the political impact of China's engagement with the continent, saying Beijing's investments were helping "float despots and silence intellectuals." Cudjoe emphasized the importance of grand bargains, properly weighing what Africa would gain and lose in its exchanges with the world.

"At some point in the future, our resources will be depleted," Cudjoe said, "and when they run out, what you're left with is your own people. They are your ultimate resource. What we have to do is be sure that we are getting maximum value for our natural resources so that we can take care of our human resources, and the China deals are not doing that."

"China needs us for our resources much more than the West does now," said Bentil. "We may be getting a bad deal, but I think eventually this can be turned around. The West, on the other hand, needs us for our people," he said, citing the aging demographics of Europe. "I, for one, don't believe in brain drain. If Ghanaian doctors are leaving the country, what we should do is train more doctors. We need to make that a business of the future."

———

Before leaving Ghana, I squeezed in visits with friends, like Albert Osei, a Ghanaian national who had been country director for the World Bank in Guinea and in Burkina Faso. Albert lived well, on an elevated plateau a good ways outside the center of Accra. He had built his immaculate white retirement villa near the University of Ghana's Legon campus. He received me in a spacious living room brimming with books and music.

"The fear that China is going to come here and rape us of our resources is nonsense," he said. "The Chinese need our resources and the key questions are what price we get for them and how much transformation is done locally. All the rest is meaningless."

To get the best deals for themselves, Albert said, African countries had to stop dealing with China single-handedly. "With fifty-four countries in Africa, there's not much leverage that any single one of us can have. But if we work to cut deals together we can get much better terms. We can also enlist China to help us build an infrastructure that lets us trade much more with each other."

Leverage was the key concept, he said, and it worked in other ways, as well. "China's involvement should help us change the terms of engagement with the West, in order to gain greater equity, more parity. If the West is jealous of China, we should say to them, Train our people and give them a bigger role in your companies. Don't complain about the Chinese. Help us move up the value chain. Do this, and we will love you."

I had just enough time at my hotel to chat with Seth Dei, an incredibly sharp Ghanaian business executive who had been friends of my parents in Côte d'Ivoire in the 1970s and 1980s. We talked about lots of things, and the conversation inevitably turned to the Chinese. "I think the Chinese are incredible people," Dei exclaimed. Then he told me a story.

"One day it was raining heavily [in Accra] and people were crowding into a bus stop for shelter," he began. "A Chinese couple approached and began to nudge their way into the crowd seeking cover. The Ghanaians began to grumble among themselves. 'Who are these people? Why are they bothering us?' they said. At that point, the Chinese man spoke up in Twi [Ghana's near universal lingua franca]. 'Ade?' [Why?] 'Aren't we people, too?'"

PART THREE

Happy Family

CHAPTER NINE

Saints of the Household

I stopped in Tanzania, on the east coast, on my way from West Africa back to southern Africa, giving myself time to explore Dar es Salaam for a few days before returning to Mozambique. It was in Dar, Tanzania's sprawling, seaside economic capital, that I had begun reporting on China's African migration boom three years earlier. I'd traveled overland to Zambia on the TAZARA Railway, which China built under Mao in the 1970s, as both a show of solidarity with the continent and a bid for influence. With that single, dramatic stroke, China successfully insinuated itself into a game that had previously been dominated by the United States and the Soviet Union.

The Chinese presence in Dar had grown enormously. In Kariakoo, a low-end commercial district of narrow, dusty streets where I'd seen scattered Chinese traders before, they were out in force now, dominating whole blocks, with their proliferating storefront shops, sidewalk stalls, and street corner hawkers.

In this bric-a-brac universe, the newcomers hawked plastic flowers, sold curtains, fresh fruit, shoes, Chinese medicines. Other stalls featured a proliferation of Chinese-made phones bearing unheard-of brand labels, or outright copies that carried fanciful combinations of well-known names, things like Nokia-Siemens, or ATT+Samsung. I priced an iPhone knockoff called the G-Tide at $7, and when I turned to walk away, the clerk proffered another, even cheaper copy, a Panda, which he said I could have for $5.

Tamimu Salehe, the assistant secretary general of the Tanzanian Union of Industrial and Commercial Workers, complained to me that petty commerce, the first rung on the economic ladder for most city dwellers, was being taken over by Chinese newcomers.

"This is the question we ask in Tanzania. Why do they give such room to the Chinese? We are a trade union, and we ask this of our government. Why give them space to play in a sector where locals should be the main players? But the government is quiet on that. They give no answer."

Salehe had an answer for his own question, one that echoed an explanation I had heard from the former Zambian finance minister, who had told me that officials in Beijing had urged his government to tread lightly on enforcing immigration laws with Chinese nationals, as a matter of "friendship."

"This is happening because the Chinese government is helping this government with loans, with construction, and with assistance of various kinds," said Salehe, "and the Chinese use this as camouflage for immigration. It is true that we get aid from the Chinese, but if you turn the coin over, you will see that they are benefiting at our expense. The Chinese will take over all the business in Tanzania. In ten years, if nothing changes, there will be nothing left."

I asked him why Chinese should be regarded any differently from Indians, who had dominated the retail sector and much else in Tanzania for decades. He ignored my question and repeated some of the standard complaints about the Chinese newcomers.

"As a trade union, what we see is that they are taking the employment opportunities of the Tanzanians, and it is very hard to organize workers for Chinese employers. They have been very rude with the unions. They have given conditions to their workers, saying that if you belong to a union we will fire you—on the spot. That is illegal according to Tanzanian law, but they pretend not to know the law, and we have many, many cases."

The flight from Dar to Maputo followed the coast of the continent southward past some of Africa's thickest forests, its richest fishing waters, and over some of its most beautiful and unspoiled beaches. Seemingly forever, Mozambique has been one of the world's ten poorest countries, but in addition to these already considerable natural assets, it is now estimated to have the world's largest untapped coal deposits, as well as some of the biggest offshore natural gas reserves—all discovered recently. In 2012, four of the five largest gas finds in the world were in waters off Mozambique.

On my first trip there I had set off almost immediately for the countryside. For most of its history Mozambique had scarcely been an afterthought in the global economy, but now, as much as any country in Africa, it was clearly and stirringly in play, and I was returning because I needed to see more of the country and talk with more people to understand what was going on.

The Chinese were not the only ones drawn by Mozambique's new-found bounty. Bangladeshis were now turning up to do commerce in small towns scattered throughout the countryside, and Indonesians, drawn by a booming and scarcely regulated logging industry and by semiskilled jobs in the oil and gas industries, were helping sell out the seats on most flights into the country.

Most strikingly, the boom here was also attracting large numbers of Portuguese, Mozambique's onetime colonial masters who were now residents of one of Europe's poorest countries and among the hardest hit by financial crisis. Between 2009 and 2011, the number of Portuguese officially registered with their embassy increased by over 20 percent, with 23,000 of them thought to be living in Mozambique's two biggest cities, Maputo and Beira. The Portuguese were every bit as clannish as the Chinese, keeping their own company in favorite home-style restaurants in Maputo, or gathering around tables in private homes. Together, they ritually bemoaned the stagnation of the old country while plotting moves forward. Portugal and China shared a history of sending emigrants around the world to establish new communities. One had done so because it was a perennially poor land at the margins of Europe, and the other because it was a poor and overcrowded land in the heart of Asia.

At a Portuguese dinner for recent arrivals, I sat next to a doctor who had somehow found his way into the warehouse business here. He invoked an old proverb to explain his decision to come all this way to build a new life. "The saints of the household have no powers to bless you. It is only the saints of faraway lands that can help." I suspected that any Chinese emigrant would understand the sentiment.

An element in my decision to return to Mozambique was a desire to visit the far north. It was easily the poorest part of the country, and yet as is common in conflict-prone African societies, it was also the most richly endowed with almost all of the country's main resources. The north had been the stronghold of the RENAMO rebels during the long civil war, which ended in 1992. Ever since, it had been largely frozen out in terms of politics and patronage, compounding its poverty. Not incidentally, the north also seemed to be favored by many Chinese migrants, who carved out big chunks of the forest for logging, and who worked the country's waters for prized, industrial catches of shark, shrimp, and squid.

As it happened, my visit coincided with an extraordinary spate of reports in the local press about Chinese depredations in the north. These ran from an epidemic of major bribery cases involving customs agents to the seizure of illegal fishing boats from Chinese operators. The most spectacular item, though, was an investigative report in the Mozambican newspaper *O País,* about the impounding of six hundred containers of illegally logged old-growth mahogany and other hardwoods by Chinese operating in the northern forests. Following their initial scoop, journalists were not allowed to inspect the seized wood, and people in the know in Maputo told me that this probably meant that all but a symbolic quantity of the timber was probably quietly sold back to the Chinese loggers, or else auctioned off to other exporters by officials who then pocketed the profits.

Views like this were of a piece with the extraordinary pessimism that hung over the society about its ability to harness its resource wealth. The role of China and its migrants was a key element in the dire outlook.

Simon Norfolk, who runs a small NGO called Environmental Justice with his Mozambican wife, does not entirely share the pessimism. I talked with him in the villa where he lives in a leafy residential neighborhood. The walls of the foyer were decorated with block-cut socialist realism propaganda posters from the liberation struggle days.

He told me of a road trip he had taken just a month earlier, from Nampula and Nacala, another city in the north. "We broke a cardinal rule and traveled by night," he said. "Normally you would expect roadblocks all along this route, but this time there weren't any. What we saw instead was lots of trucks filled with unmarked logs, which means they were illegal. This can mean only one thing: that a phone call went through."

Norfolk made no overarching claims about the Chinese role in Mozambique, nor was there any stress on the blame that should be apportioned to them; that he reserved mostly for the government, which he, as many others, saw as the key to misuse of the land and to corruption. A London-based group, the Environmental Investigation Agency, estimated that in 2012 China imported between 190,000 and 216,000 cubic meters of illegally exported timber from Mozambique, worth roughly $130 million.

"The collusion of local authorities is probably less important than the collusion of national figures," Norfolk said. "It is not uncommon to hear stories of foreigners who go to local government for permission to log and are refused. Then they go to the national level, and the central government people put pressure on the local folks to issue a license. The local official will literally receive a phone call telling him what to do, leaving him no choice.

"We talk to local officials all the time and they throw up their hands and say there is nothing they can do, because we've got this national elite that's having a party with the buyers of our resources."

In the past, he said, logging and land deals had gone through the prime minister, whom he called the "go-to person" for Chinese doing business in the country. "She got sacked, though, and [President Armando] Guebuza took over all of this business for himself. It's not subtle, and it is going to get worse, because Guebuza has gathered his family and told them he has two more years in office, so this is the time to make money."

Norfolk's story was an illustration of the classic presidential clan rentier capitalism that has ravaged any number of African countries, and the Wild West atmosphere surrounding the country's forests was being replicated along the coast with the country's sea resources. This rentier system also governs Mozambique's management of its immense, newfound reserves of coal and natural gas. The state clings to the practice of contract secrecy, which allows it to hide the terms of foreign investment, along with any revenues, from its own citizens. This helps explain an apparent paradox widely observed in Africa: poverty is declining much faster in countries without mineral wealth than in those that are richly endowed in natural resources. For years, Western countries have provided huge amounts of budgetary support to Mozambique, and by not demanding an end to this practice they have arguably served as accomplices.

João Pereira, a former journalist, was director of a group called the Civil Society Support Mechanism, one of a handful of indigenous NGOs that were struggling to make inroads against the culture of corruption in Mozambique, a formal democracy that, like many African countries, was still more or less run like a one-party state. The picture Pereira painted of his own society reminded me of the struggles over the control of natural resources among big foreign interests in Liberia, Guinea, and Sierra Leone. Here, as in West Africa, China was battling to make inroads against giant, privately owned Western mining companies.

In the early going here, the big prize had been something called the Nacala Corridor. This was the name given to a prospective link via railroad between the deepest natural port in East Africa, in the northeastern city of Nacala, to the world-class coal reserves of Tete province, in western Mozambique. Along the way, it would pass through some of Africa's most valuable prime forests. The corridor project was mainly conceived to give landlocked Malawi and Zambia a cheaper route to the sea, and had remained on the drawing board, collecting dust, for years. But two events had recently come together to give it urgency: an understanding of the extent of Mozambique's vast coal deposits, and soaring demand for fossil fuels in both India and China.

As to the coal, in the early going at least, according to Pereira, the Chinese had lost out to Vale, Brazil's global mining powerhouse. The Chinese strategy, he said, had initially focused on co-opting certain key ministers in the government, along with a number of influential generals from FRELIMO, the victors in the civil war. Vale, however, had prevailed via an even surer route: winning over the president himself.

I heard stories from a man named Dino Foi about how the Chinese astutely went about working President Guebuza's personal network to improve their prospects. Foi, who boasted an MBA and Ph.D. in business earned in Taiwan, had run a company called Focus, whose mission was to serve as a conduit and facilitator for prospective Chinese investors. Foi told me that the company's principal owners were four of the president's children. He had left Focus to form his own business, hoping to earn big commissions servicing Chinese investors, instead of working for a salary. He estimated that there were 100,000 Chinese living in Mozambique.

If the Chinese had lost out in Nacala, Pereira said, they were doing whatever they could to make up for it. Doors to other opportunities were steadily being opened for them through their work in the road-building sector. The government was allowing Chinese road builders to bring in as many workers as they liked, Pereira said. Some of the Chinese workers went into business for themselves and sank roots in the country, while others saw Mozambique as a relatively easy back door into the promised land of prosperous South Africa, next door.

"Each of the companies that comes here acts like a private intelligence operation and they inform their embassy about all of the resource and business opportunities that might interest China," Pereira said. "They do some good things. They are providing some jobs. They are adding to the budget. They are building roads, and they do it quickly. But if you compare the negative to the positive, the negative is much greater. It's not part of the public agenda, though, because of the party's relationship with the Chinese over the years, and because Chinese business has captured our elites.

"Their impact on the environment is a complete disaster," he said. "They take everything down, from the big trees to the small trees, and they don't do any replanting. When you speak with a Chinese company, as I have with the directors of timber companies, they'll say, 'Our problem is not your environment. Your environment is a question for your future, not mine. Talk to me about money. I came here to make money and I have brought money to your country.'"

As I talked with Pereira, a wealthy-looking man swept past us in the hotel lobby. He was large, tall, and impressively dressed in an expensive, tailor-made suit. In one giant hand he carried four cell phones clutched together. Pereira identified him as the minister of trade, commerce, and industry, someone he had grown up with.

"He comes from the same class as me, but within three years of getting his minister's appointment, he had three homes in Maputo, each of which is worth more than a million dollars."

Pereira said the last time they had met, he had asked the minister why he had never been invited to any of his new homes, and then scolded him, saying that such acquisition of wealth didn't reflect the values they were both raised with. Pereira said the man replied, "If you want to be stupid, then you will remain poor."

As we parted company, Pereira said grimly that with the country given over to illicit enrichment, lawlessness, and exclusion on such a vast scale, all signs pointed not to economic takeoff for Mozambique, but rather to yet more war.

Late one chill, sunny morning, I made my way to a relic of a building in an old, low-lying quarter by the bay called Baixa that housed the office of João Carrilho, a top official in a government agency called the National Directorate of Lands and Forestry. The Portuguese, who first arrived in Mozambique in the late fifteenth century, and began a formal colonization process three hundred years later, sending settlers there by the thousands, had not reconciled themselves easily to the idea of relinquishing their hold on this land. The handsome buildings they built here for their own use, like this one, full of fine ironwork railings and huge windows, were striking testament to this. The gentle, filtered light and the soothing colors inside reminded me of Old Havana as I made my way through the faded hallways to Carrilho's office.

Carrilho, a mixed-race Mozambican with a face as loose-skinned and wrinkled as a Shar-Pei's, was dressed jauntily in a green sport coat and thick gray-and-black scarf, which he wore wrapped around his neck against the chill. He is a man who enjoys his own rhetoric.

Land management was in a grave state of crisis in Mozambique. An immense and irresponsible selloff of land was taking place, run by corrupt officials high and low. Many people had emphasized to me that forestry, usually a euphemism for clear-cut logging, was one of the biggest drivers of the crisis. And nearly everyone had told me that Chinese operators were at the very heart of the phenomenon. Carrilho, however, began by denying there was a land rush at all, before falling back to the slightly more defensible claim that it "has been contained."

"We've achieved that through zoning," he said, "which we've carried out in the entire province of Zambezia, where only 10 percent of the land has been made available. I think we've learned from other places, say, Sudan. News travels rather quickly nowadays, and the state has reacted to the advance warnings we've had about this problem from other countries, and because land rights groups here have been so active."

As for the disturbing forestry problems, "The main problem is the way that the Chinese pursue exploitation of timber resources. We have a law that promotes the transformation of the wood [meaning milling and other ways of adding value], but for some reason they are always trying to export wood in the form of raw timber." Carrilho professed befuddlement as to why Chinese loggers were so desperate for his country's hardwoods. "The first thing we need to understand is the incentives that these people have in China to get our logs. Because we find containers where in the middle you have logs surrounded by all sorts of other goods to hide them. They must suffer to do this sort of thing. You wonder why they go to such lengths?"

Carrilho went on to speak grandiloquently about lessons absorbed from other countries. "In Brazil for many years they were cutting the Amazon without any controls. Now they are controlling it. That's due to citizen empowerment, greater knowledge, democratization, better enforcement, more laws, etc. Maybe we will get there someday, too, and our grandchildren will be able to enjoy these resources in the future."

I suggested that much depended on the kind of leadership the country had, and said that the political class, particularly FRELIMO Inc., as many called the robber barons of the ruling party, was the principal beneficiary of the big land selloff.

He argued that people who focused on elite corruption were missing the picture. "We know that elites exist and try to take advantage of things, but certain practices go all the way down to the watchmen in the street who sell parking spaces," he said. "You can give twenty bicycles to a local chief and get a big piece of customary [tribally held] land. This is why we need to work with the Americans and see that everyone has a title. That way it will be a lot harder for people to come in and take over their land."

Here he was referring to another Millennium Challenge Corporation project, like the one in Mali that aimed to strengthen property rights, especially for peasants. In fact, the American program would be rolled up after five years, and in any case it only concerned a tiny fraction of the country.

"Listen, I know very well that in my life span this will not succeed," said Carrilho, "no way. But we have to do something, and we are not heroes. In thirty years, what is certain is that we'll be facing the same problems."

Not really. In thirty years, Mozambique's old-growth forests will be all but gone.

I reached the office of the Chinese commercial attaché in Mozambique after a long uphill walk along a broad, heavily trafficked avenue in the quarter of the city called Miramar, which overlooks the Indian Ocean. I was escorted across the flagstone garden path into a glum office that was sunk below the level of the gardens outside. Liu Xioahui, the attaché, entered presently and slumped into his armchair. He was well into his fifties, wore dark cotton pants and a gunmetal-colored windbreaker of a type much favored by men his age back home. It was a flawlessly sunny afternoon, but he kept it zipped to the neck.

He gave me a kind of greatest hits version of China's economic relationship with Mozambique, full of numbers and dates, and even a quote affirming that "we are good brothers, good friends, good partners," using the same words China's then president, Hu Jintao, had used in a recent speech. Two-way trade between the countries had stood at $1 billion in 2004, he said. In 2011, he said with a twinkle in the eye of a face that had hitherto looked tired and entirely impassive, it was approaching $7 billion.

Liu ticked off things that Chinese companies had built—a new forty-thousand-seat stadium, a new airport terminal, an international convention center. "These buildings are the pride of the country," he said. "They are the calling card of the country now. Do you understand the meaning of calling card?"

Referring to a continent-wide tournament that would take place in the stadium a few months hence, he added, "You don't know how much that means to a country this poor."

Liu talked about agriculture, remarking with raised eyebrows,

"This is a country that can't feed itself. You think about a place so rich in land, and it makes you wonder."

I asked what the obstacle was.

"It's cultural. Chinese people can really *chi ku* [eat bitter], and that's not just spoken from the end of my lips. It's a real difference. In Chinese we say that if you are hungry or cold you have to do something about it. Here they don't have that problem. They get food easily and a few clothes suffice them.

"Chinese people are in a hurry to work, to earn money, to get rich. If they are farmers, they make every day count. Here, it's not the same. Africans like to dance. That's their specialty. They may be poor, but they are very happy."

How many times had I heard these very words, or variants thereof? As we've seen, in Africa, China has rolled out a special vocabulary of friendly partnership, of marching together fraternally along the path of development, and, above all, of "win-win," the anesthetizing catchphrase that is attached to nearly everything it does. In Liu's remarks, echoed in a thousand other similar conversations I'd been a part of, though, one glimpsed a darker truth. China had not so much broken with the paternalism of the West that it so often decried, as replaced it with a new one of its own. Africans were not really brothers. Not at all. Behind the fraternal masks, Chinese officials thought of them as children, capable only of baby steps, to be brought along with sugary inducements and infantilizing speech.

I told Liu that I'd heard stories about lots of Chinese setting up farming homesteads in the countryside or engaging in forestry. He said that he was unaware of any private Chinese investors to speak of in agriculture.

Two hours after I had left Liu's office, I received a call from the Chinese embassy: the ambassador wanted to see me the following day and announced the hour when I should present myself.

At the embassy I was greeted by the ambassador's aide, a young woman who was unusually smiling and friendly. She ushered me into a waiting room decorated with Chinese landscapes and offered me a cup of fine tea. Moments later, when the ambassador was ready to receive me, she escorted me into a large formal room decorated with gorgeous porcelains and ink-and-brush paintings in the classical style—originals, for all I could tell.

Huang Songfu, the ambassador, was a hale, almost beefy man of fifty-seven who wore his black hair brushed carefully backward in the same impeccably dyed and waxed-in-place style favored by many of China's top leaders. We sat stiffly, side by side, in cushioned chairs with straight but low backs, with a side table between us, as if I was a visiting foreign dignitary. I was confronted with an aspect of the country's soft power that had always impressed me. Every bit of decoration in the room spoke to the longevity and wealth of Chinese civilization and to the seemingly unfathomable depths of its culture.

The ambassador began with much practiced small talk, telling me that he had arrived in Mozambique a year earlier from Brazil, where he had worked for many years. "My feeling about this place is better than what I imagined. The environment here, the city's atmosphere, they are all better than what I had imagined."

Next, after inquiring a bit about my work, Huang said to me, "So tomorrow you are flying to Nampula," signaling that he knew all the details of my schedule. He then retraced the same general outlines of my conversation with Liu the day before, beginning with a blizzardlike recitation of business and cooperation in Mozambique. He boasted that Chinese construction was the best in the world. "We're doing good work, and we keep our promises. If we say two years [for a job] it's two years."

I didn't point out that in China, the very week before, its ambitious high-speed railroad program had suffered a fatal accident so embarrassing that the government had tried to cover it up by burying the trains before there could be an investigation. Nor did I say to him that almost everywhere I'd been during my travels, Africans had questioned the quality of Chinese construction. On my most recent visit to Mozambique, the first of Maputo's Chinese-built international airport terminals had already suffered serious flooding in the earliest days of its use.

Liu, the economics counselor, arrived mid-conversation and installed himself in a chair on the far side of the room near the entrance, exclaiming, "Oh, Mr. French, you are here," with faux surprise.

Ambassador Huang then turned his attentions to agriculture, just as his colleague had. He said that with Chinese technique, productivity could be doubled, adding that private investors would have an important role to play. "Mozambican land is incredibly good, so these are some of the things we are working on. The problem is that there is not enough of a business culture. We have to help the peasants understand markets.

"There are so many black people who don't know how to do anything," Huang said. "We offer training in every industry and it is depending on their needs. It varies from a few months at a time to two or three years. Starting next year we will begin a new program for university students. We will show them how China itself has developed. . . . This is what we Chinese did, ourselves, as we began our reforms. We sent all kinds of officials overseas to developed countries to see the difference, the gap in development, and to understand the experience of developed countries. This, too, is a kind of training.

"We have two aims, to show Mozambicans that they can have big goals—not just to feed themselves, but also to sell what they produce overseas."

Huang had spoken almost nonstop for two full hours, leaving me little opportunity to ask a question. When at last I got my chance, I asked him how many Chinese lived in Mozambique.

"Maybe five thousand," he answered with a smile. "It is always changing. What is certain is that from one year to the next it is always rising. The environment here is good. They are open to investment, and there are lots of vacant areas." His figure was a twentieth of the number for Chinese living in the country that I had heard from reliable sources.

I told Huang that I had heard that his countrymen had become big players in fisheries and in timber, and for the very first time he grew defensive. "Fish is not a big problem here, and the amount exported is not large. If there is a problem, it is not a big problem. These exports have just started.

"As for wood, I've heard about it in the papers. Mozambique has wood, and China has markets, but these are not state companies involved. They are private citizens, but there may be two reasons behind any trouble. One is that they [the Chinese] may not in fact actually be following the law altogether. The other is that Mozambicans are selling them wood. Our position is to insist that our businesspeople respect local law."

I waited for my flight to Nampula in the crowded old domestic air terminal, which was due to be replaced soon by the latest Chinese-built marvel, which was rising next door. A gauzy documentary began to play on the large TV screen that hung from a post in the hall just above us. It was an idealized gloss on China's ancient history, a procession of ruling dynasties. There are all kinds of ways to bid for soft power, I thought to myself.

At my hotel in Nampula the next afternoon, I received a visit from Calisto Ribeiro, a local civil society activist who worked in the countryside, educating peasants about their rights. He looked younger than his forty-four years, had a broad, open face and dark complexion, and wore his hair cropped very short on the sides and piled thick and high on top. He offered to give me a tour of the city, which I'd scarcely seen, and we set off in his large SUV.

In the downtown area, such as it was, a dreary main avenue ran up a slight, steady incline, bisecting Independence Square, whose fenced-off interior contained an ungainly abstract monument to the country's liberation by FRELIMO. A mural in bold blues, greens, and reds on a wall facing the square showed scenes of iconic battles against the Portuguese, with heroic pride of place given to the early independence leader Samora Machel. A Marxist slogan there proclaimed the revolution's creation of the New Man.

A huge advertisement in the unmistakably bright red tones of Vodacom, the global mobile phone giant, looked on this tawdry scene. It read to me like a distilled message about the only values that remained in this country, whose leaders were once committed Marxists: money and power. Up the hill, along the main drag, on either side of the trash-strewn road stood blocks of stolid mixed commercial and residential properties, with musty shops on the ground level and apartments up above. This would have all been strikingly new forty or fifty years earlier, late in the colonial era. Now this commercial district resembled nothing so much as a plant that had failed to take root. It was once someone's idea of modernity; now it was just a tattered and forlorn place, where there had been no real economic growth in years. Global-ization had passed it by.

Nampula is a new city, founded in the 1960s by the Portuguese, who despite their long history in the country had built little outside Maputo and Beira, especially here in the north. It was meant to be both a garrison town and a model city, part of a strategy whose intended message to northerners was that under Lisbon's rule modernization for all was within reach.

"They [the Portuguese] built a lot of things here for show—housing, a university, an airport," said Ribeiro, "thinking they should take on the rebels right where they came from."

The showcase town thinned out surprisingly fast as we drove down a boulevard where the storefronts gave way to roadside commerce, with small traders dealing from stands, including Chinese here and there, and poorer ones spreading out their goods for sale on the ground. In the distance beyond loomed spectacular, scattered mountains with towering karst formations bathed in the softening light.

Drawing on his work in the countryside, Ribeiro painted a pic-ture for me at length of Chinese domination of the timber trade. He described areas he'd visited in Zambezia province that were still famous the decade before for their formidable stands of thick forest and their giant old-growth trees, little of which remained. His bigger worry, though, was agriculture. Lots of Chinese were now looking for places to grow rice.

"The Chinese are not big landowners yet, but their presence on the land is growing rapidly," he said. "Five years ago you couldn't find them at all here, but now they are farming in almost every district."

European companies were so far responsible for the major land takeovers, or "land grabs." Lurio Green Resources, of Norway, for example, had paid $2.2 billion to gain control of more than 100,000 hectares (220,000 acres) in this region to farm eucalyptus trees for industrial purposes, and according to Ribeiro it had sidestepped many legal procedures.

Ribeiro described how the country had begun to sell things off in the early 1990s, when once socialist Mozambique began to liberalize under former president Joaquim Chissano and quickly became a dar-ling of Western donors in the process.

"By now we have reached the point of no control," he said. "The government has no capacity to control the exploitation of land and natural resources. Anyone can come and take whatever they want from Mozambique, and when the government does control some small area, it is itself involved in the exploitation. If your question is Why?, I think the first problem is illiteracy. Everything here happens from the top down, starting right from the presidency. You get a piece of paper that says you can exploit this or that, and that's all the authorization it requires."

With its sudden, newfound resource wealth, Mozambique was hurriedly building *things,* Ribeiro said, but it was doing far too little to invest in education or, to use the development industry buzzwords, build capacity. "In order to have a good outcome here, people need to know their rights. They need to know how to negotiate. Unless we get stronger participation from people at the grassroots level, the natural resources of this country will all be gone soon. There may come a day when people open their eyes, but by that time it will be too late."

That evening, I ventured for dinner to the Copacabana, a thatched-roof restaurant compound that Ribeiro had recommended. At one table sat a bright-faced, young Chinese woman I'd seen in the hotel lobby a few hours earlier, when we had sat on adjacent sofas using the WiFi. I'd seen her check into the hotel that morning with the same two Chinese men in their thirties who accompanied her now. As they waited for their elevator, I saw her point in surprise to a large poster that stood off to the side advertising the on-call massage services of a young Chinese woman. I couldn't hear their conversation, but it was a safe bet that she was registering how China's giant prostitution trade had reached this distant and unlikely shore.

I had briefly struck up a conversation with her while we used the WiFi. She had seemed a little bit uncertain about whether it was okay to be friendly, but told me that she was from Guangzhou, and that it was her first time in Africa. On her way to Mozambique, she had stopped in Kenya "to see the animals." When I asked what she was planning to do in Nampula, she was vague.

"I'm here to visit friends," she answered simply.

I did not talk with her in the restaurant that evening. The next morning, when I went for breakfast in my hotel, there she sat, alone at a nearby table. Halfway into the meal, our glances met, and I said good morning, to which she reciprocated, flashing a friendly smile. We talked across tables for a few minutes and then she asked if she could join me.

She introduced herself as Song Jie, and said she was an office worker in China. She also told me she was due to leave for Nacala the next day: "My friends do business there."

"What kind of business?" I asked.

"They are shipping wood, selling trees," she said. "I really don't like it. But this place is full of Chinese people in the forestry business. Or they come here to look for business, and that's what they all end up in."

"Why do you oppose that?"

"They are taking original growth trees. They're cutting down old forests—lots of them, and this is going to destroy the environment."

I asked if she had expressed her disapproval to her friends.

"I've told them. Maybe they can change, but it will take time. First they have to make enough money." They had been at it for three years.

That afternoon, I had an appointment with Chen Jun, the head of the association of Chinese residents of Nampula. We met at the Pensão Parque, a cheap pension hotel and restaurant that stood at the lower end of the grubby, main downtown drag. Going by the name and the cafélike terrace-style layout, I'd assumed it was owned by a Portuguese holdover from colonial days. I was quickly disabused. There was a Chinese short order cook on duty and the friendly waiters told me the owner was Chinese, too. In fact, the man I was meeting owned the place.

Chen looked world-weary as he chain-smoked. He was forty-three, but easily looked a decade older. He was born in Shantou, a city in southeastern Guangdong province, long a traditional source of emigrants, where he had attended university before getting into his province's booming import-export business.

Chen said his arrival in Nampula eleven years before brought the number of Chinese in town to three, and by his estimate their ranks had since grown to four hundred. "There are Chinese people all over the north now, not just Nampula. We were all from Guangdong at first, but the newer ones come from everywhere in China."

There was a familiar story about the pull factor of a successful acquaintance, one of those three original pioneers, now long gone, who had urged him to come join him in Africa. Chen "wanted to go to the U.S. to study, but said you can make money in this place, even if it is really poor. At first I was selling TVs, and because this is the economic center of the north, you could get by okay as a trader. When I got here I couldn't believe it. The black people were so primitive, you know, the way they work. Not like us Chinese. We're in a hurry."

He told me he came from a family of migrants going back several generations, with relatives in Thailand, Indonesia, and Burma. The Pensão Parque had been one of his early business ventures, but things began to pick up for him in earnest, he said, only around 2004, when he began to diversify into shipping, imports, and "various things." His best business was fish.

"I've got a license now. I can sell to anywhere; not just to China, but to America, Canada, Europe—anywhere," he said.

Chen's pudgy-cheeked, sixteen-year-old son had sat quietly across the table from me, playing games on his telephone, and when I inquired about him, Chen bragged that the boy could speak English well and embarrassed him by urging him to demonstrate. His son had gone to elementary school in Nampula but had since returned to China to live, visiting his dad in Nampula during the summers.

"I want him to go to America. It's free. The laws are clear there. You have liberty." He was happy to stay in Mozambique and would remain here "until I get old," a time he calculated would begin sometime in his sixties. "This country is developing fast now and that's because foreigners are coming and investing. The place is opening up. Nowadays, you see a lot of poorer countries getting richer like this."

Chen offered to drive me around town. We had to stop at a couple of scantily stocked drugstores on the main drag, both owned by foreigners, like every other shop on the strip. I remarked to Chen that development would be difficult in a place where the locals are not involved in business.

"The blacks don't have any qualifications," he said. His son, speaking up for the first time, added, "They don't have money."

Chen ran the air-conditioning constantly, even though it was cool by now. He told me that he had been robbed several times, the last time at gunpoint at his home, when he lost $20,000 in cash. "It was part of a wave of attacks on Chinese here. We signed a petition to the Chinese embassy in Maputo and they put pressure on the local authorities, and that worked for a while. Things quieted down. But just the other day, a man from Pakistan was robbed and killed in the street. Shot in the head.

"Look at this place," he said as we drove down the main avenue. "They haven't built anything here."

I remarked that the physical landscape was left by the Portuguese, who hadn't done much to develop their colonies anywhere in Africa. "They themselves were a poor people, the worst of the colonizers, and a very small country, at that," I said. "Less than ten million people."

This struck a sudden chord with him, producing an insight about his own country's history. "Yes, I see the pattern," Chen said. "Look at rich South Africa, colonized by the British, and look at this place. It's just like Hong Kong and Macau. The Portuguese did nothing with Macau.

"How do you expect a country to develop if every time a foreigner walks down the street, either they get robbed or the police stop them and ransom them for money or haul them away?

"Deng Xiaoping opened our country up to foreign investors: You want land, you want to build factories? We are open for business. They don't understand that here. The leaders are not developing this country. Everything requires a payment, and it's all for them. They pocket it." He paused, and then added, "I am sure you know that in China it's like that, too. Hu Jintao can't control corruption. Everything works on money there, too, but fortunately we started developing the country before things got totally out of control."

When he dropped me off at my hotel, he invited me to a special gathering of Chinese the following night at the Pensão Parque.

When I arrived at Chen's restaurant the next evening, its familiar entrance was closed with a locked grille, which I hadn't seen before, and a watchman shooed me away as I approached. Looking inside, I could see it was a Chinese-only crowd. I told the guard I was invited, but he shouted at me to leave. Luckily, Chen was sitting near the door and must have overheard our exchange. He ordered the watchman to let me in.

I immediately became the center of attention at the party, as heads swiveled my way and jaws dropped, the Chinese guests clearly surprised by the arrival of a *lao wai*, an outsider, a foreigner. Chen made dual victory signs as he waved his hands like a campaigning politician, announcing with distinct pleasure above the murmuring crowd: "We have an American friend with us tonight, but don't worry, he speaks Chinese."

"It's the first Chinese wedding here in Nampula," he explained to me. "We've had children born, people come and go, and even a death, but never before has there been a marriage."

The entire restaurant had been reconfigured for the celebration. Six large round tables were clustered together in the center of the space, and every seat except the one I was ushered to was taken. At the back of the room, furthest from the entrance, I could make out the guests of honor, the bride and groom. They looked to be in their early twenties and beamed impressive smiles from surprisingly innocent and unformed faces.

Chen described them as members of a new generation, one that was unlike his and every other Chinese generation in memory because they had never known severe hardship, they had never eaten bitter. The pretty bride, who wore a blue satin dress and white shawl, seemed incapable of breaking out of a permanent, deeply dimpled smile. The groom, equally attractive, was a tallish five feet eleven or so, and stick-thin in his loose-fitting dark suit, white shirt, and narrow tie. He seemed incurably earnest and far less at ease than his wife. The couple were from Fujian province, and almost all of the guests were from China's south, with most, like Chen, from his native Guangdong.

Before long, a huge array of food, wine, and Chinese spirits was laid out by Mozambican waiters who were on the trot the whole night to keep up. There were four different kinds of seafood, including lobster, shrimp, and fish, and copious meat dishes. There were dumplings, steamed vegetables, soups.

Midway in, the toasts began. They were simple expressions wishing happiness and good fortune, and urging the couple to remember that others would always be there for them. To cheers, the bride was called upon to speak and did so movingly, with an utterly Chinese frame of reference. "I can never forget that I am Chinese, and that everyone here, because [he or she is] Chinese, is part of one united family." The young groom, a bit unsteady on his feet, droned on a bit woodenly with his words of thanks, especially directed, he said, to the *hui zhang,* the head of the association, Chen.

At that point there were calls for me to make a toast, but feeling awkward, I resisted. Most of all, I didn't want to serve as an exhibition, the exotic *lao wai* on display. A bit later, I approached the couple at their table to express my best wishes. The moment I drew up alongside them, there was a riot of camera flashes, and the crowd urged us to pose together, and I obliged. Next the couple sang familiar songs of devotion, karaoke style, to each other. She knew the words perfectly, but he, by now woozy, needed both her support and guidance.

Most of those seated with Chen and his son at my table were workers in their thirties, who were Chen's employees. Chen's elder brother asked me questions over the din about the finer points of American immigration law and the workings of the TOEFL exam, an English language test given to foreign students. We discussed Africa cursorily, and I told him my first trip to Africa was in 1975. Seizing on my familiarity with the continent, the older brother asked me if I would work for him traveling together to the countries I knew best to introduce him to people and to business opportunities.

He was visiting Mozambique for the second time, and had traveled from Shantou, the brothers' hometown, where he owned a small hotel and hot springs resort. The big new thing in his life was Mozambican seafood. Chen had told me previously that *he* had entered the business, but he'd said little more. "This place is incredibly rich in seafood, particularly in shrimp," the elder brother said.

Using his chopsticks, he pointed to the big, fleshy pink-orange steamed shrimp that glistened on a plate before us, and said, "In China we don't have shrimp like this anymore. Naturally raised shrimp are almost all gone. What we have there is farmed shrimp. Do you know what shrimp like this would cost in China? Roughly 150 renminbi [about $22] for ten. Do you know what my costs are here? Less than a quarter of that. My business is as simple as that: a play on the difference between cost and sales price. It's a fantastic margin, that's why we've bought a big boat." He grinned at the thought.

"What about overfishing?" I said. "I hear that's a big threat here."

He waved my question off with one hand. "There's enough seafood in these waters to last fifty years, if not a hundred."

I asked what kind of opportunities there were for Mozambicans to be in the business. One of the younger men at our table said, "The crews are Chinese. We can train Mozambicans, but it will have to be bit by bit."

A few minutes later I asked to be excused and expressed thanks all around for the hospitality and conversation. People insisted on a couple of final toasts, and then Chen, his brother, and his son, along with a handful of others, walked me out to the sidewalk, where I had asked my taxi to wait for me. The older brother asked me, "If you could put yourself in the place of the American government, what impression would the Chinese in Africa make on you?"

Most of the Chinese I met in Africa had expressed a sure and easy self-righteousness about their country's place in the world. The older brother's question represented the first time anyone had shown any curiosity about others' views of them.

I could only share my own personal point of view, I explained. "China is a country that was shut off from the world for a long time," I said. "Now it is in a great hurry. It wants to expand its reach and grow and enrich its people as fast as it possibly can."

He nodded enthusiastically. "We want to make a great leap," he said. "We are in a big hurry, you are right. But it is win-win. Double happiness." The characters for those two words had been stamped on all the red lanterns hung for the wedding banquet. "Win-win," he repeated. "Don't forget that."

CHAPTER TEN

Fat of the Land

I was the first American Hou Xuecheng was going to meet, and he was the first person I called when I got to Namibia, far down on the Atlantic coast. We had been in touch for a while via the Internet, where I had found him through a Chinese online discussion group, and he, along with a man named Xie, picked me up straightaway at my hotel. Hou was in his thirties and was dressed simply in a button-down shirt and plain cotton trousers.

The route he took quickly got us out of Windhoek's old city center, with its odd mix of faded, Miracle Mile storefronts and newish office buildings, and put us briefly onto a very modern, looping expressway. Then Hou pulled into a drab complex of warehouses and unfussy, depotlike shops. I missed the sign that hung high above the entranceway announcing that this was the city's Chinatown.

Hou pointed to his store, just in from the street, but he drove on until we had reached the back of the large compound, filed with parked cars. Several of them—including a big, four-wheel-drive Toyota pickup and a late-model, top-of-the-line Volvo—were his.

"In China, I was a nobody," he said, "but now I am rich. Things are smooth for me now. Do you think if I were in China I could have cars like these?"

We climbed the steep staircase to the upper floor of one of the warehouses and entered a spacious meeting room, where a handful of Chinese men sat drinking tea amid wafting clouds of cigarette smoke. Hou introduced one of them, Lin Jindan, as the *hui zhang*, the head of the association of Chinese businesspeople in Windhoek. Every city seemed to have one. Lin was alert, suspicious, and wizened well beyond his fifty or so years. He was hostile to me at first, then softened, but was never welcoming.

Lin told me he had arrived from Fujian in 1996 and gone back home only once. He called himself a member of the first wave of Chinese in the country, whose number he put at ten thousand. I mentioned the young woman from Fujian I'd met one night in a little village in Mozambique, where she lived alone, making her living as a small-time merchant. He nodded in a kind of recognition.

"That's our specialty," he said. "We are assiduous, hardworking, and here in Namibia you can find at least two Chinese in every locality."

This was precisely the proposition that had drawn me to this place, a seldom-heard-from country that is as large as France and Germany combined, but contains only slightly more than two million people, in part because it is largely desert.

As a percentage of the indigenous population, ten thousand Chinese residents, which many Namibians say errs on the low side (common estimates ran as high as forty thousand), arguably represents China's largest footprint in Africa. For that reason, Namibia may in some sense be a bellwether of China's ongoing migratory push into Africa.

Lin said he had started out simply, selling shoes and clothing by the piece, but now he had many businesses, including the warehouse on the ground floor, below where we sat.

"Most of the Chinese people here want to go back to China eventually. They are basically here to make money." A substantial minority, though, try to stay on, he allowed, investing the required minimum of $30,000 to qualify for immigrant status, and then hiring lawyers to push their cases forward. Of all the applicants, maybe three hundred had succeeded so far. "They are particularly strict with Chinese," he said. "They spend a lot of time investigating whether you've really opened a factory or not."

Lin put these attitudes down to the country's wealthy white minority, saying that the white people in Namibia disliked the Chinese and felt threatened by their competition. Somehow, he said, they managed to influence blacks to be prejudiced against them, as well.

It turned out Hou had arranged the courtesy call with Lin because without his consent, Hou wouldn't have been allowed to talk with me.

Before coming to Namibia, Hou had been kicking around in his native Hubei province, in China's north, following his release from the People's Liberation Army. He was the product of a farming family with no money and few prospects, he said, and he initially settled on employment in an auto garage. "When I looked around me, though, it was clear that none of the people in my circle were going anywhere." That led him to the idea of going to Africa, and then, with further research, settling on Namibia. "I couldn't find any good work in China. I had no capital, and it seemed like I had no possibilities. But I heard stories about business that people were doing here, and I had faith that with just 10,000 Namibian dollars [$1,200], I could get rich."

Wealth hadn't come easily for Hou here, though. On the first trip to Namibia, his money ran out around the same time as his visa, and the immigration police soon came knocking. He had neither the means to bribe them, as some friends advised, nor to hire a lawyer, as others suggested. So he went back to China dejected but not defeated, and immediately began saving money in order to return to a life of petty commerce in Namibia that he believed would lead to bigger things.

In his second coming, by the time his visa was nearing expiration, Hou had put enough aside to hire a lawyer and pay court fees. The immigration police were unrelenting in harassing him, though, and his lawyers constantly came up with reasons why they needed more money. "The problem with them is corruption. The lawyers are connected to the judges and most of the time they are just splitting the money, which makes it impossible to satisfy them."

Hou was eventually reduced to hiding out in friends' homes to evade deportation. "The police started arresting anyone I called on the phone, so I had to stop talking to people." The tightening noose made it impossible to work, so reluctantly he resigned himself to returning home to China once again.

I asked why he had persisted in the face of such difficulties just in order to stay in Namibia.

"I'm Chinese," he answered, "and we have an expression that says you leap forward if there's an empty space. Empty spaces are there to be filled."

Hou saved up again and returned the following year. This time, rather than wait until his visa was nearly expired, he hired an immigration officer almost immediately for advice. "He said the only way to solve my problem was to marry a Namibian woman, so I began looking around," said Hou, who was already married. Marrying local women as an immigration ploy had become common among Chinese newcomers. "I looked into a lot of women. Finally, I met one who seemed right, and I called my wife in Hubei and told her that I needed to marry her. She told me that if it was for practical reasons and not for love, she could accept this.

"We had a huge traditional wedding, with lots of guests, and slaughtered animals and had plenty of drink, and of course we started living together. We even got a nice house." But after a year or so, Hou said the two of them began to have trouble because his Namibian bride and her family wanted the new couple to produce children. "I didn't want a child, because I was worried about the reaction of people back in China to a mixed-race baby. They would look down on it. I also didn't feel love."

Hou's marriage allowed him to regularize his immigration status, and then he decided to bring his original wife from back home to Windhoek.

"That's when the really big trouble began," he said. "My in-laws began threatening me, saying that they would go to the immigration people and tell them that I had arranged a marriage just in order to get a residence permit." To buy them off, he gave his Namibian wife their new home and a lump sum payment whose amount he didn't disclose. "My experience is like a TV movie," he said.

Hou drove us into a quarter named Katutura, whose existence one would never have suspected from the confines of the dowdy but prim downtown Windhoek. It was a world of flimsy shacks, all with roofs made of zinc sheeting, that were draped over hills as far as the eye could see, and glimmered dazzlingly in the sun. Here and there, little children played in the narrow-gauge streets, and as I looked around I was struck by the proliferation of beauty salons, almost all rudimentary affairs with hand-painted signs, that sprinkled every block, sometimes numbering as many as one out of every five shacks.

These were the city's newest residents and they were among its poorest, lacking electricity and plumbing. Windhoek was small by the standards of African capitals, a mere 230,000 people, but internal migrants were flooding in from the countryside, swelling this city just as surely as almost every other city in Africa, where urbanization was proceeding at a breakneck pace.

As rain clouds gathered and the light grew soft and pastel, the road dipped down into a close little valley, where Hou forded a small creek, plunging us into a rural setting. We stopped on a hillside and Hou sounded his horn. It drew a strongly built Namibian man in his twenties who came hurrying out of the shack that sat on the crest of a hill surrounded by rows of planted vegetables.

This was Hou's farm. He briefly busied himself pacing the rich, black soil between the rows of beans and cabbage, pointing out to his Namibian employee little things—like a handful of yellowing lettuce leaves—that he found amiss.

"It would cost me 3,000 a month to employ a Chinese to oversee this farm, but a black person only costs 1,000," he said in a satisfied tone. The Namibian man was "basically" competent, he added.

Xie, the withdrawn, slightly shabbily dressed man who had ridden quietly with us from the outset, spoke up for the first time. "These vegetables are really good quality, and that's why he's doing such a good business in them," he said. "Even the whites have started buying them. Vegetables protect your body against harmful substances. They're good for your health and they help keep you going. I don't know why the blacks don't eat them. They just don't get it. All they are interested in is meat."

After a few minutes, we left the farm and drove back into the neighborhood of shacks with zinc rooftops. Hou said his watchman lived there. "He has ten children. Can you believe that? He makes 1,500 a month, and his money runs out before the end of each month, so he has to come borrow from me to make ends meet."

We climbed out of the car and walked toward the shacks, met halfway by a tall man in his late forties. He greeted us with a powerful handshake and a gentle smile, and accompanied us to the threshold of his home. His children poured out of their two-room tumbledown to greet us. The eldest was a cute, skinny seventeen-year-old girl who had inherited a lot of her father's height. Hou spoke teasingly with her, almost flirting, in his broken English, and she giggled bashfully. Her mother stood just behind her, in the entranceway, never quite emerging from the darkness.

We drove on to a gated expanse of land that Hou also owned. It was much bigger than the first, but not yet planted. There were two buildings here, a rambling wooden villa and a blocky, functional-looking structure intended for storage.

An alert Namibian man in his twenties emerged to greet us from the second building. I noticed big scars along his neck and arm—signs of a knife attack. Hou told me that the villa, which he was slowly renovating in order to move into it, had been robbed recently. "They even took the bricks and roofing, and of course anything else of value they found inside." He seemed strangely at ease about this, as if it merely represented a small cost of doing business.

I asked him why he was so determined to live outside China.

"You know, in my circle of friends back home, very few people were able to even afford a car. None of them became bosses. I had to leave China in order to achieve this."

We returned to the little Chinatown just before dark, and when Hou pulled up alongside his home, just across from the supermarket he owned, two small children greeted us on his side of the car, jumping up and down and shouting, "Daddy! Daddy!" Hou pointed to his wife, who stood over a bucket, hand-washing some clothes nearby. She was a plump, plainly dressed woman with a ruddy, slightly weather-beaten face. I greeted her very briefly in Chinese, which drew no response. Then Hou announced he was going to take me to the "Chinese club" for dinner.

After a short drive in the dark we pulled into the Windhoek Country Club, a big casino complex with a gaudy, over-the-top entranceway lit up with Las Vegas–style neon. Hou walked with a little strut as he led me into the complex and up a winding flight of stairs, where around the first bend I could make out the unmistakable wash of bright red decorations that signifies a Chinese cultural zone.

Chez Wou, which was guarded by two large ceramic lions, was the complex's one Chinese restaurant. It served as a popular gathering place for Chinese people in the country. There were perhaps thirty red-covered tables in the place, but on this evening only three of them were occupied. When the menus were delivered, he asked me to order, which I resisted, but he was persistent and said, "Whatever you want, whatever you want."

While I studied the menu, he turned his attention to business talk with occupants of an adjacent table. His interlocutors struck me as a little rough around the edges, both in their style of speech and in their slightly worn, ill-fitting dress. "They're farmers," Hou whispered to me.

Their talk was full of complaints about workers—about *hei ren*, a phrase they used incessantly, meaning black people. There was no great sting to this, in part because I was so accustomed to hearing it from Chinese, but also because it didn't carry the same history with it, the way, say, *nigger* might in the United States. Still, there was no escaping the fact that this was race language, too. Nobody said the Africans, or the Namibians, or even the locals. Among Chinese, it was ever and always *hei ren*.

When he broke off from his neighbors, I asked Hou if Namibia would develop, to which he answered a confident yes. When I asked whether its native citizens would get rich, too, Hou paused, picking at the garlic cucumbers and salted peanuts before us, and then shook his head. "It's difficult for them. I don't think so. It hasn't happened after all these years, so I don't see them getting rich."

I asked him how long he thought he would remain overseas. "I'm not going back to China," he announced flatly. "Why should I?" A string of laments about the pressures and hardships people had to put up with back home ensued. "It's not a pretty picture," he said, before complaining about soaring real estate prices, the seizure of land, arbitrary acts by local governments, and the corruption of officials, which he said fueled all of these phenomena. "What's a peasant if he doesn't have land? That's what you call a poor person. He has no more life."

Hou and Xie both had complained about corruption in Namibia, so I asked what was so bad about China.

"Yeah, I give some gifts to people here. That's the way things work. But it's nowhere near as heavy-handed or unpleasant. In China, you have the Party controlling you all the time." He reached his hand out as he said this, in a grabbing gesture. "They're always squeezing you for more and more money."

As we worked our way through the meal, Hou continued to speak about the pressures of Chinese society. There was the merciless business competition. There was the lack of space, both personal, in terms of what an American would call privacy, and physical, as in public space. There was pollution. There was food safety. Hou sighed deeply as he took his last mouthful and patted his belly, complaining that he had put on weight—twenty-five pounds, to be precise. I told him he should get some exercise, and he nodded wearily, answering, "There's no time."

Everyone knows the stock story of China's breathtakingly fast growth and of the country's seemingly irresistible rise. It was this less familiar underside of the country's recent experience, though, that was helping drive migration. Encounters like this one were reminders that huge numbers of Chinese had not boarded the up escalator, or at least they did not feel they had. To the contrary, they felt crushed.

Meanwhile, uncertain and insecure in a strange new environment, Hou lived in a grimy little Chinatown, right by the shop. There were world-class beaches in Namibia, but Hou had never been. Some of the world's best game parks were here, too, but he'd never seen those, either. For all of his cars and the money, this was a curious form of success.

Hou said his children would eventually be sent to China for school. What would they remember of Africa? What would they have really known of it, beyond memories of the house girl who helped look after them?

On December 30, my brother, Jamie, flew in from Johannesburg, where he lives, to join me. We planned to drive 450 miles north to the border with Angola. There was an important Chinese community in Oshikango, a little frontier town right on the border, and they were said to be doing a huge business servicing the southern part of oil-rich and spectacularly corrupt Angola, in everything from heavy machinery and trucks to household appliances and dry goods.

By the standards of the region, Namibia was a very lawful place, and the Chinese in Oshikango were getting rich by leveraging the good business environment to cater to Angolans who drove south across the border to conduct their trade. I had been warned that the Chinese community in Oshikango was virtually impenetrable and no one there would speak to outsiders, or if they did, they would say little that was candid. Hou Xuecheng, who had businesses of his own on the border, had been kind enough to provide me some contacts.

Jamie and I had recently lost our mother, and the trip offered us a chance to reflect on our family life together. It was also a sort of reprise of a formative adventure we had shared more than thirty years earlier, when we had wandered by road from Abidjan, Côte d'Ivoire, far north into Mali.

It was well into mid-afternoon when we set out and we soon became entranced with the landscape, immense stretches of flat, open land that glittered as if peppered with gemstones, punctuated by heavily worn mountain chains. The two-lane highway was ruler straight for long stretches and devoid of traffic, making it easy to put the driving itself out of mind as we talked over the high-pitched little car engine.

Several hours into the trip, the skies suddenly grew dark and unleashed an immense downpour. Dry riverbeds all about us flash-flooded and water stood inches thick on the road, causing the little car to hydroplane and forcing me to drive slowly. Fierce lightning exploded over the terrain from time to time and the occasional tractor-trailer seemed to bear down on us terrifyingly from the oncoming direction on the unlit road.

Around 10 p.m., we pulled into Tsumeb, an old mining city that was a gateway to Etosha National Park, one of the continent's premier wildlife reserves and a staple of TV nature documentaries I'd watched over the years. Tsumeb, with its rail line, had also been a staging point for South Africa in its long, apartheid-era war, sometimes by proxy, sometimes direct, against the Marxist government of Angola.

We refueled at a gas station that would seem familiar to any long-distance American driver, with its giant, canopied pump islands and big convenience store, where I bought food and caffeinated drinks. The station doubled as a gathering spot for youths, who bought snacks and hung out in the parking area and chatted over the rap music that played on the station's loudspeakers, like the Snoop Dogg number that played as we drove off.

It was very late by the time we pulled into Ondangwa, a city that the maps suggested was perhaps a half hour from Oshikango and the border. This was a bigger town than Tsumeb, built along several axes instead of just one, and there were better hotels here, along with a new, slate gray Chinese-owned mixed office and shopping center named Times Square that looked all the more impressive for the way it towered over the one-story town.

The next morning, I called some of my Chinese contacts. We agreed to meet in the late afternoon for New Year's festivities, where I would be their guest. I also called Taara Shaanika, the CEO of the country's Chamber of Commerce, to see about meeting him back in Windhoek a few days hence. Shaanika told me he was nearby, visiting his hometown, which was just a twenty-some-odd-mile drive from where I was staying.

Our agreed meeting place was a sprawling, one-story shopping mall across the road from a large state hospital in the nearby town of Oshakati. Jamie and I parked in front of a busy KFC, where there was heavy, incessant foot traffic of people making last-minute New Year's purchases, and young people who mostly strolled about, working their cell phones. This was a side of Africa that one seldom saw in Western depictions of the continent: a booming modern commercial sector, with modern consumerism built on what might be called the American model. Shopping centers like this were still rare just fifteen years earlier, when I last lived in Africa, and now they were to be seen everywhere. Here was one located in a smallish city in the furthest northern reaches of lightly populated Namibia.

Shaanika was over an hour late, but then pulled up in his white Mercedes. We drove to a smaller, nearby shopping complex where we ended up eating lunch at a Wimpy's restaurant.

Shaanika, who was short and had close-cropped hair, was dressed in tan pants and an open-collar linen shirt. He spoke rapidly and with authority between multiple incoming calls on his BlackBerry.

"China is a major player in the global economy," he said, "and there is no way that any country is going to avoid its impact—whether it's Chinese products, Chinese investment, or Chinese immigration, especially for smaller countries, where you don't have a strong industrial base, or a strong business tradition.

"Before independence, twenty-one years ago, we had no Chinese presence in our country. I can't remember even seeing a single Chinese individual. Of course [China is] one of the countries that supported us in the liberation struggle, but because Africa has so many untapped resources, I think Chinese policy is actually to dominate us, especially through trade relations, and immigration plays an important part in that."

He said that most of the Chinese companies of any size were government-owned, and their access to the resources of the Chinese state allowed them to dominate competition all over Africa. "Even the companies that are not state-owned seem to have the backing of the state—especially if they are exporters."

He described a phenomenon of ultra-competitive bidding aimed at winning contracts at any cost; people had spoken of the same thing on previous stops. "We can't build infrastructure for ourselves, because if we bid 200 million, they will offer to build for 100 million. Yes, the state saves money, but the negative consequence is that the private sector here is killed off." A solution, he said, would be to require Chinese companies to form joint ventures with local partners. "They should bring Namibians aboard, so that we can build up our society and benefit from its wealth. Otherwise in ten years we will see that only the Chinese have benefited and Africans remain poor. Unfortunately our leaders in Africa don't have a very good understanding of this."

Shaanika spoke at length about the arrival of small-time Chinese traders, who could be seen by the roadside throughout the north nowadays grilling meats for sale on charcoal fires, Namibian-style. Many others, he claimed, were cannibalizing the local arts and crafts trades, copying local designs of woodcarvings and traditional cloth and having them mass-produced in China. These, too, had been the subject of widespread complaints wherever I went.

A few months earlier, he said, local anger over such practices had caused the government to bar foreign "investors" from the small business sector, but he said enforcement had been lax. Public opinion nearly reached the boiling point when Chinese obtained investor visas for opening up beauty salons. The labor minister had to plead with the public not to attack Chinese people in the country.

I told him I would be visiting Dragon City, the popular name of the Chinese border enclave in Oshikango.

"If you go there you will find that it is 100 percent Chinese, and there is a lot of resentment at the way they have been allowed to come in and buy up land like that for their exclusive use.

"In Namibia, we have a place called Swakopmund. It is a German town; every second person you pass there is German. The Germans even have their own schools there. We don't need more of this kind of thing in our country. We have already experienced apartheid here before, where black people were not even allowed to enter into certain sectors—mining, banking, insurance. This kind of influx, in my opinion, needs to be curtailed. It is not good for Namibia. It is not good for our future, and if it is not stopped, what we will find before long is that many towns here will have their own Chinatowns."

Jamie and I were now on our way to Dragon City. Someone at our hotel that morning had said we would have to drive sixteen miles back to Ondangwa, the town where we had slept, in order to take another road for the thirty-seven-mile ride to Oshikango.

The traffic was heavy in mid-afternoon on New Year's Eve, though, and using Google Maps, Jamie found what looked like a much shorter route. So we barreled down a road that was well paved and traffic-free, flying past occasional villages, which were cordoned off by carefully tended briar patch barriers. Here and there on the dusty earth that stretched into the distance stood the simplest of small, concrete buildings, all brightly painted and bearing fanciful names, advertising bottle stores or barber shops or other forms of trade. They didn't look old, but they were all abandoned, the stunted outcroppings of local commerce, before the arrival of the malls and of what locals called the China shops.

Hou had told me that Xie would be our guide in Oshikango, so I called him as I drove. His instructions for when we reached the border town were strikingly simple: "Just look for the place where there are lots of Chinese. You can't miss it. Give me a call, and I'll come and get you."

A few more minutes down the road, what had been smooth enough sailing turned into the beginning of a nightmare. It had been raining heavily throughout the area recently, and the roadbed turned cratered, and then waterlogged, and finally treacherous, almost like quicksand in spots. For long stretches, any sense of a road or even of a pathway vanished altogether. People had been scarce for most of the way, but when we came upon a villager, I stopped and asked him how to reach Oshikango. There was a gentle reproach in his voice as he answered: "Now it is the rains. Why are you taking this road?"

Wiser words had never been said.

Moments later, I ran over a jagged, eight-inch-wide tree stump, violently tossing us in the car and producing a loud boom. "We're fucked," we both said at the same instant. We stopped to inspect the damage, and saw that the rim was badly bent and the tire was mauled, missing a big chunk of rubber. Somehow it had not gone flat, though, so on we went, the road still worsening.

The sun was beginning to set now and I worried that we would be stuck out in the dark. Soon, though, we came upon a couple of villagers who indicated a shortcut through some nearby farmland that would allow us to avoid the badly flooded route that stood directly ahead of us. We followed their advice, and ten minutes later we emerged on an asphalt road, rejoining the excellent highway we would have taken if I had just followed the ordinary route.

Oshikango materialized promptly in all its two-dimensional glory. Even from those first glances, it was clearly not an organic town, but rather a transnational outpost: not really Namibia, certainly not Angola, and not quite China, although with signs of China and of Chinese capital, its lifeblood, everywhere. At the entrance to the town sat an immense depot of Chinese-made tractor-trailers, earthmoving equipment, and other heavy machinery for sale. I followed that road, discovering that it was the settlement's one and only street, running straight and true, its margins decorated with ornamental concrete globes, evenly spaced every few feet.

We were looking for Xie and following his instructions, but things were not as obvious as he had led us to believe because Chinese people and Chinese shops were everywhere. It was the end of the day, and businesses were closing for New Year's Eve, so we drove along the street for the length of the town, ending up at a gated complex of the Ministry of Finance. It was the national customs bureau, and on the other side of the barrier, visible just ahead, lay Angola.

We doubled back, looking at the Chinese shops on either side of the road, with their odd English names, selling auto parts, building supplies, home electronics, you name it. I got Xie on the phone again and he said he was waiting on the street in front of the compound where we were expected. I spied a group of Chinese women emerging from the first walled compound we encountered, and asked them if they could speak with Xie on my phone to help us get our bearings. They obliged and quickly sorted things out. We were close to where we needed to go, and a few moments later we spotted Xie, who waved us down an alley and past an open steel gate.

There, inside, was a large group of Chinese whose party was well under way. There were a few dozen of them, mostly young people in their twenties and thirties, including a few couples, and they were swilling Windhoek Light beer and feasting on roasted pork, which was sliced from a hog that was turned on a spit under the cooling evening skies. As Xie escorted Jamie and me into their midst, I said, "Hello everyone," producing the usual murmurs. Beyond that, though, the reception was distinctly chilly. In those early moments it felt like we were a foreign body that had been detected by an organism that was marshaling its immune response.

In contrast to the other partygoers, who all wore their weekend best, Xie was dressed in faded clothes, his floppy, faded printed shirt half unbuttoned as if by oversight. He escorted us to two orange plastic chairs placed in the midst of the crowd and began plying us with food and drink.

Directly across from us sat a showy young couple that conveyed the feeling of being socially exalted within this crowd. I felt an odd dissonance as they commented about us in Chinese from just a few feet away as if there were no chance we could understand.

To break this strange spell, I addressed them in Chinese, producing a surprised response from the girl. As if by point of pride, though, her boyfriend replied to me in patchy English, refusing to engage in his own language or even acknowledge that it was being spoken to him.

A feeling of pointlessness washed over me, and I began plotting an early exit. We had secured invitations to a local New Year's party, too, and I figured that if this one was a bust, the other one might still prove interesting.

Xie now presented us to a man whom he seemed to almost grovel toward, introducing him as the dean of the Chinese community, the *hui zhang* of Oshikango and one of the two founders of the Chinese enclave here, Chen Qingping. He was a fit man in his late fifties with a thick shock of black hair. He wore a yellow tennis shirt, white Nike shoes, and a very large gold Rolex.

Handing me a business card that identified him simply as "Chairman," he told us of arriving nearly two decades earlier with 50,000 Chinese renminbi (about $8,000 nowadays) in capital that he had borrowed from friends.

"When I first got here, there were only five hundred people in this town; I mean Africans," Chen said emphatically. "Back then, I lived in a little tiny place, almost like a tent, and when it rained heavily, even cows and goats would wander in. It didn't matter to me, though, because I had customers all the time from Angola. Angola was still emerging from war, and there was still shooting all the time. But because of the war there, I knew there were opportunities, and I didn't mind taking on debt because I knew how to do business. And after a single year here, I was rich."

Chen, who was from Jiangsu province, near Shanghai, had worked for twenty years as a manager for a manufacturing company there before setting out for Africa. "I never had enough money to buy a house. I had to hand over our profits constantly to the Communist Party. In China, the system is built for the Party and not for the businessman, and whatever else happens, it is always the Party that gets rich."

With that, a weathered, slightly older man who had sidled up to us began to insinuate himself into our conversation. He had had too much to drink, but his clear aim was to restrain Chen from speaking too freely, and he muttered something about how Chinese people were transforming Namibia, while gushing about Shanghai. When that didn't work, he turned to Chen and flatly pronounced the familiar line that it was best not to discuss politics.

Chen began to boast about the many businesses he had built; he seemed to have a hand in every line of commerce. He even owned ranchland, a favored investment of the old moneyed classes in Namibia. He told us there were other ways to measure his success, proudly proclaiming that he had fifty-three family members living in the country. The preening and standoffish young man who had sat near us with his girlfriend a few minutes earlier was his son and designated successor in business here.

"I think that after a little while I am going to go back to China. China is doing well now. It is advancing very fast. When I came here, Namibia was richer than China," he said, laughing. "Here, I am a very rich man. But in the China of today, there is nothing remarkable about me at all."

I asked him whether he worried that there were too many Chinese in Namibia already.

The problem was not the numbers of Chinese, Chen said, but the behavior. Newcomers tended to be lower-class, with big ambitions but little finesse or manners. "They make no effort to speak the language. They begin bossing people around. And they behave very arrogantly."

By way of illustration, he said that if he caught a thief among his Namibian workers, he wouldn't make a big deal of it. "But some of these newcomers might go so far as to beat the person. They feel that they have saved their money and come all this way to invest, and it makes them angry and entitled to take matters into their own hands."

I asked him if crime was a big problem.

"Ninety percent of Africans are thieves," he said.

As Chen accompanied us to the driveway where I had parked I asked him whether the Chinese government was helping businesses like his in this frontier export zone. He laughed, saying that Chinese state banks constantly offered easy money to finance trade. "The credit requirements are ridiculously easy. You hardly have to document anything," he said. "China has too much money, with all those American dollars we are holding. There's so much money that they don't know what to do with it."

Reflecting on this enclave of Chinese operations, Jamie and I talked about the *comptoirs* or trading stations and depots that European powers had established up and down the West African coast centuries earlier. They had been important forerunners of colonialism, introducing Africans as much to the unfamiliar ways as to the shiny new wares of the grabbing outsiders. They created appetites, and with them markets. And in time they extended credit and contracted debt.

The moves toward full-fledged colonialism would await the ideological softening up of the indigenous peoples through religion, along with a change in the balance of forces, created by the growth in the number of Europeans on the ground, and especially by a stepped-up security presence, whether through the fort or the Gatling gun. By the time the Africans realized what was happening to them, in most places the game was already up. This was the process that famously lay at the heart of the Nigerian author Chinua Achebe's classic novel, *Things Fall Apart*.

"The white man is very clever," says its hero, Okonkwo. "He came quietly and peaceably with his religion. We were amused at his foolishness and allowed him to stay. Now he has won our brothers, and our clan can no longer act like one. He has put a knife on the things that held up together and we have fallen apart."

To be sure, the parallels were more approximate than exact, and China protests vehemently that it is anything but the new colonizer. But everywhere I went in Namibia, I heard these concerns from locals who felt disempowered by the Chinese as they watched these foreign workers and traders flock to their country and flout their labor laws, or as they watched their government, the inheritors of Namibia's liberation struggle, defend the outsiders and do their bidding. These complaints, as we've seen, are rife in Africa.

Some young people at our hotel had invited us to a place called Benny's Entertainment Park, in the nearby town of Ongwediva, to celebrate New Year's Eve. A little bit before midnight we left the car in a puddle-filled parking lot out front, and joined a long, lively line of teenagers and people in their early twenties at the entrance. From the immense size of the crowd, it seemed a safe bet that this must have been the biggest celebration in all of Ovamboland, the narrow, fertile strip of Namibian territory that runs parallel to the Angolan border. It had certainly captured an entire demographic.

The young people were dressed sharply in fashions that felt oddly familiar, given the remote location. The girls wore slinky pants or glittery dresses, with a heavy accent on cleavage. The guys without dates strutted around striking macho poses. Some wore dark, large-framed sunglasses or had hair dyed blond. Many of these youths came from reasonably prosperous middle-class families that sent them off to school in Windhoek; they were home now for the long Christmas holiday.

After a long wait before the closed entrance gate, some in the crowd started pushing. Security guards emerged and began flogging people with truncheons, causing the girls to scream and those in striking range to scatter. Midnight struck amid a shower of fireworks while we were still outside. When we were allowed in, we discovered a giant complex swarming with people, complete with multiple bars, thatched-roofed paillotes, and a large, lit swimming pool.

I was carrying a camera and Jamie had both his camera and a computer bag. On top of that, I'd forgotten to remove my money belt, which contained upward of $5,000 in cash. As we walked forward into the crowd, a man flashing an exaggeratedly clownish expression stepped in front of Jamie, shifting right and left to block his way forward. I recognized the gesture immediately as a robbery attempt of a type usually attempted by a team of two, with the clown acting as a distraction.

Things were happening fast, and there was no time to speak to Jamie, so I engaged the eyes of the clown with a stern expression meant to say that I was on to him, and stepped forward briskly. My brother was shouting at the man, and at the accomplice whose presence he had detected. "Get your hands out of my pocket, motherfucker!"

There was a brief tugging to and fro involving the four of us, and then just as abruptly as it had begun, the incident was over; the robbery attempt aborted.

We had arrived late in the beauty contest, which had been billed as the highlight of the evening; we approached the staging area in the rear of the complex at the very point when they were whittling the selection down from five girls to three finalists. It was time for the round of interview questions that were meant to show that beauty contests are not just about faces and flesh.

One of the girls, tall and needle thin, with shimmering dark skin and a confident smile, was asked about recent events in faraway Côte d'Ivoire, where there had recently been an election with disputed results, and the vote had come fresh on the heels of a long period of civil violence. Two men now claimed to be president. How should the situation be resolved?

"I would request that another election be held, so that the will of the people is respected," the girl said, smartly.

From there, the event wended its way through its final moments and the crowning of the queen. We were witnessing perfect mimicry of a form of American popular culture.

This event was quickly followed by a local rap group that skipped and skittered out onto the stage. They wore ghoulish masks and black gowns, their hands jerking all the while back and forth sideways. The music was local, but both it and the dance would have fit in comfortably on the Black Entertainment Television network's programming back home.

I had spent most of the day thinking about a new Chinese colonialism. Amid all of these flourishes of Western culture, the evening was ending with an African equivalent of video night in Katmandu.

Jamie and I spent two days driving through spectacular countryside and braving more occasional torrential rains, all the while praying that the little car's gored tire would hold up. The constantly changing landscape shifted from ancient, eroded mountains to dry, rolling scrublands, and jewel-like little German towns, including one where we stayed. The residents of these hermetic places were the descendants of white settlers, and the surviving old buildings, which bore the mark of their culture, gave them the feeling of lost relics.

Toward the end of the drive, we made a long climb onto a high desert mesa, where the terrain consisted of vast, sandy wastes, and the air was as hot and dry as in Death Valley. Here and there, just off the side of the road, lay some of the world's biggest open uranium mines—one of Namibia's principal sources of income—including one that had just been acquired by Chinese interests.

Lastly came the twenty-mile descent to the coast and more precisely to Swakopmund, a prosperous resort city of 42,000 founded by Germans a little over a century ago. Throughout this last leg, all the traffic was headed in the opposite direction on the immaculate two-lane highway. The cars were full of whites headed back to Windhoek after sun and sand holidays, playing on the gorgeous beaches here and in the area's towering dunes. Namibia no longer had apartheid, to be sure, but the stark separation of races that still prevailed could be seen in the two very different vacation scenes we had witnessed: all black in the north and all white here.

My main order of business in town was to speak with Kauko Nishikaku, an electrical engineer at one of the big mining companies nearby who was a prominent critic of the Chinese presence in his country. We met for lunch on a cloudless day at a beach restaurant that looked out on the South Atlantic, where whale sightings were said to be common.

Nishikaku was a member of the country's smallish black professional class, and he spoke in an articulate and impassioned way about the rising number of Chinese in Namibia and of their business practices. He was not a race baiter, though; his principal grievance wasn't against the Chinese at all. Rather, echoing complaints I have heard often, he blamed his government for selling out to Chinese interests, for corruption, and worst of all, for a lack of vision for his country. He cited a famous story in the country based on WikiLeaks documents that Chinese officials had negotiated the writing off of an unspecified amount of Namibian debt in exchange for five thousand passports and immigration permits for Chinese nationals.

"I don't blame the Chinese for taking over the sale of our traditional goods in the countryside if this is true," he said. "It is the government that is responsible for destroying our small and medium-sized enterprise sector and preventing the growth of a middle class here."

Beyond the WikiLeaks affair, he said, the Chinese had routinely won contracts through bribery and by flouting the country's labor laws. They showered gifts on members of the political elite, almost all of them members of SWAPO, the ruling party that had fought and won the country's liberation war, partly due to Chinese assistance.

"Have you heard about the provision of scholarships given to the children of senior politicians?" he asked me. "This includes the daughter of the president. They are sent to China for schooling. These are just some of the political favors that are given in order to influence our leaders. I think that any normal country would respond strongly to something like this. Can you imagine something like this coming out in America? Here, when it surfaced, though, there was nothing."

For Nishikaku, the scandal over scholarships was merely one of myriad ways in which new Chinese interests in the country had bought influence in Namibia.

"They say that we live in a global village and we need to cooperate with everyone. They say that we stand to benefit strongly from China. But here, I am personally not sure. The terms are always favorable to them. Take for example our labor laws, which are very strict in Namibia. They govern hiring, wages, working conditions, etc., but they are never applied to Chinese companies. Somehow they are exempted.

"Our labor unions complain about everyone else in this country. They are usually no-nonsense and can be quite militant, but they have nothing to say about the Chinese. This tells me there are bigger forces at play behind the scenes. People are bribing the leaders to make sure their interests are protected."

I knew the main unions in question in Namibia to be virtual extensions of SWAPO. Arrangements like these were not uncommon in Africa, particularly in countries governed by parties that had won power as victorious liberation movements.

I asked Nishikaku where I could get some corroboration for his charges. As we have seen, China's most steadfast claim in Africa was that it refrained from interfering in the internal affairs of other countries. The contacts he provided led me back to Windhoek, and to Herbert Jauch.

Jauch had emigrated from Germany to Namibia in the 1980s. He was a founder and senior researcher of the Labour Resource and Research Institute, a local think tank that has studied Chinese employment practices in the country. I asked him why Chinese companies should deserve any special attention in the country compared to other foreign employers.

He responded by saying that by virtue of their political relationship with SWAPO, many Chinese interests here had received preferential treatment of one kind or another, starting with the government's own rhetoric. "They say that workers should not demand too much, that we must be happy that the Chinese are here. They say that we should look past our cultural differences and take a long view. What is striking is that this is almost exactly what the Chinese embassy here says."

Amid rising tensions between Chinese employers and Namibian workers, Jauch's group had been commissioned by the main labor union to conduct a study of Chinese employment practices in the construction industry. The union got cold feet about the report, though, as its damning findings began to trickle in.

"They seemed to lose interest, to go a little soft," Jauch said. "The suspicion was that behind the scenes they were asked to treat these issues gently." He said his investigation had documented how "Chinese builders were deciding wages based on their own sense of worker productivity. What we found is that they are frequently paying as little as one-third of the legal wage, and for some people here this feels like a new form of colonialism.

"If the practices of the Chinese firms had been engaged in by other companies there would have been a severe crackdown. What is most interesting is the Chinese don't deny that they aren't paying minimum wages here and yet the government is still willingly issuing them tenders. This is just unacceptable."

After his report came out, Jauch said he was received by the Chinese embassy in Windhoek. He said they were "very unhappy. They told me I didn't understand, that their investments must be given time to grow, and that the Chinese were not here to exploit people."

Paulus Mulunga, a good-looking and sharp-minded young man who had returned six months earlier from a Chinese-funded scholarship studying at the University of Geosciences in Beijing, presented a different point of view. He came from what he called "a business family." He was dressed neatly in a white button-down shirt when we met for drinks. He has smooth, dark skin, bright eyes, and a deep voice for someone his age.

He said he had gone to China because he wanted "to understand how they had achieved 10 percent annual growth. I wanted to see what the differences were between the two economies. And I wanted to know more about the Chinese." During his three years in the country, Mulunga had learned Chinese well enough to study in the language. He said he had learned to ignore the staring of strangers in China and the occasional racist comments thrown his way and attempts by some at bars or parties to bait him into physical confrontation. All was not ostracizing and hardship, though. He'd also enjoyed the company of Chinese girlfriends during his time in Beijing.

Mulunga had, in fact, returned high on China and generally positive about its relationship with Namibia. Nowadays he got occasional work with Chinese companies and he eventually saw career possibilities for himself along these lines, so it is impossible to discount self-interest altogether in these views. Still, he came across as sincere and genuine.

"It is important if you engage in business with the Chinese to understand their culture," he said. "I don't know if you have heard the Nuctech story, but if you don't understand them, you are more prone to this sort of thing. They are very tricky people. There are elements of trust that arise with them all the time, but if you understand them, at least you stand a better chance."

Nuctech was a Chinese company that sold airport scanners, and there had recently been a scandal in Namibia over bribes it reportedly paid in order to win a major contract. "Nuctech sold scanners to the Namibian government at inflated prices, and there were kickbacks involved," he said. "The machines were billed at $55 million, but the correct cost was really $40 million, so that's quite a big difference."

This story was of more than passing interest because the son of Chinese president Hu Jintao was the CEO of Nuctech, and very embarrassingly the son had been invited for questioning by Namibian investigators over the affair. For a time in China, in order to quash discussion of the matter, censors had gone so far as to block all Internet searches involving the word Namibia.

I asked Mulunga if the Nuctech story didn't prove the pessimists' point about China's incursions in Africa.

"The Chinese relationship is benefiting us," he insisted. "They are building infrastructure, they are building hospitals, and they are providing loans, so I am generally optimistic, but cautiously so. They are helping us, but at a cost, and it is not all smiles. This means we have to give something back. They won't do any favors for you unless they get something from you. This means we have to relax some laws for them. We must steer some tenders their way. It may seem unfair, and I don't like it, but what can you do about it? Beyond the unfairness, you have to understand what they are bringing, which is a lot of development, which African countries probably wouldn't get otherwise."

His optimism sounded to me more like a lack of options.

"I think that if Namibians get to work with the Chinese, after twenty years or so we will have a better chance with them than we had with the Afrikaners," he said. "Africa cannot make it by itself. The world is moving too fast. Where are we going to get the education? Where will we get the capital? We've tried everyone else already, and we were left for dead."

Justina Jonas, a labor union activist I'd met on a previous visit to the country, had risen up through the rank and file and hence did not owe her place to political patronage. Her union's workers had gone on strike against a big Chinese construction firm for failure to pay the legally established wages, which they eventually won.

Jonas was a well-spoken and engaging thirty-year-old. She was dressed in a black leotard top and big silver earrings when I walked into her simple branch office. She had a soft, easy smile, but there always seemed to be a touch of sadness to it when she spoke. She had become a labor activist almost by accident.

"In 1999, I was an assistant clerk for a construction company, and I really didn't know anything. But because I talk too much, perhaps, I was chosen to represent the union at a labor conference in Durban [South Africa]. I was supposed to be representing women, but the whole thing really opened my eyes, and I learned a lot."

As a young union official, she was moved around the country before making her way back to the capital, where she acquired a reputation as a force to be reckoned with in a union that had generally played its politics cautiously. In recent years, she had made her reputation in particular for taking on cases involving complaints of unfair Chinese labor practices. She denied being hostile to the Chinese.

"We want to bring them aboard. We want them to help empower us. We want them to embrace a real skills transfer."

Weren't they already creating lots of jobs? I asked.

"That may be true," she said. "But if you are employing people you have a social responsibility toward them. The people employed by the Chinese are the most exploited workers in Namibia. Their laborers are paid as little as 2 Namibian dollars per hour [21 cents], which is far from the minimum wage of 9 Namibian dollars per hour [95 cents]. We are not against the Chinese, but those are not wages someone can survive on, and they must respect our laws."

The first time I met Jonas, she was still reeling from a conference her union organized that was intended to clear the air between Chinese contractors and Namibian unions. The construction industry was on edge with talk of an industry-wide strike. Jonas said that the union representatives had pleaded for respect of the law, saying they were working to protect the interests of future generations in the country. A Chinese speaker then stood up, she said, and complained that Namibian workers were lazy. "He said flatly that we don't know how to work, and that they were going to pay people whatever they felt they deserved." An angry shouting match ensued, causing a representative of the Chinese to stand up and say, "You can say whatever you want, but there is nothing you can do to us."

"We cannot tolerate someone coming into our country like this; coming into someone's home and doing whatever they like," Jonas said.

At the end of that first conversation with her, she spoke in terms of profound powerlessness and discouragement, and asked me to help find a spot for her at an American university, ready to become another casualty of the continent's brain drain. Soon afterward, the country's president, Hifikepunye Pohamba, had said publicly that his countrymen were too busy complaining about the Chinese, forgetting how they had helped Namibia obtain independence. The president ended his aside by telling his countrymen to get over their disgruntlement, because the Chinese weren't going anywhere. That is what stung many Namibians the most.

In March 2011, five hundred Namibian construction workers had walked off their jobs with one of the big Chinese contractors, complaining that they were being paid at only half the rate they were legally entitled to. The Chinese company, feeling sure of its position in the country, filed a complaint against the workers for an allegedly illegal strike, and the company prevailed, allowing it to dismiss all of the striking employees.

The affair had not ended there, though. The strikers began marching in the streets, a relative rarity in this quiet, highly consensual society. What is more, the marchers wore T-shirts with the president's likeness on them, citing his scornful words that Namibians are "too busy complaining." A placard carried by many read, "If we owe the Chinese anything, let us pay it back. Let them respect our laws." This had hit a nerve. The president's senior aides soon settled the matter.

The dismissed workers were reinstated and promised their due pay. The government made clear that a condition of the settlement was that protests end.

"Why is everything involving the Chinese so sensitive?" Jonas asked me. "This is something that you and I cannot answer."

Jamie and I spent three days driving to Johannesburg at a leisurely pace, sleeping on the Namibia-Botswana border one night under one of the starriest skies I have ever seen. We had ventured out into some of the most sparsely inhabited terrain in all of Africa, and, for most of the drive there were only tiny towns flung many miles apart, with only ostriches, baboons, and the occasional aardvark to capture our attention.

When at last we crossed into South Africa, the first sizable settlement we reached was Zeerust, a pure frontier town with a Wild West flavor not unlike others in northern Namibia, only bigger. We pulled over on the main street so I could buy a new SIM card. As I looked around, I noticed that almost every shop along the stretch was owned by Chinese immigrants. (Later I learned they were nearly all recent arrivals.) I went into one of them out of curiosity and observed a young mother in her twenties with a baby talking by QQ to her folks back in China, as two brothers tended the cash register. My brother came in search of me as I talked to the shop owner in Chinese. When he saw Jamie, he said in his spotty English that this was the first time a foreigner had spoken to him in Chinese here. "A foreigner! First time!" he shouted enthusiastically.

I was struck by the irony of what it meant to be a foreigner, and thought to myself, not for the first time, how thoroughly the world can change.

Epilogue

Any act of generosity can only be properly understood by considering the motives of the would-be benefactor.

As it has made big inroads in Africa, China has gone to great lengths to say that its project bears no resemblance to the Western imperialism of the not-so-distant past. And as we have seen, Chinese authorities have developed their own solipsistic language about their engagement with the continent in order to press this point home.

What one must grant is that every imperial project throughout history is distinctive, and in this sense, whatever China is doing in Africa today is undoubtedly different from the behavior of other powers that have preceded it along this path. The question that will continue to be debated remains whether what we are witnessing today merits this label at all.

Imperialism, for me, inevitably involves some form of foreign domination, which results in substantially altering the target population or polity; either gradually or suddenly it loses the ability to resist. In *The Abacus and the Sword,* his account of Japan's takeover of Korea, which was launched at the end of the nineteenth century, Peter Duus wrote that imperialism requires "an available victim—a weaker, less organized, or less advanced society or state unable to defend itself against outside intrusion."

Familiar examples are more readily drawn from the historical experience of the West, about which Eric Hobsbawm wrote in *The Age of Empire:* "Between 1876 and 1915, about one quarter of the globe's land surface was distributed or redistributed as colonies among a half-dozen states."

Describing this process, Duus writes:

Industrialization upset the technological balance of power between the Europeans and the rest of the world, and this imbalance made possible rapid European successes in conquest and domination. . . . The peoples of Africa, South and Southeast Asia and Oceania were no more able to withstand the impact of Western traders bearing machine-spun cotton yarn than they were able to resist Western troops armed with repeating rifles and Gatling guns. The penetration of distant markets went hand in hand with political dominion.

For many, at first blush, it will be the dissimilarities with these examples that spring to mind, whether Japan's efforts to take over large parts of the Asian mainland at the point of a bayonet, or the much broader Western push for global markets, for conquest, and ultimately for domination. For one thing, as Beijing frequently and not unreasonably points out, what has been called China's embrace of Africa clearly does not involve colonies. Beijing's strides thus far, moreover, have unquestionably been peaceful, and for the most part welcomed by the governments of Africa, even though here it should be said there are growing signs that for some the honeymoon is over.

It is worth keeping in mind, though, that the nature of empire has changed dramatically over time depending upon the circumstances. In the sixteenth and early seventeenth centuries, for example, the Portuguese, Spanish, English, and Dutch set up imperial trade outposts around the world, scarcely bothering themselves with the then prohibitive notion of controlling overseas territory or governing alien peoples. Barely a century later, lopsided technological advantages—steam, rail, and especially increasingly advanced weaponry—came into play for the Europeans, making possible, or perhaps inevitable, Hobsbawm's mad scramble.

Even within the history of late Western imperialism the variation has been so great as to include such things as outright colonies, indirect rule, spheres of influence, protectorates of various kinds, and an innovation sprung by the West on China itself—zones of foreign commercial and administrative control known as concessions.

For all the obvious dissimilarities with patterns like these, a few important features do seem to link China's current involvement with Africa to broader historical trends.

A consistent feature of imperialism, especially in its later manifestations, is the linkage between political and economic competition among contending powers. And China, for all its denials of any global ambition that could be likened to hegemony, is clearly competing with someone and for something—global preeminence.

The signs of this are omnipresent in Africa, where Beijing has exhibited a preference for giant projects that serve as constant, highly visible reminders of China's reach, its power, and of its supposed generosity and solicitude. China claims, for example, to have built forty-two stadiums and fifty-four hospitals on the continent. A June 2013 tweet from *China Daily,* an official, English-language newspaper, captured the spirit behind this succinctly: "In the last decade, China's investment in Africa has grown to $2.9b from $75m, and China's influence can be seen everywhere."

Speaking with me in a moment of unguarded self-satisfaction, Beijing's self-confident and affable ambassador to Zambia, Zhou Yuxiao, indirectly revealed the importance of this symbolic competition to China, saying that he saw his American counterpart around Lusaka from time to time, and couldn't help feeling a little sorry for him, because the man had so few projects that he could point to.

"You employ local people and place them as observers at each and every polling station," Zhou said with a little mocking laugh. "What else? I haven't seen any roads being built by [the Americans], any schools, any hospitals that really touch people, that can last, that can serve society for long. Maybe training election people is your biggest contribution."

When he finished, I asked him if he was familiar with an American program called PEPFAR, and he shook his head. Then I told him that through this program, the United States had spent about $1.5 billion in Zambia since 2004 to fight HIV, whose transmission rate had been brought down dramatically over the course of a decade. This American funding had played a big part in guaranteeing daily antiretroviral treatment for nearly 500,000 Zambians. (To be sure, like anyone's, American aid also has motives worth examining.) Zhou's entire response consisted of a nod.

China's competitiveness and search for national influence can also be seen in the way it is investing massively in African media. The state broadcaster, CCTV, is building what it hopes will become a continent-wide television powerhouse in Nairobi. The official Xinhua news agency has teamed with African mobile phone companies to supply news via cell phone. And *China Daily* has launched a supplement, *Africa Weekly,* for wide distribution on the continent. At the same time, Beijing is funding Confucius Institutes, a very rough equivalent to the Alliance Française or Germany's Goethe-Instituts, all over the continent. Nominally this is in order to train Chinese speakers, which African countries can certainly use and benefit from, but one would be naive to ignore Beijing's other clear and very old-fashioned purpose: expanding its influence.

Other features of Chinese activity in Africa also inevitably recall the patterns of empires past. The most frenzied period of imperial expansion the world has ever seen was not driven by arms alone, but also by an unprecedented expansion of global trade between the mid-eighteenth and early twentieth centuries. The new manufacturing centers of the West were only able to sustain growth of this magnitude by continually opening up new markets and inundating them with their goods. To do so required new infrastructure, and today one easily forgets that ports, railways, roads, and the administrative districts that became the downtowns of capitals around the world were built on an extraordinary scale all over the world by Westerners in the driven pursuit of their own interests. As manufacturing powers, they needed their goods to circulate, and they needed the raw materials from far-flung places in order to make them. Seen in this light, it scarcely seems coincidental that China, a country that has surged from near autarky to becoming the so-called factory of the world in the space of a mere generation, has quickly become the most ambitious builder of infrastructure in Africa, the world's fastest-growing region, both demographically and economically, and the source of a disproportionate share of the globe's natural resources.

In my belief, however, it is the human activity, migration, that provides the most striking parallels with imperial patterns of the past. No one knows how many Chinese have set themselves up on African soil in recent years, but if anything, the widely used figure of one million, which I myself have adopted here, seems quite conservative. It is even more reasonable to expect these numbers to continue growing, perhaps even dramatically. The arrival of these newcomers on this scale is arguably the latest chapter in a very long narrative of empire construction through emigration.

Portugal began sending settlers to distant Mozambique early in the sixteenth century, relying on them, rather than any extensive administration, as a cheap way of opening up new areas to trade and to assure a semblance of order favorable to Lisbon and its interests.

In one of the most recent examples that world history provides us, in the early 1930s, Japan (a country with one-tenth China's population) sent a million of its people, including very large numbers of shopkeepers, entrepreneurs, and agricultural emigrants, to settle Manchuria, in northeastern China. Tokyo's plan, never fully realized, was to eventually send five million people "to create a new generation of 'continental Japanese' who would secure a more thorough domination of colonial society," wrote historian Louise Young in *Japan's Total Empire: Manchuria and Culture of Wartime Imperialism.*

In my view, both of these examples, as different as they are, have a relevance to what is taking place between China and Africa today. Long before they had contemplated anything resembling modern colonial rule, the Portuguese had understood the potential of a diaspora in a faraway land to build up favorable trading networks, to extend political influence, and even to reduce problems back home, by giving marginal elements of the society a shot at wealth and redemption.

Since that time, the Chinese have arguably developed the concept of diaspora more fully than any other people.

In some ways for me the Japanese experience is most compelling of all, and this is not at all intended as a provocation. Imperial Tokyo and the Japanese emigrants to northeastern China mythologized Manchurian land as fertile and almost endlessly abundant, and more important still as all but empty and begging for cultivation by their modernizing hand. They glorified the hardy settlers with something akin to the Chinese tales we have heard here of eating bitter. And they even vowed to build a *shintenchi*, a new heaven on earth in Manchuria—but not just for themselves. In their era's version of win-win, the Japanese saw themselves as elevating the much poorer and woefully disorganized Chinese. In their own solipsistic telling, they were going to open a path for their Chinese brothers never offered them by the cruel and exploitative West: to dignity via modernity and civilization.

The movement of people from China to Africa obviously shares nothing with Japan's militarism. So far, it can only be said to be top-down in organization in the fuzziest of ways. Indeed, what often impressed me most about the stories of the new Chinese in Africa I met was the almost haphazard quality to the life stories that had landed them in places like Mozambique, Senegal, Namibia, and elsewhere. There was little hint of a grand or even deliberate scheme, but in the end, that's not so important. As the outraged Ghanaians who seem to have awoken one recent day to the discovery that thousands of Chinese newcomers were scrambling illegally to take control of their country's lucrative gold mining sector, digging up the countryside, despoiling the land, and bribing local chiefs and police officials in the process, might say, it is outcomes that count.

Acknowledgments

By way of a long and winding path, whose destination I by no means envisioned at the outset, this book grew from the kernel of work I began doing on the topic of China's relationship with Africa for *The New York Times* in 2007. I am thankful to my editors and collaborators back then, in particular Fan Wenxin and Lydia Polgreen.

The very next year, I left the *Times*, where I had worked since 1986, mostly as a foreign correspondent, to join the faculty of the Graduate School of Journalism of Columbia University. Soon afterward, I got an assignment from *The Atlantic* to take a deeper look at the Chinese presence in Africa, and I benefited greatly from my collaboration with Don Peck, a staff editor at the magazine.

My *Atlantic* work on this topic drew the attention of the Open Society Foundations, which granted me a fellowship in 2010–11. Without that generous support, a project like this, with its vast amount of travel, simply would not have been possible. I would like to express particular thanks to Leonard Benardo and to Stephen Hubbell, whose persistent encouragement early on, and knack for patient and probing discussion, served as a critical catalyst for nearly everything that followed.

I overcame an initial inhibition to take on the fieldwork that went into this book alone and unassisted on the ground, only by virtue of work on my previous book of documentary photography, *Disappearing Shanghai,* and by studying with Wang Zhao over a long, hot summer in that city. In its final phase, just before beginning work on this book, the aforementioned photography project required me to negoti- ate my way into the homes of working-class Chinese people and persuade them to allow me to photograph their lives. Almost every day for an entire summer, I knocked on the doors of strangers in this pursuit, and little by little gained enhanced confidence in my ability to have lengthy, unscripted conversations in Chinese, like the ones that fill this book.

I have been fortunate in life to have a number of great language teachers. I first got to know Wang Zhao in this capacity, as my tutor, meeting her many mornings that summer for lessons in which she pushed me hard, but with humanity and great humor. Wang Zhao later moved to New York to pursue postgraduate studies in linguistics, where for a time she continued to tutor me. After I had completed many of my interviews for this book, in an act of immense kindness from someone I count now as a friend, she transcribed some of them for me in Mandarin.

No one collaborated with me more closely in this work than Li Zhen, who cannot be thanked enough for her steadiness, her integrity, and her resourcefulness as a researcher, as well as for her sincere friendship over the years. As *New York Times* bureau chief in Shanghai, I hired her in her first job out of college, one of the best decisions I have ever made. Working from her native Chengdu after leaving the newspaper, she helped me find many of the most interesting Chinese characters I met during my long wanderings in Africa.

Two of the wisest friends I have, Peter Rosenblum and Daniel Sharfstein, both read early drafts of this book, and were wonderfully generous with their feedback and unstinting, when need be, with their criticisms.

Sun Yiting, one of my most impressive students at Columbia, who has gone on to work as a reporter in West Africa, also generously assisted in transcription, checked some of my translations, and also helpfully offered perceptive critical advice about portions of the book. Joanna Chiu, another former student, also read portions of the book and offered incisive feedback.

For all of the assistance and advice I have been fortunate to receive from these people and from many others, helping to strengthen this account, any errors and shortcomings are entirely mine.

Many friends put me up, put up with me, or otherwise helped sustain me on the road, thereby immensely easing the burdens of travel, including isolation. I would like to give particular thanks to Tiébilé Dramé, Erick Kabendera, Francis Kpatindé, Paanii Laryea, Aaron Leaf, Jonas Masjop, and Patrick Slavin. Many other friends all along the way, old and new, were also generous with their time, their insights, and their camaraderie. They include Loveness Kabwe, Clair Macdougall, Pax Mwandingi, Magano Ndjambula, and Marta Nhumaio, and many others who must go unnamed.

Thanks also go to Ben Berg, a pulmonologist based in Hawaii and friend since our teenage years who monitored me via Skype through a major respiratory episode that dogged me for weeks in eastern and southern Africa, causing me to break a rib from violent coughing and to be hospitalized briefly in a tiny clinic in northern Mozambique. I am also deeply grateful to Dr. Agostinho, who treated me there with care and who knew his stuff.

A special word of appreciation goes to my brother, Jamie, who joined me in Namibia, Botswana, and South Africa, for the latest resumption of a shared lifetime adventure of Africa.

Finally, and perhaps most important of all, I wish to thank the many, many people, Chinese and African, who opened their lives to me. Without them, there is no story.

Notes

Introduction

4 For a key Chinese industry like construction: "New Challenges Arise as China-Africa Ties Deepen," *Oxford Analytica,* January 21, 2013, http://www .oxan.com/Analysis/DailyBrief/Samples/CHINA-AFRICATies.aspx?WT.mc _id=TWT.

6 40 percent of global growth: David Shambaugh, *China Goes Global: The Partial Power* (New York: Oxford University Press, 2013), p. 156.

6 According to the International Monetary Fund: Lucas Kawa, "The 20 Fastest Growing Economies in the World," *Business Insider,* Oct. 24, 2012.

7 By century's end, demographers predict: *World Population Prospect, the 2010 Revision,* United Nations Department of Economic and Social Affairs.

PART ONE: Manifest Destiny

CHAPTER ONE: Mozambique

12 build thirty hospitals: David Shambaugh, *China Goes Global,* p. 110.

12 But according to Fitch Ratings: Mike Cohen, "China's EXIM Lend More to Sub-Saharan Africa Than World Bank, Fitch Says," *Bloomberg,* Dec. 28, 2011.

12 A research group called AidData: "Tracking Chinese Development Finance to Africa," http://aiddatachina.org/. Beijing itself claims that as of 2011, over a course of decades, it had committed $37.7 billion in official development aid globally: see Deborah Brautigam, "Rubbery AidData Numbers Surface in Beijing," *China in Africa: The Real Story,* May 16, 2013.

19 Year on year, China's trade with Africa: "African Trade to Surpass EU, US," *China Daily,* Oct. 13, 2012.

CHAPTER TWO: Behold the Future

42 Today, China alone accounts for 40 percent: Jack Farchy and Javier Blas, "Chinese Buying Drives Copper to Record with More Rises Expected," *Financial Times,* Nov. 12, 2010.

43 In 2013, meanwhile, the World Bank: "Africa Continues to Grow Strongly Despite Global Slowdown, Although Significantly Less Poverty Remains Elusive," press release, World Bank, April 15, 2013, http://www.worldbank.org/ en/news/press-release/2013/04/15/africa-continues-grow-strongly-despite -global-slowdown-although-significantly-less-poverty-remains-elusive.

44 Scenes like this are being played out: Shantayanan Devarajan and Wolfgang Fengler, "Africa's Economic Boom: Why the Pessimists and the Optimists Are Both Right," *Foreign Affairs,* May–June 2013.

47 "probably one of the greatest copper fields": Frederick Russell Burnham, "Northern Rhodesia," in Walter H. Wills. "Bulawayo Up-to-date: Being a General Sketch of Rhodesia" (London: Simpkin, Marshall, Hamilton Kent & Co., 1899), p. 179.

61 Prices for the metal soared in the 1960s: Index Mundi: http://www.index mundi.com/facts/indicators/NY.GDP.PCAP.CD/compare?country=zm# country=br:kr:my:tr:zm.

61 Kaunda's first approach was to try to raise taxes: "You'll Be Fired If You Refuse: Labor Abuses in Zambia's Chinese State-Owned Copper Mines," Human Rights Watch, Nov. 4, 2011.

61 The second half of his long tenure: Index Mundi, Zambia's GDP: http:// www.indexmundi.com/facts/zambia/gdp-per-capita.

62 "We were told by advisers" : Khadija Sharife, "Who Will Help the Zambians?," *The Zambian Economist,* June 7, 2011.

62 And by 2010, according to the Chinese newspaper: *Southern Weekend,* April 8, 2010.

62 "Almost immediately after production began": "You'll Be Fired If You Refuse: Labor Abuses in Zambia's Chinese State-Owned Copper Mines," Human Rights Watch, Nov. 4, 2011.

65 "I don't like what happened there": *Zambia Post,* http://www.postzambia .com/postread_article.php?articleId=14832.

65 "When [the Chinese businesspeople] treat Zambian workers": "Is China's Africa Policy Failing?," *Global Voices,* Aug. 15, 2012.

67 For one worker, Hedges Mwaba: Alexander Mutale, "Zambia's New President Sata Sets New Mining Rules for China," *The Christian Science Monitor,* Sept. 28, 2011.

CHAPTER THREE: Friendly Gestures

75 "Oh, that's easy!": Ezra F. Vogel, *Deng Xiaoping and the Transformation of China* (Cambridge, MA: Belknap Press of Harvard University, 2011), p. 342.

75 These early, classified warnings: "China Outmaneuvering Taiwan in Africa," classified diplomatic cable, WikiLeaks, Aug. 8, 2005.

75 "It is important to African governments": "US Tells Africa to Reject 'Cheap' Chinese Goods, Labor," *allAfrica*, Nov. 24, 2011.

PART TWO: The Devil and the Deep Blue Sea

CHAPTER FOUR: Liberia: *Small Fates*

95 "There seemed to be a seediness about the place": Graham Greene, *Journey Without Maps* (Garden City, NY: Doubleday, Doran, 1936), p. 20.

CHAPTER SIX: Freetown: *Instruments of Magic*

131 He quickly invested £6.6 million: Dan Box, "Sierra Leone Diamond Float on AIM," *Sunday Times* (London), Nov. 7, 2004.

131 Timis's new company may have had no cash flow: Saeed Shah, "From Penniless Refugee to Buccaneering Entrepreneur," *The Independent* (London), June 7, 2005.

CHAPTER SEVEN: Why Mali?

143 The poky, old Bamako: *The World's Fastest Growing Cities and Urban Areas from 2006 to 2020*, City Mayors Foundation.

146 Vaclav Smil, a prominent environmental scientist: Vaclav Smil, *Global Catastrophes and Trends: The Next Fifty Years* (Cambridge, MA: MIT Press, 2008), pp. 136–37.

164 Its main proponent: "Destined to Fail: Forced Settlement at the Office du Niger," *Journal of African History*, 42 (2001): 239–60.

169 "'You can never beat China'": Henry Sanderson and Michael Forsythe, *China's Superbank: Debt, Oil and Influence—How China Development Bank Is Rewriting the Rules of Finance* (Singapore: Bloomberg Press, 2013), pp. 101–2.

169 As a result of this passing: According to the China International Contractors Association, China dispatched 4.91 million workers abroad between 1978 and 2009. "Cheapness Alone Won't Cut It for China's Overseas Worker: Interview with Diao Chunhe," *Global Times*, Nov. 20, 2009.

170 "Africa has a population": Han Wei and Shen Hu, "Animal Instinct and China's African Odyssey," *Caixin Online*, April 1, 2012.

172 "In the current economic climate": *Beijing Cultural Review*, Aug. 2011. For an English language account, see Antoaneta Bezlova, "Latest Africa Foray: Altruism or Hegemony?," *IPS*, Nov. 9, 2009.

CHAPTER EIGHT: Ghana: *Habits of Democracy*

188 "The process for accessing World Bank and IMF credit": Henry Sanderson and Michael Forsythe, *China's Superbank*, p. 112.

192 "Do we look like colonists?": Leslie Hook, "Synohydro Shrugs Off Africa Criticism," *Financial Times*, April 10, 2013.

PART THREE: Happy Family

CHAPTER NINE: Saints of the Household

212 Seemingly forever, Mozambique has been one: "Vale, Rio Tinto Slammed over Mozambique Resettlements," Agence France-Presse, May 23, 2013.

213 In 2012, four of the five largest: "Natural Gas Discovery Promises a Boon for Eni and Mozambique," *The New York Times*, Dec. 5, 2012.

213 Between 2009 and 2011, the number: "Portuguese Head to Former African Colony to Escape Euro Crisis," *The Washington Post*, Nov. 11, 2012.

214 The most spectacular item: "Contentores suspeitos contêm madeira em toros," *O País*, July 8, 2011.

215 A London-based group: "Mozambique Loses a Fortune to Illegal Timber Exports," Environmental Investigation Agency, Feb. 7, 2013.

215 This helps explain: "Africa's Pulse," World Bank, Oct. 2012.

225 European companies were so far responsible: "Government Approves Eucalyptus Plantations," ClubofMozambique.com, Dec. 25, 2009.

CHAPTER TEN: Fat of the Land

243 The labor minister had to plead: Chamwe Kaira, "Namibia Bans Chinese Investment in Beauty Salons," *Bloomberg*, Feb. 22. 2010.

252 He cited a famous story: "Namibians Want Answers," *The Namibian*, Dec. 15, 2012.

252 "scholarships given to the children of senior politicians": "It's a Scramble for Chinese Scholarships Among Country's Top Brass," *Informanté*, Oct. 15, 2009.

255 For a time in China: Jamil Anderlini, "China Orders Internet Purge," *Financial Times*, July 22, 2009.

257 That is what stung many Namibians: Jo-Maré Duddy, "Business Grills President over Chinese," *allAfrica*, March 22, 2011.

Epilogue

259 "an available victim": Peter Duus, *The Abacus and the Sword: The Japanese Penetration of Korea, 1895–1910* (Berkeley: University of California Press, 1998), p. 21.

259 "Between 1876 and 1915": Eric Hobsbawm, *The Age of Empire: 1875–1914* (London: Little, Brown, 1989), p. 59.

260 Industrialization upset the technological balance: Peter Duus, *The Abacus and the Sword*, p. 6.

260 for some the honeymoon is over: In an op-ed published March 11, 2013, in the *Financial Times*, for example, the governor of Nigeria's Central Bank wrote: "It is time for Africans to wake up to the realities of their romance with China. . . . China is no longer a fellow under-developed economy—it is the world's second biggest, capable of the same forms of exploitation as the West. It is a significant contributor to Africa's deindustrialization and underdevelopment."

261 The signs of this are omnipresent: David Shambaugh, *China Goes Global*, p. 204.

263 "to create a new generation": Louise Young, *Japan's Total Empire: Manchuria and the Culture of Wartime Imperialism* (Berkeley: University of California Press, 1999), p. 4.

Index

A NOTE ABOUT THE AUTHOR

Howard W. French is an associate professor at the Columbia University Graduate School of Journalism, where he has taught since 2008. After teaching at the University of Côte d'Ivoire in the early 1980s, he began his journalism career as a freelance reporter covering Africa for *The Washington Post.* In 1986, French joined *The New York Times,* and served as the newspaper's bureau chief for Central America and the Caribbean, West and Central Africa, Japan and Korea, and Shanghai. He has reported from six continents, both as a senior writer for the *Times* and as an independent journalist. The author of *A Continent for the Taking: The Tragedy and Hope of Africa* and *Disappearing Shanghai: Photographs and Poems of an Intimate Way of Life,* with Qiu Xiaolong, French is the recipient of two Overseas Press Club awards and is a two-time Pulitzer Prize nominee. He was born in Washington, D.C., and lives in New York, with his wife, Avouka.

A NOTE ON THE TYPE

This book was set in Minion, a typeface produced by the Adobe Corporation specifically for the Macintosh personal computer and released in 1990. Designed by Robert Slimbach, Minion combines the classic characteristics of old-style faces with the full complement of weights required for modern typesetting.

Composed by North Market Street Graphics,
Lancaster, Pennsylvania

Printed and bound by Berryville Graphics,
Berryville, Virginia

Designed by Betty Lew